T0319808

Women's Entrepreneurship in a Turbulent Era

IN A TURBULENT ERA SERIES

These are turbulent and changing times. The longer-term effects of phenomena such as pandemics, the climate crisis, disruptive technologies, war, rising inequality, and shifts in global influence and power, on business, the economy and geo-politics are still unknown. Given these rapidly changing economic and social norms, businesses, organisations and institutions must be nimble to thrive. Focusing on one area at a time, this series seeks to investigate best practice, cutting-edge research and new ways of operating in this turbulent era.

For a full list of Edward Elgar published titles, including the titles in this series, visit our website at www.e-elgar.com.

Women's Entrepreneurship in a Turbulent Era

Edited by

Colette Henry

Head of Department of Business Studies, Dundalk Institute of Technology (DkIT), Ireland, and Griffith University, Australia

Joan Ballantine

Department of Accounting, Finance and Economics, Ulster University Business School, Ulster University (UU), Northern Ireland

Shumaila Yousafzai

Graduate School of Business, Nazarbayev University, Kazakhstan and Cardiff University, UK

Roshni Narendran

Tasmanian School of Business and Economics, University of Tasmania, Australia

IN A TURBULENT ERA SERIES

Cheltenham, UK • Northampton, MA, USA

Cover image: Johannes Plenio on Unsplash.

Published by
Edward Elgar Publishing Limited
The Lypiatts
15 Lansdown Road
Cheltenham
Glos GL50 2JA
UK

Edward Elgar Publishing, Inc.
William Pratt House
9 Dewey Court
Northampton
Massachusetts 01060
USA

A catalogue record for this book
is available from the British Library

Library of Congress Control Number: 2024939201

This book is available electronically in the **Elgar**online
Business subject collection
http://dx.doi.org/10.4337/9781803920825

ISBN 978 1 80392 081 8 (cased)
ISBN 978 1 80392 082 5 (eBook)

Printed and bound by CPI Group (UK) Ltd, Croydon, CR0 4YY

Contents

Figures

Tables

Editors

Colette Henry is Head of Department of Business Studies at Dundalk Institute of Technology, Ireland, and Adjunct Professor – Department of Business Strategy & Innovation – at Griffith University, Queensland, Australia. She is also an Affiliated Researcher with Jönköping University, Sweden. Her previous roles include Adjunct Professor of Entrepreneurship at UiT–The Arctic University of Norway; Norbrook Professor of Business & Enterprise at the Royal Veterinary College, London, and President of the Institute for Small Business & Entrepreneurship, UK. She is the founder of the Global Women's Entrepreneurship Research Network (Global WEP) and Founding Editor (and former Editor in Chief) of the *International Journal of Gender & Entrepreneurship*. She has published on entrepreneurship education, gender, the creative industries, and veterinary/rural business. In 2015 she received the Diana International Research Project Trailblazer Award, and in 2017 received the Sten K Johnson European Entrepreneurship Education Award from Lund University, Sweden. Colette is a fellow of the Royal Society, the Higher Education Academy, the Academy of Social Sciences, and the Institute for Small Business & Entrepreneurship. She is currently leading a series of Global WEP publications and has published, with the OECD, *Entrepreneurship Policies through a Gender Lens* (OECD–GWEP, 2021). Her current interests have taken her into the world of creative writing. One of her short crime stories – *Betrayal* – was broadcast by BBC Radio Ulster and BBC Sounds in 2023.

Joan Ballantine is an accounting graduate and Fellow of the Association of Chartered Certified Accountant (FCCA). After working in industry, she took up her first lecturing position at Queens University Belfast and subsequently joined Warwick Business School, Warwick University. During her ten years at Warwick, Joan gained her doctorate and was actively engaged in delivering executive education/consultancy to a range of private and public sector organizations. She returned to Northern Ireland to take up the post of Senior Lecturer at Queen's University Belfast before being appointed to her current position as Professor in Accounting at the University of Ulster in 2008. She currently teaches on a range of Masters' courses in the areas of strategic management accounting, accounting and finance and research methods. She is an active researcher working in the broad areas of education, gender budgeting, entrepreneurship and gender, and gender in senior management. She has published widely in national and international peer-reviewed journals. She sits on a number of editorial board positions and has examined numerous doctorates. Joan holds a number of board positions, including Board member at Banbridge District Enterprises and Cancer Fund for Children. She is also an Independent Assessor for the Commissioner for Public Appointments for Northern Ireland which regulates appointments to the boards of public bodies.

Shumaila Yousafzai is Associate Professor of Entrepreneurship at Graduate School of Business, Nazarbayev University, Kazakhstan and a Reader (on Leave) at Cardiff Business School, Cardiff University, UK. She is the Founder and Director of Nazarbayev University Research Centre for Entrepreneurship (NURCE). Her research interests include entrepreneurship (women and disabled), critical management studies and entrepreneurship in circular economy. She has published widely in international scholarly journals and her work has appeared in *Human Relations*, *Entrepreneurship Theory and Practice*, *Psychology and Marketing*, *Technovation* and *Entrepreneurship & Regional Development*, among others. She has edited ten volumes on topics including women's entrepreneurship, disabled entrepreneurship, sustainability and technological leapfrogging in Africa.

Roshni Narendran commenced her career at an autonomous government body, focusing on regulating public sector units in India. This professional background inspired Roshni to delve into research on how governmental interventions could influence entrepreneurial activities. Roshni has contributed to diverse disciplines, including pharmaceutical marketing, pedagogical teaching methods, tourism and female entrepreneurship. With a primary research interest in gender and entrepreneurship, Roshni's doctoral thesis delved into the institutional constraints faced by women. Her study further explored the impact of the caste system and government programmes on female entrepreneurs. While there is a growing emphasis on studies about women entrepreneurs, Roshni believes that other segments of the population are not receiving adequate attention in academic literature. Recognizing the need for a broader voice, her research extends to entrepreneurs in the transgender and other LGBT+ communities.

Contributors

Nurlykhan Aljanova is a Research Fellow, Nazarbayev University Research Centre for Entrepreneurship. She holds a PhD in Cultural Studies and a Master's degree in Religious Studies from Al-Farabi Kazakh National University. Her research focuses on the Kazakh Identity, Creative Industry, Cultural and Religious Entrepreneurship, and Religious Studies. Along with several published articles on Religion and Entrepreneurship, Semiotic Aspects of Kazakh Traditional Culture, she co-authored some books on Cultural Monuments and Symbols. She is an Editorial Board Member of the *Eurasian Journal of Religious Studies* and *Bulletin of Indonesian Islamic Studies*, and has held numerous positions, including Research Fellow at the Qazaq Research Institute for Future Studies (2019–2020), Secretary of the High Qualification Committee of the Ministry of Education of the Republic of Kazakhstan (2018–2021) and Deputy Head on Science, Innovations, and International Cooperation (2016–2022). Nurlykhan has had research internships and served as visiting professor at Madrid Complutense University within project One Asia Foundation, the One Asia Community in Cross-cultural Dialogue with Europe II.

Bettina Lynda Bastian is a researcher in entrepreneurship and focuses on the intersections of gender, culture, governance, policy, and organization associated with new ventures and innovation. Her research is internationally recognized for translating social science into work policies and practices that promote entrepreneurship and sustainable business, especially women's development and capacity building. She has worked in senior university roles promoting entrepreneurship, innovation, gender equality and sustainability/ESG. She served as Dean of the College of Business and Law at the Royal University for Women in Bahrain; she was Head of Academic Programs in Entrepreneurship and Innovation at the Holy Spirit University of Kaslik, Lebanon (USEK), and Head of Business Ethics programmes at the American University of Beirut (AUB). Currently she is building her own educational consultancy, and she works as adjunct associate professor at the American University of Bulgaria.

Siegrun Brink is a research associate at the Institut für Mittelstandsforschung (IfM) Bonn. After completing her apprenticeship as a bank clerk, Siegrun studied business administration at the Georg-August University in Göttingen and then worked as a research assistant at the Chair of Business Administration, specifically in Human Resource Management and Organization, Schumpeter School of Business and Economics at the University of Wuppertal, where she received her PhD in 2009.

Gray Cavender was Professor Emeritus of Justice & Social Inquiry in the School of Social Transformation, Arizona State University (ASU). His interests focused on corporate crime and regulation, punishment, media, and gender studies. His extensive record of professional service included serving as the founding director of ASU's pioneering interdisciplinary PhD programme in Justice Studies in 1985. Most recently, he was a member of the International advisory board for the journal *Crime Media Culture* and served as associate editor for the *Oxford Research Encyclopedia on Crime, Media, and Popular Culture*. His academic books include *Parole: A Critical Analysis* (Kennikat Press), *Corporate Crime Under Attack* (Anderson, Routledge, two editions), *Entertaining Crime: Television Reality Programs* (Aldine De Gruyter), and *Provocateur for Justice: Jane Tennison and Policing in 'Prime Suspect'* (University of Illinois Press). His fiction books include *Death of the Ayn Rand Scholar* (Amazon) and *The Pandemic Casebook of Jillian Warne* (Amazon), and another book of stories (forthcoming). He died on 8 August 2023, with his family by his side.

Luisa De Vita is an Associate Professor in Economic Sociology at the Department of Social Science and Economics, 'Sapienza' University of Rome. She directs the PhD programme in Applied Social Sciences and has joined several research projects at national and international level. Her current research concerns inequalities, gender policies, diversity management, labour market and working conditions, with a focus on self-employment and women's entrepreneurship.

Spinder Dhaliwal is a Reader in Entrepreneurship at Westminster University Business School, UK, and leader of the Entrepreneurship Research Group. Her research expertise is female entrepreneurs, Asian entrepreneurs, and Entrepreneurship Education. She is the author of *The Millennial Millionaire: How Young Entrepreneurs Turn Dreams into Business* (Palgrave, 2017). Spinder has written extensively about entrepreneurship and the business community and compiled the Britain's Richest Asians list, reflecting her long-held interest in the field. Her previous book, *Making a Fortune: Learning from the Asian Phenomenon* (Capstone, 2008), has been noted widely. Her earlier book, *Silent Contributors: Asian Female Entrepreneurs and Women in Business* (Roehampton Institute, 1998), illuminates the complex role of Asian women in business.

Elisa Errico is a PhD student at the Doctoral School of Social Sciences and Economics at Sapienza University of Rome. Female entrepreneurship and women's business associations are among her main research interests. Her PhD research project focuses on the green transition of SMEs in Italy, including social impacts and gender inequalities.

Maryam Fozia is an independent researcher residing in the Middle East. She obtained her PhD in Business from the Aligarh Muslim University, Aligarh (India) in 2019. Her research focuses on assessment of entrepreneurial processes and the aspect of decision-making by entrepreneurs. She is currently engaged in a research project focused on migrant and under-privileged entrepreneurship, family business succession and women entrepreneurship in the Middle East region. In addition, she is an active member of Society for Effectual Action (SEA) and is currently engaged in studying philosophical questions around 'World Making' and 'Use of symbols' in the field of entrepreneurship.

Richard George is a Senior Lecturer in Tourism & Hospitality Management at ICON College of Technology and Management in Whitechapel, London, UK. He obtained his PhD in Marketing from the Faculty of Commerce at the University of Cape Town (South Africa). His research interests are in the field of tourism management: travel influencers, tourism crime-safety, and entrepreneurship in tourism. He is the author of *Marketing Tourism & Hospitality: Concepts and Cases*, second edition (Palgrave Macmillan, 2024) and several research papers on tourism topics.

Navid Ghannad is an Assistant Professor at Halmstad University. He holds a PhD in Business Administration in international Entrepreneurship (2013) and has published articles and book chapters mainly within the field of entrepreneurship, international marketing, and management. His research interests include business growth, strategy, sustainability, and higher education.

Nelia Hyndman-Rizk is an organizational anthropologist who specializes in intercultural management, new digital technologies, entrepreneurship, and innovation. Her research interests include mobility studies, the Lebanese diaspora, gender, and cross-cultural competency. Her current research focuses on digital nomads, entrepreneurship, and the future of work.

Nancy C. Jurik is Professor Emerita of Justice & Social Inquiry in the School of Social Transformation, Arizona State University. Her interests focus on work organization, entrepreneurship, and media constructions of gender and work. Her books include *Doing Justice, Doing Gender: Women in Legal and Criminal Justice Occupations* (Sage), *Bootstrap Dreams: U.S. Microenterprise Development in an Era of Welfare Reform* (Cornell

University Press) and *Provocateur for Justice: Jane Tennison and Policing in 'Prime Suspect'* (University of Illinois Press). She has received distinguished researcher and mentoring awards from Arizona State University and several professional associations. She is a Global WEP member.

Rosemarie Kay is Deputy Managing Director at the Institut für Mittelstandsforschung, a research institute focusing on small business and entrepreneurship. She completed her doctorate at Freie Universität Berlin in 1998. Her research focuses on business start-ups, business succession and hybrid entrepreneurship. She has published numerous reports and papers in these fields, including articles focusing on the gender and the origins of founders and successors.

Saskia de Klerk (SFHEA) is the Discipline Lead for the Marketing, International Business, and Tourism disciplines at the University of the Sunshine Coast, Queensland, Australia. Her research interests include mapping, developing, and advancing entrepreneurial and networking skills and regional entrepreneurial ecosystems. She is interested in supporting this transition to entrepreneurship by non-traditional participants, minorities, and disadvantaged groups by using a gender-lens and inclusive approach. She has authored many research articles/chapters and reports.

Alena Křížková is Head of the Gender & Sociology Department of the Institute of Sociology, Czech Academy of Sciences. Her focus is on economic and social justice, gender wage gap, gender in organizations and in entrepreneurship, on ageing and digitalization and recently on the impact of the Covid-19 pandemic on gender equality. She conducted a Fulbright Fellowship at Arizona State University for comparative CZ–US research on the entrepreneurship environment for disadvantaged populations and gender equality. She is the Czech country expert in the 'scientific analysis and advice on gender equality in the EU' (SAAGE) for the European Commission and executive member of Global Women's Entrepreneurship Policy Research network (Global WEP).

Melissa Langworthy is a feminist economist specializing in inclusive and sustainable development, gender equality, and economic justice. She has 15 years of experience working on women's empowerment, decent work, and capacity building for NGO, government, and corporate social programmes, including for Facebook, UN Women, Oxfam MENA, and the European Commission. Through her many publications, policy papers, and a forthcoming book, she continues to define and argue the terms and support needed to drive promotion of high quality, sustainable, and innovative women's enterprise.

Yelena Muzykina is a fellow at the Center of Postnormal Policies and Futures Studies and a trainer at the Academy of Public Administration under the President of Kazakhstan. She is a certified futurist and also holds a PhD in Islamic Studies from Al-Farabi Kazakh National University, a Candidate of Science in Social Philosophy from the People's Friendship University of Russia, a Master's degree in Cross-Cultural Studies from Andrews University (USA), and a few degrees in History, English, Economy, and Theology. Yelena worked as Assistant Director at Qazaq Research Centre for Futures Studies, responsible for research, business development, and education. Her academic interests focus primarily on Futures Studies and Foresight as well as Postnormal Times, Sociology, Comparative Studies, and Theology.

Parisa Nakhaei recently completed a PhD in economics at the University of New South Wales' School of Business. Her PhD focused on women home-based business entrepreneurs in Iran, conducting a comparative case study of home-based businesses in informal and formal economies. She holds Master's and Bachelor's degrees in development studies and social science, and possesses extensive experience in social, economic, and business research. Her research interests encompass Gender and Development, Women and Entrepreneurship, Women's Economic Activities and Employment, Gender and Addiction, Informal Economy, International Migration, and Development Studies.

Marie Pospíšilová is a Postdoctoral Fellow at the Gender & Sociology Department at the Institute of Sociology of the Czech Academy of Sciences. She focuses on gender and entrepreneurship, the impacts of the Covid-19 pandemic on businesses, vulnerable groups, and on widening inequalities. She is interested in both the impacts on labour and domestic spheres and the division of labour between partners. She also focuses on digitalization, ageing, and digital interactions.

Nadeera Ranabahu is a Senior Lecturer in the UC Business School at the University of Canterbury in New Zealand. She obtained her PhD in Business from the University of Wollongong in 2018. Her main research interest is entrepreneurship in minority groups such as refugees, immigrants, low-income people, and women. She also studies social entrepreneurship and social innovations and the intersection between microfinance and sustainability.

Markus Rieger-Fels received his PhD from Bonn Graduate School of Economics in 2014. He worked as a postdoctoral researcher at Karlsruhe Institute of Technology and Dortmund University (TU) before joining the Institut für Mittelstandsforschung Bonn in 2021.

Susanne Schlepphorst studied business administration at the University of Applied Sciences (FHDW) Gütersloh. From 2008 to 2013 she was a research assistant at the Chair for Entrepreneurship and Family Business at the University of Siegen, where she received her PhD in 2016. In 2014, she joined the Institut für Mittelstandsforschung (IfM) Bonn team as a research assistant.

Anna Sörensson has a PhD in Business Administration within international marketing (2014) from Åbo Akademi, Finland. She is an Associate Professor at Mid Sweden University in Östersund, Sweden and at Inland School of Business and Social Sciences in Rena, Norway. She has published articles and book chapters mainly within the field of marketing, entrepreneurship, tourism, and sustainability. Her research interests are broad and include nature-based businesses, sustainable development, and education.

Rebecca Weicht is an entrepreneurship researcher whose work focuses on self-employment and entrepreneurship education. She received her PhD from Manchester Metropolitan University and was a researcher at Institut für Mittelstandsforschung.

Friederike Welter leads the Institut für Mittelstandsforschung, a research institute on small business and entrepreneurship, and holds a professorship at the University of Siegen. Her main research interests, on which she has published widely, are contextual entrepreneurship, entrepreneurial behaviour, women's entrepreneurship, and entrepreneurship policies. She is Senior Editor of *Entrepreneurship Theory and Practice*. For her research work, she has received several honours, recently as a member of the 21st Century Entrepreneurship Research Fellow and the Academia Europaea.

Bronwyn P. Wood has a PhD in Marketing from Otago, in her native Aotearoa New Zealand. She currently teaches in the UAE, has a consultancy, www.MuslimMarketingMatters.com, and is a Field Editor for the *International Journal of Gender and Entrepreneurship*. With publications across the business spectrum, particularly in Islamic Marketing and Women's Entrepreneurship, Dr Wood applies her varied experience to perceptual and epistemological discussions of meaning and well-being. Interest areas are non-hegemonic methodologies, decolonization, social justice, and social and economic sustainability.

Shumaila Yousafzai is Associate Professor of Entrepreneurship at Graduate School of Business, Nazarbayev University, Kazakhstan, and a Reader (on Leave) at Cardiff Business School, Cardiff University, UK. She is the Founder and Director of Nazarbayev University Research Centre for Entrepreneurship (NURCE). Her research interests include entrepreneurship (women and disabled), critical management studies and entrepreneurship in circular economy.

She has published widely in international scholarly journals and her work has appeared in *Human Relations, Entrepreneurship Theory and Practice, Psychology and Marketing, Technovation* and *Entrepreneurship & Regional Development*, among others. She has edited ten volumes on topics including women's entrepreneurship, disabled entrepreneurship, sustainability, and technological leapfrogging in Africa.

Dongling Zhang is Assistant Professor of Criminology in the Department of Global Languages, Cultures & Societies at Webster University. His research focuses on microenterprise development programmes in urban China, women's entry into entrepreneurship in post-1978 China, and women micro-entrepreneurs' experiences of gender-based domestic violence. He is the first editor of a peer-reviewed editorial volume titled *International Responses to Interpersonal Violence: Gender-Specific and Socio-Cultural Approaches* (Routledge).

Foreword

Candida G. Brush

The post-Covid-19 pandemic years have caused global economic turmoil, manifested by disruptions to all business sectors, as well as significant shifts in our personal and family lives. For entrepreneurs, the consequential effects of supply shortages, school closures, layoffs, remote work, shifting consumption patterns, new health regulations and technology have simultaneously sparked innovation and created structural and policy challenges. However, for women entrepreneurs, the challenges in business and family are more dramatic. Worldwide, women are primarily responsible for caring responsibilities and managing their households; they faced psychological and emotional challenges in juggling family responsibilities in addition to the trials of pivoting their business models and maintaining business legitimacy. While the Covid pandemic caused unprecedented global turmoil and challenges for women in particular, women entrepreneurs have also had to navigate and redefine their roles during other turbulent times, including wars, conflicts, pandemics, regime changes, environmental disasters, and climate change.

Scholarship outlining both the challenges and innovations of women entrepreneurs during and after the pandemic, together with other turbulent environments, is still emerging. However, a comprehensive examination of the challenges, innovations, adaptation strategies, and social impact has not been systematically explored.

The first part of this volume uncovers some of the unique challenges faced by women entrepreneurs, which, without the pandemic and other turbulent times, may not have come to light. For example, the challenges of institutional and structural factors such as work permits, licensing, and tax policy are more apparent. Further, singular constraints for women such as stereotype bias, family expectations and societal expectations for women to conform to gender norms are more visible. Given these challenges, the second part of this book presents the strategies that women used to pivot their business models and capitalize on opportunities, often innovating using digital platforms and social media. The rich stories and interviews offer lessons for what we can learn from women entrepreneurs about how to successfully deploy feminine capital (e.g., collaboration and empathy), to persevere, be resilient and resourceful, and leverage networks when faced with a business crisis.

The third section of the text highlights societal and global contexts, illustrating how women entrepreneurs are often stabilizers or shock absorbers within their business and communities. In some cases, turbulent times have diminished gender equality due to economic circumstances. Notably, each chapter proposes future research directions and suggestions for how policies might be created or amended to better ensure effectiveness and success of women entrepreneurs and their businesses.

This volume, led by Professors Colette Henry, Joan Ballantine, Shumalia Yousafzai and Roshni Narendran marks the 2nd Global Women's Entrepreneurship Policy Research network (GWEP) collection focusing on women's entrepreneurship policy. I am personally gratified because the efforts of the GWEP initiative emerged from scholars who originally attended our first Diana International Research meeting in Stockholm, Sweden, in 2003. This network of research scholars from across the globe has catalyzed a review and critique of entrepreneurship policy with a gender lens.

It is notable that this book features a very distinguished group of authors from a variety of disciplines, experiences, backgrounds, and countries. This has resulted in a colorful and nuanced tapestry of women's entrepreneurship providing insights into what entrepreneurs can learn from women when operating in an era of turbulence.

Candida G. Brush, Franklin W. Olin Professor of Entrepreneurship
Faculty Research Director – Diana International Research Institute
Babson College, USA

Foreword

Tim Vorley

The role of entrepreneurs in pursuing future growth opportunities has long been an area of academic interest. This role is particularly acute during economic downturns, where entrepreneurs serve as catalysts to the recovery and resilience of economies. It is not simply about how entrepreneurs navigate economic uncertainties, global crises, and technological change, but how they adapt in turbulent times and go on to shape the future.

Entrepreneurship is about identifying, evaluating, mitigating, and managing risk in the pursuit of potential opportunities. Yet, to successfully navigate turbulent times, entrepreneurs face greater uncertainty and heightened risks, with the result that bold decision-making is even more critical. Indeed, it is often in challenging times that the resilience of entrepreneurs sees their creativity and innovation prevail in identifying and pursuing opportunities in adverse conditions. However, entrepreneurship is not a neutral concept, but is affected by social factors and their intersections, including gender, diversity, and the socioeconomic backgrounds of entrepreneurs. Women entrepreneurs often face additional challenges compared to their male counterparts. Formal challenges range from equal access to finance, to regulatory barriers around starting a business. The nature and extent of such barriers are often context specific, highlighting women's entrepreneurship itself as highly heterogeneous.

Beyond the business of entrepreneurship, women also face a wide range of social and societal challenges. From the prevailing gender stereotypes of 'who is an entrepreneur', which can create biases and discrimination towards women entrepreneurs, to the realities of work–life (im)balance where women often take on the role of primary carers, which can constrain their time and flexibility to pursue their entrepreneurial endeavours.

In unpacking these inequities there is a need to focus on the experiences of women entrepreneurs as individuals as well as the entrepreneurial ecosystems in which they operate. Entrepreneurship requires agility and resilience, and this is particularly true of women entrepreneurs given the systemic disadvantages they encounter. How women entrepreneurs respond to and overcome such disadvantages, particularly in turbulent times, demonstrates their entrepreneurial acumen.

Entrepreneurs identify opportunities and develop solutions to adapt to and address challenges that emerge during periods of uncertainty. Such solutions are often closely associated with entrepreneurship, through the process of bringing ideas to market. The adversity encountered by entrepreneurs in turbulent times can also serve as a stimulus to innovate in a way that may appear counter intuitive. Whether the nature of crisis is a recession, pandemics, conflicts, wars, or environmental disasters, the ability to innovate is more likely to see entrepreneurs succeed and outperform their peers.

Despite the undoubted strengths of women entrepreneurs who prevail, there is an urgent need to address the disadvantages experience by women entrepreneurs more broadly. This is a deficiency of the entrepreneurial ecosystem and the societies in which they operate. There is a need for policymakers, investors, business leaders, and business support organizations to understand this more fully and to address this inequality. At its core, this means creating a more inclusive and equitable entrepreneurial ecosystem, by challenging gender biases, promoting diversity and empowering women entrepreneurs to succeed with access to support and resources.

The journey of women entrepreneurs does not start with parity, and any inequity is exacerbated through the social systems in which they operate. It is important to illuminate and understand the systematic disadvantages facing women entrepreneurs; such disadvantages are often invisible or overlooked and are undoubtedly amplified in turbulent times. This book not only highlights the nature of the challenges faced by women entrepreneurs in turbulent times but also the strategies they employ to manage, mitigate, and overcome them.

The rich collection of chapters contained in this book spans different countries and contexts impacted by different forms of turbulence. The value of the collection is not only in the insights themselves, but also in the visibility the collection gives to delving deeper into the issues and questions raised in relation to women's entrepreneurship. The collection highlights the importance and dynamism of women entrepreneurs, but also the nature and extent of the disadvantages they face.

The book also highlights the need to make entrepreneurial ecosystems more equal and inclusive. Neither gender nor other characteristics should be discriminating factors in determining entrepreneurial success, regardless of whether entrepreneurial endeavours occur in turbulent times. Therefore, this book is important not only in terms of its focus but also in highlighting the need for more equal and inclusive entrepreneurship that embraces and builds on the strength of diversity.

Professor Tim Vorley, OBE
Pro Vice-Chancellor and Dean
Oxford Brookes Business School, Oxford, England

About Global WEP

The Global Women's Entrepreneurship Policy Research Network (Global WEP – www .globalwep .org) is a group of established researchers from over 30 counties. Its goal is to examine, internationally, support policies for women's entrepreneurship, and to identify explicit or implicit gender biases within public policies. Global WEP also seeks to identify effective policies or practices that are potentially beneficial to other countries in supporting women's entrepreneurial activities. Global WEP scholars exchange policy knowledge and share policy data for collective publications and report dissemination. In so doing, Global WEP adds value to extant policy scholarship and informs policy development.

Founded and launched by Colette Henry at the 2014 Diana International Research Symposium in Stockholm, Global WEP is supported by an Executive Team and an International Advisory Panel. Global WEP members comprise researchers from Africa, Asia, Australasia, Europe, North America and South America. In addition to hosting by-invitation and open-door workshops, Global WEP has published a number of internal reports, conference papers, books, book chapters and peer-reviewed academic journal articles. The Global WEP network and its members have also led several special issues in leading journals such as the *International Small Business Journal*, the *International Journal of Entrepreneurial Behaviour & Research*, and the *International Journal of Gender & Entrepreneurship*. Global WEP members have also presented at the Diana International Research Conferences, Institute for Small Business & Entrepreneurship Conferences, United Nations Conference on Trade and Development (UNCTAD), and the T20 Conference. We have also led and/or contributed to several webinars for the Organisation for Economic Co-operation & Development (OECD), Diana International Research Institute (DIRI), WEIForward, Centre for Innovation Management Research (CIMR) at Birkbeck, and the International Council for Small Business (ICSB). In 2017, Global WEP published a comparative study of women's entrepreneurship policy in 13 countries in the *International Journal of Gender and Entrepreneurship* (Henry, Orser, Coleman and Foss, 2017). The research was based on analyses of 38 policy/policy-related documents, across Africa, Asia, Australasia, Europe and North America. This 13-country study was followed by more in-depth studies, such as that of Coleman, Henry, Orser, Foss and Welter (2019) in the *Journal of Small Business Management*. Drawing on institutional and feminist theories, this study provides a critique of policies and programmes to increase women entrepreneurs' access to capital in five economies: Canada, Germany, Ireland, Norway and the USA.

In 2021, in conjunction with the OECD, we published a report exploring entrepreneurship policies in 27 countries in Europe, Africa, Asia, North America, South America and Australasia. Findings revealed countries with no dedicated women's entrepreneurship policy; countries where there were policies without programmes, and countries where there were programmes but no policies. Women-focused entrepreneurship policies often referred to women as 'minority', 'lacking skills', 'in deficit' and needing to be 'fixed'. Access to financial capital was identified as one of the most significant barriers to women's entrepreneurship, and there was a general lack of monitoring and evaluation mechanisms.

Collectively, these studies reveal that authorship of women's entrepreneurship policy documents is often anonymous, rarely gender-balanced, and sometimes predominately by men. The analyses suggest that many government policies relegate women entrepreneurs to minority or disadvantaged group status, hence restricting access to resources or overtly privileging traditional men-dominated industry sectors. Few policy documents explicitly state a theoretical foundation or rationale for intervention, or describe evidence-based inputs and outcomes to inform future policy development. Many policies appear to be pilot or ad hoc initiatives. When such policies are considered within their national and institutional contexts, there is often evidence of a mismatch between official policies on the one hand, and practices and funded programmes on the other.

Accordingly, many women's enterprise, small business and entrepreneurship policies have made only modest contributions to the economic welfare and security of women. Opportunities remain for policymakers to do more.

As the new co-chairs of Global WEP from 1 January 2024, Professor Tim Vorley and Dr Beldina Owalla at Oxford Brookes University are committed to the network's further development and expansion.

Introduction to *Women's Entrepreneurship in a Turbulent Era*

Colette Henry, Joan Ballantine, Shumaila Yousafzai and Roshni Narendran

In the dynamic landscape of global entrepreneurship, the surge in women's entrepreneurial activities marks a significant shift in the economic and social fabric. The Global Entrepreneurship Monitor (GEM) data, recording an impressive 163 million women-owned businesses (GEM, 2017), underscores the rising prominence of women in the entrepreneurial arena. This trend not only breaks the patriarchal norms prevalent in many industries but also contributes substantially to the global economy. The scholarly discourse around women's entrepreneurship has evolved, with an increasing critique of the masculine-centric narratives that have historically dominated the field (Ahl, 2006; Swail and Marlow, 2018). The growing use of feminist theories in entrepreneurial research reflects a deeper engagement with the complexities of women's entrepreneurial experiences (Tlaiss and Kauser, 2019; Ahl and Marlow, 2021). Yet, the journey of women entrepreneurs often unfolds in the shadows of heteropatriarchal norms, where a social system – dominated by heterosexuality and patriarchy – marginalizes alternative perspectives (Arvin et al., 2020). This dominance is evident in the parameters commonly used to gauge business success. Women-owned enterprises are frequently assessed against masculine benchmarks of profitability, sales, and workforce size, overlooking the intangible aspects of entrepreneurial endeavors, such as unpaid labor, in which women frequently engage (Marlow, 2020). The heteropatriarchal influence is so ingrained that women entrepreneurs themselves sometimes adopt feminized identities or romanticized ideals to promote their businesses (Heizmann and Liu, 2022), perpetuating these entrenched norms.

However, recent years, marked by political and economic turbulence, have offered opportunities for women to challenge or conform to these heteropatriarchal expectations. The COVID-19 pandemic, for instance, became a catalyst for many women entrepreneurs to pivot their businesses to digital platforms (Afshan et al., 2021; Manolova et al., 2020; Mustafa and Treanor, 2022). Furthermore, Althalathini et al. (2020) demonstrated how women entrepreneurs navigate patriarchal expectations to make significant social and economic contributions, reshaping their roles in society and within their families. Yet, these shifts often come with added layers of subordination and responsibility, such as balancing family care with customer health concerns (Afshan et al., 2021; Mustafa et al., 2021). Moreover, women entrepreneurs face unique challenges, including economic and mental stress, that heighten their vulnerability to domestic violence (Roesch et al., 2021).

This book aims to delve into how women entrepreneurs navigate and redefine their roles during turbulent times, encompassing wars, conflicts, pandemics, regime changes, environmental disasters, and climate change. It seeks to bridge the gap in literature by offering insights into women's entrepreneurial efforts in redefining the norms and rules in a rapidly changing world. Through this exploration, we aim to contribute to the ongoing debate on the contextual embeddedness of women-owned enterprises and stimulate further research and action in this critical area of study.

STRUCTURE

The landscape of women's entrepreneurship, particularly in times of significant turbulence, presents a diverse array of challenges, innovations, and societal impacts. This book, comprising ten insightful chapters, is thoughtfully organized into three distinct Parts, each delving into different facets of women's entrepreneurial experiences during periods of upheaval and change. These Parts collectively offer a comprehensive exploration of the various dimensions of women's entrepreneurship in the face of adversity and transformation.

Part I focuses on the challenges and resilience faced by women entrepreneurs in diverse global contexts. The chapters included here provide a nuanced understanding of how women in various parts of the world, from Russia to Iran, have navigated and adapted to the challenges posed by economic, social, and health crises. These narratives highlight the unique strategies employed by women entrepreneurs to sustain and grow their businesses amidst adversity.

Part II shifts focus to the innovative and adaptation strategies that women entrepreneurs have employed in response to the turbulent times marked by the COVID-19 pandemic. It explores how women-led businesses have adapted their business models, embraced digital transformation, and navigated financial challenges. This section underscores the agility and resourcefulness of women entrepreneurs in the face of unprecedented global changes.

The final section of the book (Part III) addresses the broader societal impact and global contexts of women's entrepreneurship. It examines the role of women entrepreneurs in stabilizing economies during crises, their efforts to maintain legitimacy in traditional gender role contexts, and the societal expectations shaping their entrepreneurial journey. This section provides a critical lens on how women entrepreneurs influence and are influenced by the societal and global dynamics surrounding them.

Each section, with its collection of chapters, offers valuable insights and contributes significantly to the understanding of women's entrepreneurship in turbulent times. As readers navigate through these sections, they will gain a deeper appreciation of the complexities, strengths, and transformative potential of women entrepreneurs across the globe.

PART I: CHALLENGES AND RESILIENCE IN ENTREPRENEURSHIP

This section focuses on the multifaceted challenges and resilience demonstrated by women entrepreneurs across various global contexts. It brings to light how these entrepreneurs have navigated through socio-political turmoil, economic constraints, and the unprecedented challenges of the COVID-19 pandemic. The narratives encompass a diverse array of cultural and geographical landscapes, reflecting the unique experiences and adaptive strategies of women in the entrepreneurial realm. At the heart of these discussions is an exploration of the resilience that women entrepreneurs exhibit in the face of adversity. From adapting business models to shifting market conditions, to tackling gender-specific barriers in traditionally male-dominated environments, these chapters showcase the ingenuity and tenacity of women in business. The resilience theme is prevalent throughout, whether it's dealing with societal expectations, balancing family responsibilities with business ambitions, or innovating in response to crises like the global pandemic.

The chapters in this section also highlight the importance of support systems – both formal and informal – in aiding women entrepreneurs during challenging times. The narratives delve into the impact of cultural norms and societal expectations on women's entrepreneurial journey. They explore how these external factors shape business decisions and strategies, and how women entrepreneurs navigate these influences while maintaining their legitimacy and business viability. This section, therefore, offers a comprehensive overview of the resilience of women entrepreneurs in the face of diverse challenges. It sheds light on their strategies for survival and growth, their ability to pivot and adapt, and the critical role of supportive networks and societal structures in their entrepreneurial journey. The narratives further include the role of professional networks, membership organizations, and micro-financing institutions in providing crucial support. These support mechanisms not only offer practical assistance but also serve as platforms for emotional and psychological backing, which is especially vital in turbulent times. Through these varied narratives, the section paints a vivid picture of the strength, adaptability, and perseverance of women entrepreneurs across the globe.

Chapter 1, 'Surviving the Storm: How Russian Migrant Women Entrepreneurs Demonstrate Agility in Turbulent Times?', authored by Yelena Muzykina, Nurlykhan Aljanova, and Shumaila Yousafzai, explores how migrant Russian women entrepreneurs adapt and innovate, transforming crisis into opportunities within unfamiliar landscapes. Utilizing qualitative research and narrative inquiry, the chapter captures the complex dynamics of their entrepreneurial experiences, emphasizing agility, resilience, and resourcefulness as key components of their success. The study delves into the internal and external drivers that spur the entrepreneurs' adaptability. It reveals how external factors like the COVID-19 pandemic and the Ukraine–Russia conflict necessitated rapid business pivots, expansion of product ranges, and the launch of new ventures. Internally, these women navigated the divide in societal support for the war, influencing their leadership and decision-making. They also embraced their feminine capital, utilizing qualities like empathy and collaboration to navigate the business environment effectively. The narratives of Anna and Olga underscore the importance of agility in improving business performance. Despite the challenges of adapting to new cultures and rebuilding networks, their strategic responses to the crisis led to diversified business offerings and sustained financial health. Their stories illustrate the multifaceted nature of agility, blending political, social, moral, and financial dimensions that extend beyond traditional internal–external dichotomies.

In Chapter 2, 'Italian Women Entrepreneurs During the Covid-19 Pandemic: Striving for a Collective Response through Female Employer and Business Membership Organizations', authors Luisa De Vita and Elisa Errico explore the response of Italian female Employer and Business Membership Organizations (EBMOs) to the challenges posed by the COVID-19 pandemic. It focuses on how these organizations adapted to meet the new needs of women entrepreneurs, providing both technical-instrumental and emotional-psychological support. The chapter utilizes a qualitative methodology, including semi-structured interviews with heads of prominent Italian female EBMOs. During the pandemic, Italian women's EBMOs witnessed a shift in their practices toward increased emotional and psychological support, aligning with previous research emphasizing the value women place on such support in professional networks. These organizations demonstrated sophisticated structures and heterogeneous relationships with various stakeholders, contradicting previous findings suggesting more informal networks. The study highlights that female EBMOs in Italy are part of larger professional organizations, enabling them to influence policymaking effectively. The research revealed that Italian women's EBMOs offered varied support during the pandemic. They provided crucial information on new regulations, business opportunities, and bureaucratic assistance, and lobbied for gendered policy tools to support women entrepreneurs. The associations showed strong cohesion among members, which facilitated tailored responses to their specific needs during the crisis. Interestingly, Italian female EBMOs reported an increase in membership during the pandemic, contrary to the trend of declining memberships observed globally. They adapted their activities, focusing on strengthening personal skills like managing uncertainty and re-conceptualizing traditional in-person activities into online formats due to financial constraints and health regulations. The EBMOs also organized recreational activities to combat isolation and stress among their members. In conclusion, the chapter reveals that Italian female EBMOs were neither structurally weaker nor less effective during the pandemic. They successfully adapted their activities to the changing needs of women entrepreneurs, exerting political pressure for positive gender equality actions. However, the lack of collaboration on joint initiatives among different EBMOs limited their potential political bargaining power. The voluntary nature of membership in these networks suggests a need for exploring other mechanisms to increase participation and reinforce the collective response of women entrepreneurs in Italy.

In Chapter 3, 'Challenges Facing Bangladeshi Female Entrepreneurs in the Brick Lane Area of East London, UK: Turbulent Times from 2019 to 2023', authored by Spinder Dhaliwal and Richard George, explores the unique challenges faced by six Bangladeshi female entrepreneurs in London's Brick Lane area during a period marked by significant economic and social changes from 2019 to 2023, including the COVID-19 pandemic. The study is set against the backdrop of the U.K.'s ethnically diverse business landscape, with a particular focus on the underrepresented segment of Asian women in entrepreneurship. These women's businesses are situated in an environment predominantly dominated by male entrepreneurs, further complicating their entrepreneurial journey. The research highlights the silent yet pivotal role that Asian women have historically played in the U.K.'s business sector. Despite facing cultural and familial constraints, these women have shown resilience in their entrepreneurial endeavors. The literature review points out the unique challenges they face, such as restricted access to resources, societal expectations, and the balancing act between their familial responsibilities and business aspirations. The study uses qualitative interviews to delve into the experiences of these entrepreneurs, examining the influence of cultural and religious factors on their business initiatives, and their strategies to overcome various barriers. Key challenges identified include stereotyping and gender bias, where women entrepreneurs are often not taken seriously within male-dominated fields, leading to struggles in establishing credibility and respect. Balancing family responsibilities with business ambitions is another significant challenge, especially accentuated during the pandemic. Additionally, language barriers and limited business skills, including marketing and financial management, emerged as critical issues affecting their business growth. Financial challenges, particularly access to finance and managing rising operational costs during the pandemic, were also highlighted as significant concerns. This chapter presents a narrative of resilience and innovation, portraying these Bangladeshi female entrepreneurs as determined and adaptable figures who strive to overcome obstacles and emerge stronger from the crisis. The study contributes valuable insights into the realm of ethnic minority women in business, specifically within the U.K. context, and calls for more inclusive and accessible support systems to aid their growth and recognition in the business community. The chapter emphasizes the need for policymakers and business support professionals to understand and address the unique challenges faced by this group, ensuring that resources and support are tailored to meet their specific needs.

Chapter 4, 'Addressing Crises through Entrepreneurial Resilience: Migrant Women Entrepreneurs in the United Arab Emirates', authored by Nadeera Ranabahu and Maryam Fozia, investigates how migrant women entrepreneurs in the UAE cultivate entrepreneurial resilience during various crises. Focusing on the experiences of two migrant women, Anna and Hina, it explores how internal and external crises affect their business operations and shape their resilience strategies. The chapter contributes to the understanding of how migrant women entrepreneurs employ both psychological and organizational resilience in navigating business challenges. Crises, as defined in this study, range from sudden, unexpected events to ongoing challenges that threaten business viability. The case studies of Anna and Hina illustrate how different crises, including geopolitical tensions, economic recession, cybercrime, and the COVID-19 pandemic, lead to diverse resilience strategies. These strategies include pivoting business models, exiting ventures, or finding innovative ways to sustain operations. Anna and Hina's narratives reveal that their psychological resilience was bolstered by personal experiences, self-efficacy, learning and development, beliefs, values, and emotional coping strategies. Organizational resilience strategies employed by both women included identifying new opportunities, pivoting their businesses, and adapting to market changes. These strategies reflect elements of resilience literature, emphasizing the interplay between psychological attributes and organizational tactics. Significantly, the chapter underscores the role of home and host country resource links in shaping entrepreneurial resilience. Anna and Hina leveraged resources from their home countries to navigate the pandemic: Anna considered relocating to the U.S.A. to run her Middle Eastern business, while Hina started a trading business utilizing contacts in her home country. Their perspectives on the host country's business environment also influenced their resilience strategies. The findings of this study provide valuable insights into the resilience strategies of migrant women entrepreneurs and offer a new perspective on how they navigate crises. It suggests that future research could expand on these findings by exploring a larger sample of migrant women entrepreneurs in the UAE and other Gulf countries, examining the resource links between home and host countries, and employing theories like the resource-based view, entrepreneurial ecosystems, or social capital theory to deepen the understanding of entrepreneurial resilience.

The final chapter in this section – Chapter 5, 'Women Home-based Entrepreneurs in Iran: Navigating a Turbulent Era', by Parisa Nakhaei, Nelia Hyndman-Rizk, and Saskia de Klerk, provides a compelling exploration of the resilience of Iranian women entrepreneurs against a backdrop of socio-political tumult and economic constraint. This chapter, through a qualitative comparative case study, delves into the experiences of 25 entrepreneurs in the garment and food industries, uncovering the tripartite barriers they face: contextual, motherhood, and individual. These entrepreneurs are navigating a landscape shaped by the lasting impacts of the Islamic Revolution and intensified by global sanctions, all of which have compounded the challenges within Iran's entrepreneurial ecosystem. The study reveals that these women often find themselves ensnared by legal and bureaucratic frameworks that hinder the transition from informal to formal business operations. Work permit requirements, guardianship laws, and a lack of knowledge about formal procedures present significant impediments, prompting many to maintain their businesses within the informal sector as a strategic countermeasure. Despite widespread gender discrimination and economic barriers at the macro level – ranging from licensing difficulties to market access and financial resource constraints – these women entrepreneurs demonstrate commendable satisfaction with their business achievements. Leveraging personal and informal networks for financial support, they craft alternative pathways to sustain and grow their ventures amidst an evolving economic landscape marked by currency fluctuations, market instability, and social media censorship. The chapter calls for targeted policy reforms to better support the transition of home-based businesses into the formal sector, highlighting the need for a streamlined registration process and enhanced government support. It suggests that acknowledging the economic value of women-led businesses through formal data can help construct a compelling business case for broader support within the entrepreneurial ecosystem. To foster a more inclusive environment, the chapter recommends reevaluating economic, social, and legal systems with an emphasis on women's rights, promoting skill development through workshops, and identifying successful role models to inspire and guide aspiring women entrepreneurs. The chapter not only underscores the importance of understanding the unique context in which Iranian women operate but also points to the broader implications for supporting women's entrepreneurship in similarly turbulent environments worldwide.

PART II: INNOVATION AND ADAPTATION STRATEGIES

This section explores the theme of innovation and adaptation strategies as employed by women entrepreneurs during the COVID-19 pandemic. This unprecedented global crisis brought unique challenges and opportunities to the forefront of the business world, significantly affecting the landscape in which women-led businesses operate. The chapters included in this section provide insightful analyses into how female entrepreneurs navigated these turbulent times, showcasing their resilience, creativity, and capacity to adapt in the face of adversity. One of the central aspects examined in this section is the impact of the pandemic on women-led businesses, particularly focusing on their strategies for survival and growth during this period. The pandemic's challenges were not uniform; they varied significantly based on factors such as geographical location, industry, and access to resources. These studies reveal how women entrepreneurs responded to these challenges with innovative approaches, rethinking their business models, and leveraging new opportunities that arose from the crisis. The chapters highlight the role of digital transformation as a key strategy adopted by women entrepreneurs. The pandemic accelerated the shift to digital platforms, and those businesses already integrated into the digital sphere found it easier to adjust to the changing market conditions. Social media, in particular, emerged as a crucial tool, enabling business communication and marketing to transcend geographical boundaries. This digital pivot not only helped businesses survive the immediate impact of the pandemic but also positioned them for sustained growth in the post-pandemic world. Furthermore, the research underscores the significant financial challenges faced by women entrepreneurs during the pandemic. The varied levels of government support across different regions meant that while some benefited from state aid, others had to rely on personal savings, family loans, or bank loans. This disparity highlights the importance of financial resources and support systems in determining the ability of women-led businesses to adapt and innovate in times of crisis.

Chapter 6, 'How Women-led Businesses Fared in the Covid-19 Pandemic', authored by Rebecca Weitcht, Rosemarie Kay, Markus Rieger-Fels, and Friederike Welter, explores the impact of the COVID-19 crisis on female-led firms in Germany, investigating if these businesses were disproportionately affected and identifying underlying causes. The study focuses on differences in how female- and male-led businesses experienced the pandemic, accounting for potential indirect effects like sector and size. It also considers direct effects, such as unique responses to the crisis and additional private obligations faced by female leaders. The COVID-19 pandemic in Germany led to swift government action, including lockdowns and substantial business support packages. These measures aimed at reducing the virus's spread and supporting businesses through financial assistance and tax relief measures. While initial research suggested that women-led businesses might have been more adversely affected due to their prevalence in hard-hit sectors and smaller size, findings were mixed. The study's findings reveal that initially, both women- and men-led businesses in Germany faced similar challenges during the pandemic. However, towards the end of 2020 and the beginning of 2021, female-led firms experienced greater hardships. This increased difficulty was not entirely due to the businesses' sector or size. Instead, it points to other factors, such as possibly more muted responses to the crisis among women entrepreneurs and a heavier reliance on government support. This suggests that the closure of schools and care facilities might have disproportionately burdened female entrepreneurs, forcing them to juggle increased care responsibilities with their business obligations. The research implies that policy measures should not solely focus on female entrepreneurship but consider sectoral and business size vulnerabilities. Policies should also support the social infrastructure, like affordable childcare, crucial for female entrepreneurs. This approach can prevent the re-traditionalization of society where women bear the brunt of unpaid labor, negatively impacting their businesses.

In Chapter 7, 'The Influence of Covid-19 Related Entrepreneurial Opportunities and Difficulties on Women Entrepreneurs' Business Models', authors Anna Sörensson and Navid Ghannad examine how women entrepreneurs adapted their business models in response to the COVID-19 pandemic. The study, based on interviews with 30 women entrepreneurs across Europe and Asia, reveals that women faced significant financial challenges, necessitating increased reliance on financial resources and risk assessments. The pandemic's impact varied significantly based on geographical location, with European women entrepreneurs benefiting from state support, contrasting with their Asian counterparts who often resorted to family loans or bank loans due to a lack of government aid. The pandemic forced many women entrepreneurs to innovate and adapt their business models. Those who had already embraced digital solutions found it easier to adjust, highlighting the importance of digital integration in modern business. Social media emerged as a critical tool, facilitating business communication and marketing across geographical boundaries. The study emphasizes the economic struggles women entrepreneurs faced, particularly in Asia, where government support was lacking. The pandemic highlighted the differences in opportunities and challenges based on geographical location, industry, and access to financial and digital resources. Women entrepreneurs demonstrated adaptability by shifting to digital platforms and reconfiguring their business models to meet changing market demands. Future research directions include exploring the long-term effects of the pandemic on women entrepreneurs' business performance and the role of financial resources in their ability to adapt and innovate. The study also suggests examining the impact of digital channel utilization on pandemic response and post-pandemic growth, as well as understanding the specific challenges and opportunities faced by women entrepreneurs in different industries.

PART III: SOCIETAL IMPACT AND GLOBAL CONTEXTS

Part III delves into the complex interplay between societal forces and the unique challenges and responses of women entrepreneurs in diverse global contexts. This section comprises insightful chapters that collectively highlight the critical role of women in stabilizing and transforming economies during periods of significant turmoil, such as financial crises, economic restructuring, and the COVID-19 pandemic. These narratives underscore the resilience and adaptability of women entrepreneurs, who often find themselves navigating a landscape shaped by gender biases, societal expectations, and institutional hurdles. A recurrent theme across these chapters is the concept of legitimacy and the strategic behaviors women entrepreneurs adopt to gain and maintain it, particularly in environments with traditional gender roles. The chapters explore how societal perceptions and expectations influence women's entrepreneurial identities and decision-making processes. They discuss how women entrepreneurs, especially in contexts with deeply entrenched gender norms, often conform to societal rules and expectations to secure their business legitimacy and ensure access to crucial resources.

Another critical aspect examined is the role of women as 'shock absorbers' in economies facing crises. Women entrepreneurs have historically stepped up during economic downturns, contributing significantly to economic recovery and stability. The chapters highlight how women have been instrumental in sectors hit hardest by crises, such as hospitality and retail during the COVID-19 pandemic. However, this instrumentalization often comes with the dual expectation of managing both entrepreneurial and family responsibilities, a challenge exacerbated by gender-biased macroeconomic policies. In addition to these themes, the chapters in this section also explore the significant shifts in business models that women entrepreneurs had to implement during the COVID-19 pandemic. These shifts reflect the entrepreneurs' ability to pivot and adapt their strategies in response to changing market demands and the challenges posed by the pandemic. The role of digital transformation, varying regional support systems, and the financial and logistical hurdles faced by women entrepreneurs are also discussed in detail.

In Chapter 8, 'Legitimacy of Women Entrepreneurs: Forced to Behave According to Rules?', authors Susanne Schlepphorst, Siegrun Brink, and

Friederike Welter explore the strategic behavior of women entrepreneurs in gaining and maintaining legitimacy, particularly in contexts with traditional gender roles. Legitimacy, defined as stakeholders' approval of entrepreneurs as competent and trustworthy, is crucial for businesses to access necessary resources. The chapter highlights the importance of legitimacy in both turbulent and tranquil times, with examples like the AIDS epidemic's impact on pharmaceutical companies and the attention to sustainability during the climate crisis. The study focuses on Germany, a context with a traditional male breadwinner model, influencing women's career choices and entrepreneurial behavior. It investigates whether gender influences entrepreneurial behavior in attaining legitimacy, particularly in dealing with bureaucratic requirements. The research suggests that while women entrepreneurs in Germany generally adhere to rules similar to men, they are less likely to engage in rule-circumventing behaviors. This compliance is seen as a low-effort strategy that aligns with cultural gender roles, implying that women entrepreneurs are more cautious in maintaining legitimacy once achieved. During crises like the COVID-19 pandemic, maintaining legitimacy is more challenging, requiring strategic behavior adaptation. The pandemic highlighted a regression in gender equality and a revival of traditional roles, impacting women entrepreneurs who juggled multiple roles. In such scenarios, legitimacy can guide women entrepreneurs in decision-making, especially when time is limited. The chapter suggests areas for future research, including exploring these dynamics in different cultural contexts and focusing on young companies' legitimacy strategies, especially during turbulent times. It emphasizes the need to understand how women entrepreneurs in different environments maintain legitimacy, considering their potential self-reinforcing professional behavior within women-dominated entrepreneurial environments.

Chapter 9, 'Women as Shock Absorbers in Turbulent Times' by Bettina Lynda Bastian, Melissa Langworthy, and Bronwyn P. Wood, highlights the significant role women entrepreneurs have played in stabilizing economies during periods of financial crises, economic restructuring, and the COVID-19 pandemic. Women have often been mobilized towards entrepreneurship as a strategy to diversify economies and relieve economic pressures. Throughout history, women have acted as a 'reserve army' of labor, supplementing the workforce during economic downturns and crises. For instance, during the 1997 Asian financial crisis and the 2008 global financial crisis, women's unpaid labor was crucial in absorbing risks and aiding economic recovery. The COVID-19 pandemic further emphasized this role, as women were disproportionately affected due to their dominant presence in severely hit sectors like hospitality and retail. Despite these challenges, female entrepreneurs have been seen as key to driving post-pandemic economic recovery. In times of economic restructuring, such as the transition of Eastern Bloc countries to liberal economies or the economic diversification in the Middle East, women entrepreneurs have played a vital role. They have created value by employing more women, innovating, and contributing to community well-being. Policies in these contexts often aim to encourage the formation of new businesses, especially by women, as a means of economic growth and private sector development. However, this instrumentalization of women comes with the expectation of their continual contribution to socially reproductive labor, maintaining family and community well-being alongside their entrepreneurial activities. This dual expectation is often reinforced by macroeconomic policies with gender biases, such as the 'male breadwinner bias'. The chapter calls for more research into the costs and patterns of women's work lives, particularly entrepreneurs, and how better support can be provided. Policy changes that could ease the burdens on women include publicly funded quality childcare, redistribution of care responsibilities, adequate social protection, and tax policies that do not reinforce gender biases. Such changes would significantly improve the working lives of women, especially those who are entrepreneurs, and help them manage their businesses more effectively during periods of economic turbulence and crisis.

Finally, in Chapter 10, 'Pivoting and Positionality: Entrepreneurship, Care and the COVID-19 Pandemic in Czechia and the U.S.A.', authors Alena Křížková, Nancy C. Jurik, Marie Pospíšilová, Gray Cavender, and Dongling Zhang examine the seismic shifts in business models that women entrepreneurs were compelled to make during the COVID-19 pandemic. This study, underpinned by 30 qualitative interviews across Europe and Asia, probes the differential impact of the pandemic on women's businesses, given their pre-existing vulnerabilities in entrepreneurial ecosystems that favor men. With diverse experiences and responses, these entrepreneurs faced significant financial challenges, with sales in certain sectors plummeting drastically. Despite this, women entrepreneurs showcased remarkable resilience, with many leveraging digital platforms to maintain customer relationships and market their products. A notable trend was the shift to social media, which proved to be a cost-effective communication channel, essential during times of limited financial resources. The pandemic catalyzed innovation and necessitated rapid adaptation of business models, with changes such as the adoption of home delivery services and the pivot to online sales channels. The study found that financial support during the pandemic varied by region, with Asian entrepreneurs lacking state support, contrasting with their European counterparts who had access to various forms of state aid. Entrepreneurs in Asia relied more on personal loans from banks or family and friends, highlighting regional disparities in support systems. For future research, the long-term impacts of the pandemic on women entrepreneurs' business performance and growth are of particular interest. There is also a need to explore how access to financial resources during the pandemic influenced their adaptability and innovation. The extent to which digital channel utilization played a role in their response to the pandemic and post-pandemic growth is another area ripe for investigation. Furthermore, examining how industry-specific challenges shaped business model adaptations during the pandemic offers another valuable research angle.

MOVING FORWARD

As we reflect on the collective insights from the chapters in this book, it becomes evident that the journey of women entrepreneurs through turbulent times is both complex and dynamic. Their experiences, challenges, and innovative responses pave the way for multifaceted implications and rich avenues for future research.

The narratives of resilience and adaptability among women entrepreneurs underline the need for robust support systems. These systems should encompass not only financial assistance but also extend to mentorship, networking opportunities, and specialized training programs. Such initiatives must be tailored to address the unique barriers that women face in business, particularly in male-dominated sectors.

Addressing societal norms and gender biases that often constrain the potential of women entrepreneurs is crucial. This requires concerted efforts in education and awareness campaigns aimed at reshaping societal attitudes and perceptions towards women in business. Such initiatives should seek to empower women entrepreneurs, providing them with the tools and confidence to thrive in their ventures.

The pivot to digital platforms, as highlighted during the COVID-19 pandemic, emphasizes the critical role of digital literacy and access for women entrepreneurs. Policies and programmes that facilitate their participation in the digital economy can play a significant role in ensuring their businesses' sustainability and growth.

Furthermore, the dual role of women as business owners and caregivers cannot be overlooked. Policies that provide affordable childcare and robust family support systems are essential. These measures would enable women entrepreneurs to balance their business and family responsibilities more effectively, thus enhancing their productivity and business success.

The post-pandemic recovery phase presents an opportunity for longitudinal studies to understand the long-term impact on women-owned businesses. Such research can shed light on the sustainability and effectiveness of the strategies employed during the pandemic. Cross-cultural comparisons of women entrepreneurs' experiences can provide a broader perspective on the global challenges and opportunities they face. This approach can help identify universal barriers and best practices that can be applied across different cultural and regional contexts.

Exploring the impact of digital transformation on women entrepreneurs is another crucial area. Understanding how women leverage technology for business growth and the challenges they face in this digital journey can inform strategies to enhance their participation in the digital economy. Evaluating the effectiveness of policies and interventions aimed at supporting women entrepreneurs can provide valuable feedback for policymakers. This research can help fine-tune existing policies and develop new strategies that are more responsive to the needs of women entrepreneurs.

Understanding how gender dynamics influence entrepreneurial practices, decision-making, and strategies is essential. Such studies could contribute to a deeper understanding of the nuances of gendered entrepreneurship. Investigating how women entrepreneurs navigate and leverage entrepreneurial ecosystems and networks can reveal the enablers and barriers within these systems. This knowledge is crucial for developing targeted support mechanisms within these ecosystems. Sector-specific challenges and opportunities, especially in areas where women are either prominent or underrepresented, deserve attention. Research in these sectors can reveal unique insights into the specific hurdles and prospects for women entrepreneurs. Finally, the impact of entrepreneurship on women's mental health and well-being, particularly in turbulent times, is an area that warrants attention. Understanding these aspects can inform strategies to support the holistic well-being of women entrepreneurs.

In conclusion, the journey ahead for supporting and empowering women entrepreneurs is multifaceted, requiring a combination of policy changes, societal shifts, and ongoing research. The insights from this book lay a strong foundation for future initiatives, aiming to create a more inclusive and supportive environment for women entrepreneurs worldwide.

CLOSING REMARKS

As we bring this book to a close, our gratitude goes first and foremost to all the authors who contributed their manuscripts. Their eagerness to share their insights, research findings, and diverse perspectives has been the cornerstone of this project. Their contributions are not just academic submissions; they represent a genuine desire to advance the understanding of women's entrepreneurship and its myriad challenges and triumphs. The willingness of these authors to open their work to scrutiny and discussion by their peers is a testament to the collaborative spirit that drives academic excellence and innovation. Our heartfelt thanks also extend to the reviewers, whose meticulous and thoughtful evaluations have significantly enriched the quality of this book. Their independent and critical assessments have ensured that the content not only meets high academic standards but also provides meaningful and impactful insights.

We would also like to express our deepest appreciation to Edward Elgar and their dedicated team. Their support and guidance have been invaluable throughout the journey of bringing this collection to fruition. Their professionalism and commitment have greatly facilitated the process, making it a seamless and rewarding experience.

We hope that this collection of chapters, encompassing a wide range of themes and perspectives, serves as a catalyst for further discussion and exploration in the field of women's entrepreneurship. The contextual richness and diverse experiences presented in this book aim to bridge existing knowledge gaps and inspire continued research and action. This book is more than just an academic compilation; it is a conversation starter and a call to action. We hope it resonates with readers, researchers, policymakers, and practitioners alike, encouraging them to delve deeper into the multifaceted world of women entrepreneurs and contribute to shaping a more inclusive and equitable entrepreneurial landscape.

In closing, we express our sincere hope that this book not only informs but also inspires. May it be a valuable resource for those committed to understanding and supporting the unique journeys of women entrepreneurs across different contexts and challenges.

REFERENCES

Ahl, H. (2006). Why research on women entrepreneurs needs new directions. *Entrepreneurship Theory and Practice*, *30*(5), 595–621.

Ahl, H., & Marlow, S. (2021). Exploring the false promise of entrepreneurship through a postfeminist critique of the enterprise policy discourse in Sweden and the UK. *Human Relations*, *74*(1), 41–68.

Afshan, G., Shahid, S., & Tunio, M. N. (2021). Learning experiences of women entrepreneurs amidst COVID-19. *International Journal of Gender and Entrepreneurship*, *13*(2), 162–186.

Althalathini, D., Al-Dajani, H., & Apostolopoulos, N. (2020). Navigating Gaza's conflict through women's entrepreneurship. *International Journal of Gender and Entrepreneurship*, *12*(4), 297–316.

Arvin, M., Tuck, E., & Morrill, A. (2020). Decolonizing feminism: Challenging connections between settler colonialism and heteropatriarchy. In Carole McCann, Seung-kyung Kim, & Emek Ergun (Eds.), *Feminist Theory Reader* (pp. 169–180). Routledge.

GEM (2017). Global Entrepreneurship Monitor, Women's entrepreneurship 2016/17 report. Available at https://www.gemconsortium.org/report/gem-20162017-womens-entrepreneurship-report.

Heizmann, H., & Liu, H. (2022). "Bloody Wonder Woman!": Identity performances of elite women entrepreneurs on Instagram. *Human Relations*, *75*(3), 411–440.

Manolova, T. S., Brush, C. G., Edelman, L. F., & Elam, A. (2020). Pivoting to stay the course: How women entrepreneurs take advantage of opportunities created by the COVID-19 pandemic. *International Small Business Journal, 38*(6), 481–491.

Marlow, S. (2020). Gender and entrepreneurship: Past achievements and future possibilities. *International Journal of Gender and Entrepreneurship, 12*(1), 39–52.

Mustafa, F., Khursheed, A., Fatima, M., & Rao, M. (2021). Exploring the impact of COVID-19 pandemic on women entrepreneurs in Pakistan. *International Journal of Gender and Entrepreneurship, 13*(2), 187–203.

Mustafa, M., & Treanor, L. (2022). Gender and entrepreneurship in the New Era: New perspectives on the role of gender and entrepreneurial activity. *Entrepreneurship Research Journal, 12*(3), 213–226.

Roesch, P. T., Velonis, A. J., Sant, S. M., Habermann, L. E., & Hirschtick, J. L. (2021). Implications of interpersonal violence on population mental health status in a low-income urban community-based sample of adults. *Journal of Interpersonal Violence, 36*(19–20), 8891–8914.

Swail, J., & Marlow, S. (2018). 'Embrace the masculine; attenuate the feminine': Gender, identity work and entrepreneurial legitimation in the nascent context. *Entrepreneurship & Regional Development, 30*(1–2), 256–282.

Tlaiss, H. A. & Kauser, S. (2019). Entrepreneurial leadership, patriarchy, gender, and identity in the Arab world: Lebanon in focus. *Journal of Small Business Management, 57*(2), 517–537.

PART I

Challenges and resilience in entrepreneurship

1. Surviving the storm: how Russian migrant women entrepreneurs demonstrate agility in turbulent times

Yelena Muzykina, Nurlykhan Aljanova and Shumaila Yousafzai

1. INTRODUCTION

Entrepreneurship is a challenging activity that requires specific skills to ensure the survival and growth of a business. This challenge has grown exponentially as humanity has entered into a period of what is known as the 'permacrisis.' Permacrisis is an extended period of instability and insecurity that poses financial and reputational threats to an organization's operations (Coombs, 2007; Shariatmadari, 2022). The risk of loss that stakeholders can tolerate, whether physically, emotionally, or financially, is also increasing, leaving entrepreneurs to face perpetual uncertainty and instability. Uncertainty is often undervalued within various cognitive, scientific, and organizational paradigms, as people have a natural desire to control their environment. Researchers have suggested that a sense of control, whether real or illusory, is essential for maintaining mental health (Taylor & Brown, 1988). However, it is becoming increasingly difficult to control unknown situations in current times.

As stated by Sardar (2010, p. 435), the *espiritu del tiempo* or spirit of our age, is marked by 'uncertainty, rapid change, power realignments, upheavals, and chaotic behaviour.' This spirit is a breath of our 'in-between time,' 'where old orthodoxies are dying, new ones have yet to be born, and very few things seem to make sense' (Sardar, 2010, p. 435). This time is called 'postnormal' (Sardar, 2010) and easily generates such a concept as 'permacrisis' characterized by diverse nature: intentional or unintentional, internal or external, violent or non-violent, technical or economic, social, political or organizational. In postnormal times characterized by complexity, contradictions, and chaos – also known as 3Cs (Sardar, 2019, p. 7) – crises can arise due to various factors of different scales, from a mere rumor, an accident, or a local scandal, to war, social unrest, political upheaval, economic recession, or technological turbulence (Coombs, 1995, 2007; Doern et al., 2019; Mitroff et al., 1988). Nevertheless, despite the prevailing negative attitude toward crises, it is important to recognize that 'every crisis is also an opportunity' (Harari, 2020) and can greatly shape and reshape business performance, agility, adaptability, and resourcefulness (Bodlaj & Čater, 2019; Liu & Yang, 2019). The COVID-19 pandemic serves as a recent example of how some entrepreneurs successfully adapted to rapidly changing circumstances by exploring online options, adjusting marketing strategies and target audiences, and capitalizing on emerging opportunities (Khurana et al., 2022). However, entrepreneurs were also confronted with internal challenges during and after the pandemic. Both internal and external crises have proven to be complex and multifaceted in postnormal times, and therefore, solutions and answers need to be equally multifaceted.

Entrepreneurs operating in the context of postnormality face uncertainty and unpredictability, and their ability to react correctly, effectively, and efficiently is referred to as organizational agility (Ashrafi et al., 2019). Different groups of entrepreneurs navigate these challenges in different ways. The concept of agility has been defined in various ways. Still, one of the most comprehensive definitions is by De Smet and Aghina (2015), who defined it as 'the ability of an organization to renew itself, adapt, change quickly, and succeed in a rapidly changing, ambiguous, turbulent environment.' Understanding how different groups of entrepreneurs demonstrate their agility is crucial for shaping the development of theory, policy, and practice.

This chapter focuses on a situation that clearly has a postnormal nature and was caused by a postnormal event, addressing our key research question: How have Russian migrant women entrepreneurs exhibited adaptability and resilience in navigating their businesses during times of postnormal crises? We examine the challenges faced by two women entrepreneurs who had to leave Russia and start businesses in new and unfamiliar environments amidst the permacrisis. By exploring the experiences of these entrepreneurs, we hope to gain insights into the strategies and skills necessary for navigating uncertain and volatile business environments.

The research sheds light on migrant Russian women entrepreneurs who have not been previously examined and whose difficult situation arose as a result of the recent Ukraine–Russia conflict outbreak in February 2022. The chapter contributes to the understanding of migrant women entrepreneurs' response to crises in two ways: first, it explores how the war has impacted the business environment in which women entrepreneurs operate, and second, it investigates how these entrepreneurs exhibit agility in the face of postnormal conditions, characterized by complexity and contradictions, to overcome challenges and seize opportunities during times of crisis.

The next sections of the chapter provide context, detail the methodology, and present case narratives of two women entrepreneurs who relocated their businesses outside of Russia. The study concludes with a discussion of the findings.

2. LITERATURE REVIEW

2.1 Agility and Entrepreneurship

The concept of agility in the context of business was first mentioned in 1982 by Brown and Agnew (1982, p. 29). They defined it as the ability of an organization to respond quickly to rapidly changing circumstances. Since then, the understanding of agility has evolved to encompass a set of capabilities to thrive and prosper in an unpredictable and fast-changing environment (Vinodh et al., 2012).

Today, agility is widely recognized as crucial for business survival in an unpredictable environment. Studies have indicated that organizations with strong agility capabilities tend to generate revenues 37 percent faster and have profits that are 30 percent higher compared to those of non-agile organizations (Glenn, 2009; Wang et al., 2014). Thus, it is clear that agility is a desirable trait and a crucial factor in determining a business's success in times of uncertainty because companies and entrepreneurs face more dynamic customer demands (Vinodh et al., 2010b) and a higher frequency of environmental changes (Ahlbäck et al., 2017), which lead to increased complexity and uncertainty in the market (Vinodh et al., 2010a). In order to achieve strong competitiveness and successful business performance, it is crucial to demonstrate solid agility. Hatzijordanou et al. (2019) recognize agility as a rewarding capability for the quick exploitation of business opportunities, while Meinhardt et al. (2018) suggest agility as a differentiation strategy in the context of an increasingly dynamic business environment.

The importance of agility in times of crisis and uncertainty has been widely recognized by managers across various industries, who consider it a vital component for success and a determinant of a company's competitive level in today's rapidly changing business environment (De Smet & Aghina, 2015; Inman et al., 2011; Vickery et al., 2010). Multiple surveys have demonstrated the effectiveness of agility in enhancing business performance, with 81 percent of participants in a recent study reporting an increase in performance after implementing agile practices in their company (Ahlbäck et al., 2017). Agility is particularly crucial for small and medium-sized enterprises (SMEs), but these organizations often face barriers to change due to rigid structures and limited resources (Bessant et al., 2000). New start-ups, on the other hand, are more adept at developing agility due to their flexibility and adaptability (Teece et al., 2016).

In her work, Anna-Theresa Walter (2021, pp. 354–357) identifies four categories essential to understanding the concept of organizational agility. The first category, called 'agility drivers,' refers to the environmental changes that push organizations into a new and vulnerable position, forcing them to search for competitive advantages. This core area includes statements and information identified as driving forces. The second category, 'agility capabilities,' refers to the specific abilities that organizations need to possess to react to changes effectively. It includes responsiveness, competency, flexibility, and speed. In other words, agility capabilities represent the company's 'fitness' to handle changes and uncertainties. The third category, 'agility enablers,' refers to the methods, tools, practices, and crucial technologies that facilitate organizational agility. These are utilized as leverage at multiple organizational levels and enable the realization of agility capabilities. Finally, the fourth category, 'agility dimensions,' refers to the various dimensions of the organization that must be agile to achieve organizational agility at a higher level. This category provides a structure for understanding which dimensions of the organization must be agile to achieve overall agility. In this chapter, our main focus is on the drivers of agility.

2.2   External and Internal Drivers of Agility

When examining the literature on agility, it becomes apparent that, prior to 2001, external agility drivers were scholars' sole focus, with an emphasis on customer-driven agility drivers. The majority of studies only considered agility drivers within the external environment. These external changes were characterized by their unpredictability and continuous occurrence, leading to a highly competitive environment with high frequency. Examples of external agility drivers included market and technology changes and globalization.

However, this focus started to shift gradually. Researchers such as Sharifi and Zhang (2001) and Bessant et al. (2001) began to include internal factors in their research, recognizing that a firm's competitive advantage in a high-velocity environment could be threatened both internally and externally. Internal agility drivers were added to the list of external drivers, including changes to the marketplace, competition, customer requirements, technology, social factors, suppliers, and internal complexity. Table 1.1, based on Anna-Theresa Walter's (2021) comprehensive review of 75 studies published between 1994 and 2018, summarizes the various agility drivers.

However, the literature rarely discussed the combination of external and internal drivers and their interconnectedness. This research gap is addressed in this chapter, which examines how both types of drivers influence the business operations of women entrepreneurs in specific critical situations.

Table 1.1   Internal and external drivers of agility

External drivers	Internal drivers
Market changes	Changes in production variables
Quicker delivery time	Workforce/workplace expectations
Increased speed of innovations	Continuous improvement strategy
Customer needs changes	Social factors
Environmental pressures	Internal complexity
Business network changes	Strategy facilitating M&A
Technology changes and innovations	New performance measurement system
Legal/political pressures and changes	Competitive strategy
Stricter financial regulations	Organizational structure
Broader product ranges	Management style
Social contract changes	Internal process changes
Intense rivalry	
Shorter product life cycle	
Outsourcing and dependence on suppliers	
Lower costs/prices	
Globalization	
IT advancements	
Individualized products and customization	
Higher quality demands	
Increased need for IT/IS safety measures	
Shorter time-to-market	

Source: Author, based on Walter (2021).

2.3   The Context: Postnormal Times and the Ukraine–Russia War

Postnormal times

In 2010, the theory of postnormal times gained public attention with the pub-lication of 'Welcome to Postnormal Times' (PNT), Ziauddin Sardar's seminal paper. Sardar proposed a new theoretical framework to better understand how change is evolving in the present day. PNT is defined as 'an in-between period where old orthodoxies are dying, new ones have yet to be born, and very few things seem to make sense' (Sardar, 2010, p. 435). Similarly, Italian journalist Ezio Mauro expressed this idea in his conversation with the late British sociol-ogist Zygmunt Bauman, stating, 'We are hanging between the "no longer" and the "not yet," and thus we are necessarily unstable' (Bauman & Mauro, 2016, p. 20). This state of transition is closely linked to the rapid pace of change that characterizes contemporary times and our ability to communicate with millions of people instantaneously through social media.

Furthermore, our world is now a globalized and highly interconnected system, thanks to modern technologies and innovations. Countless actions, interactions, and interconnections take place at every level, from local to global, every second of our lives. This generates a type of change that is unprecedented and unique, which we refer to as postnormal change. Jones et al. (2021) define the dynamics that generate postnormal change as the 4S: 'The acceleration of change is a result of the combined force of the *speed* at which change occurs, the global *scope* of this change, the fact that it can *scale* down to individual levels and scale up, and these aspects of change occur with increasing *simultaneity*' (Jones et al., 2021, p. 72).

Attributing to the 4S, the ongoing conflict on the Ukrainian frontier possesses all the characteristics of a postnormal phenomenon, unlike past wars in Syria or Afghanistan. The *speed* at which the conflict escalated was remarkable. Putin threatened nuclear retaliation a mere week after the invasion of Ukraine, in stark contrast to the slow-motion Chechen War of the early 1990s. Furthermore, the death toll in the initial weeks surpassed that of any previous conflicts. The *scope* of the conflict was unprecedented, with cascading effects felt across the globe. The Russian populace felt lost as the war waged on, while the invasion strengthened Ukrainian nationalism. The EU and U.S.A. imposed sanctions on Russia, which they had failed to achieve through decades of discussions on green economics and low carbon emissions. This led to a sense of urgency to create an energy system that relied on renewable sources. The *scale* of the conflict was also remarkable, with global economic impacts that were not seen in previous wars. The fragility of the global economy was exposed, leading to fear and uncertainty for the future. The grain shortage during the conflict caused the Arab Spring in 2011, which had a similar impact on the global food market. Finally, the *simultaneity* of the conflict is ongoing, affecting billions of lives. The Ukrainians are rebuilding their liberated cities, while Russians are still fleeing to neighboring countries. International brands have abandoned the Russian market, paving the way for local substitutes. The EU and U.S.A. continue to increase weapon supplies to Ukraine and impose sanctions on Russia, all the while grappling with internal economic and political turmoil. These simultaneous events push and pull against each other, adding to the complexity and contradictions of the postnormal phenomenon.

The theory of postnormal times also encompasses a critical set of characteristics known as the 3Cs: complexity, contradictions, and chaos. These 3Cs arise from an interconnected and globalized world, where numerous interacting elements with non-linear relationships and multiple scales result in a host of legitimate and illegitimate perspectives. PNT can be described as a system, meaning an integrated whole with interdependent, interacting components and relationships, where emergence is a critical characteristic. In other words, PNT cannot be analyzed in terms of its parts but can only be understood in its complete form. Its interacting components are self-organized and produce new patterns and structures. *Complexity* and *contradictions* generate positive feedback loops leading to *chaos*. Thus, when the 3Cs come together, a postnormal phenomenon emerges.

The ongoing war in Ukraine, referred to as a 'special military operation' by Russia, is a complex, contradictory, and chaotic phenomenon, leading to a postnormal situation. The greater the influence of the 3Cs, the higher the level of uncertainty that affects all aspects of social life. The global economy is struggling with the effects of the war, and countries worldwide are attempting to combat inflation caused by rising costs of finance, energy, and food, leading some countries to the brink of bankruptcy. Politically, Ukrainians and Russians are grappling with the chaos and complexity of decision-making. At the same time, the war's outcome will determine the West's self-belief and stature and its ability to maintain unity in the face of external threats. It will also test the West's industrial capacity as it struggles to produce enough weaponry and ammunition to help Ukraine defend itself.

From a social standpoint, as Russian tanks rolled into Ukraine, Russians were forced to make a moral decision: continue as usual or oppose Putin's 'special military operation.' Speaking out against the government in Russia was almost impossible, and even minor acts of rebellion can have catastrophic consequences. Some people chose to leave the country as a form of defiance. However, the trickle of people leaving quickly turned into a massive wave, sweeping through neighboring Central Asia. In September 2022, Putin ordered a partial mobilization of the Russian military, and ordinary men were conscripted to join the war, tearing families apart. The mood and situation in Russia shifted dramatically as the war became a reality for many. There was a violent surge of anger, conscription offices were set on fire, and crowds took to the streets for the first time in months. Many men fled to avoid being cannon fodder, leaving their families behind. Over three-quarters of a million people left after a month of mobilization, and those who left were typically people with the resources, skills, and agency to do so. Often, husbands and sons left, tearing their families apart to save themselves. Amidst this crisis, some women also chose to leave everything behind to save at least something, including the two entrepreneurs on whom this chapter focuses – Anna and Olga (pseudonyms).

The impact of war conditions on entrepreneurs: experiences, behaviors, and resilience
The impact of war on entrepreneurs and their experience and behavior is a complex and critical area of study that examines how armed conflicts and the resulting adversities shape the entrepreneurial landscape. Research in the field of entrepreneurship primarily concentrates on the consequences of war for business activities, strategies, and mentalities. It also sheds light on the challenges that entrepreneurs face and the strategies they use to navigate such tumultuous environments.

As crises have far-reaching implications, conflicts disrupt supply chains, hinder market access, and impede business operations, thus curtailing entrepreneurial endeavours (Lee et al., 2023) and forcing them to adapt and innovate to ensure business continuity. For instance, during the ongoing COVID-19 pandemic, entrepreneurs worldwide have been compelled to reconsider their business models to meet changing demands and capitalize on new opportunities, such as digital communication tools (Lee et al., 2023).

Entrepreneurs operating in conflict zones experience distinct psychological and behavioral shifts for uncertainty and risk are integral parts of war circumstances and accompany decision-making processes, causing entrepreneurs to use adaptive behaviors to survive and thrive. Studies reveal that entrepreneurs in conflict zones often display a higher level of agility and flexibility, as exemplified by Ukrainian entrepreneurs who continue to operate and contribute to societal recovery despite the ongoing Russia–Ukraine conflict (Audretsch et al., 2023). These features are vital for entrepreneurs to overcome conflict-induced disruptions.

Moreover, the background and experiences of entrepreneurs play a significant role in shaping their responses to war conditions. Previous life experience, childhood baggage, and personal narratives influence how entrepreneurs approach adversity and develop coping strategies. Some findings suggest that an entrepreneur's background can affect their internalized patterns and behaviors, leading to variations in their strategies and preferences (Ghannad & Andersson, 2012). Kwong et al. (2019) explored the experiences of displaced entrepreneurs during times of war and conflict, focusing on their responses to adversity while either setting up new businesses or continuing their existing entrepreneurial endeavours. The authors argued that while local knowledge, networks, and resources are crucial for developing ventures in these contexts, alienation from mainstream society within the original location often means finding alternative strategies and approaches for displaced entrepreneurs. Kwong et al. also suggested that bricolage – the application of broad sets of rudimentary skills and craft knowledge – can be a valuable tool for entrepreneurs in war and conflict contexts. Bricolage can help them create new products and services despite limited resources.

In conclusion, the literature on the impact of war conditions on entrepreneurs, their experiences and behaviors, highlight the multifaceted nature of these relations. War-induced disruptions create barriers to entrepreneurial activities, necessitating adaptation and innovation. Entrepreneurs' agility, flexibility, and experience are crucial in shaping their responses to conflict-caused challenges. Understanding these dynamics is essential for policymakers, academics, and practitioners seeking to support entrepreneurs and promote economic recovery in conflict-ridden regions.

3.   METHODOLOGY

3.1   The Interview Protocol

Our research question asks: How do migrant women entrepreneurs demonstrate agility in adjusting and navigating their businesses during postnormal crises? To answer this question, we utilized a constructivist epistemology and a qualitative research method, specifically narrative inquiry techniques through interviews. For our study, we chose to analyze two interviews of migrant women entrepreneurs who left Russia to start businesses in different countries. These two women were among the first wave of migrants who streamed to Kazakhstan after the Ukraine–Russia war started and re-launched their business life there. They agreed to give interviews and provide details for the purposes of the study detailed in this chapter.

Anna's and Olga's cases are similar and complement each other, providing a comprehensive understanding of the drivers of agility that influence their decisions. One of the authors of this chapter acted as the primary interviewer, contacting both entrepreneurs, providing them with study information, obtaining their consent, and conducting the interviews.

During the interviews, open-ended questions were asked to gain insights into their backgrounds, businesses, and entrepreneurial experiences, specifically regarding how their lives and businesses were impacted by the postnormal crisis that began in February 2022. Participants shared their feelings and complex dilemmas, highlighting changes in their perception of reality, personal and entrepreneurial self-efficacy, and business performance. The follow-up questions delved deeper into their uncertainty and decision-making processes. Thus, the narratives provide personal accounts of their private and business lives, with the interviewer using a semi-structured interview guide to direct the process and allow the dialogue to flow naturally.

The interviews were conducted in Russian, lasting between 45 and 90 minutes, and were subject to formal ethical review. Participants were briefed on the study's objectives, and assured of their anonymity, confidentiality, and right to withdraw from the project at any time. All participants signed a consent form, and the interviews were recorded with their consent, with word-for-word scripts developed from the recordings.

3.2   Data Analysis

The data in our research comprises the first-hand accounts of the participants who shared their life experiences and entrepreneurial journeys with us. An internal bilingual researcher transcribed and translated the interviews into

English to facilitate analysis. As we reviewed the transcripts, we discovered that the participants frequently used keywords related to complexity, chaos, and contradictions, which are hallmarks of postnormal times. Our analysis delved into each woman's crises and identified the external and internal factors that motivated their agility. By doing so, our research contributes to the understanding of the complex and contradictory nature of the challenges faced by women entrepreneurs. It highlights the importance of internal and external agility drivers. We link our findings with existing literature, discuss the implications, and outline our contributions.

4.   FINDINGS

4.1   Anna's Narrative

The happy years
Upon graduating, Anna and her classmate Dina decided to take a bold step – they wanted to create a foreign language school. They noticed a great demand for English language teachers and believed they could fill this gap. They began by opening an educational recruitment agency, without physical premises, to connect teachers and students. However, they soon understood they needed a venue for teachers and students to interact. Therefore, in 2010, they opened the first training center, aided by a language club, to encourage interaction and English practice. As word spread, students' numbers gradually increased. Finally, after two years, they welcomed a new business partner, Maria, who suggested teaching other foreign languages such as German, Italian, French, and Spanish. At first, Maria thought her partnership with Anna and Dina would be easy. But, as complexities piled up, she eventually left the school. Despite this setback, Anna and Dina continued to pursue their dream of providing quality language education to their students. They remain dedicated to their work, innovating and adapting to novel circumstances, always aiming to meet the needs of their students, launching the discussion club, introducing kid's English courses, and starting new training programs.

> Thanks to Maria's involvement, she blessed us with the gift of five languages instead of just one. It was a time when we all were carefree and childless and thought of the enterprise as an integral part of our life. But in 2014, after the birth of our kids, we had an epiphany and realized that what we were doing was more than just a hobby. It was a serious business that required professional skills and dedication. The realization hit us like a thunderstorm. But we knew we had to take a leap and transform our venture into a thriving enterprise. It was a daunting challenge, but we did it with perseverance and a lot of hard work.

This new vision caused Anna to get enrolled in an Executive MBA program. There, she learned about a new world of successful entrepreneurs expanding her business outlook beyond a visible horizon. The experience gave her confidence that 'everything is possible.' Encouraged by this newfound confidence, Anna began to take charge of the business procedures and established a strong and sustainable team. Under her leadership, the training center expanded to three locations, and the staff grew. That success proved the validity of the knowledge Anna received in the Executive MBA program.

> Looking back, I feel nostalgia. The memories flow in, and I can't help but feel a sense of longing for those days. The days when everything was perfect and happiness seemed to be the only emotion we knew. Our business was thriving, and each day brought new opportunities and growth. It appeared there were no limits to what we could achieve then. There were no setbacks, obstacles, or turbulence to restrain our progress. Looking back, I realize how fortunate we were to live through that time when everything seemed to fall perfectly into place.

Adjusting to the challenges that the pandemic brought
The COVID-19 pandemic hit Anna's enterprise like a wrecking ball, bringing it to collapse. As they were gaining momentum, everything came to a sudden halt. It looked like the end of everything when 80 percent of students demanded the termination of contracts. Anna explained, 'The education system usually practices prepayment but with no face-to-face classes, providing the services I promised our customers was impossible.'

Anna faced the gloomy reality. The once noisy corridors of the school were empty, and the sound of silence was ear-splitting. Anna sensed that a storm was coming and she needed to act swiftly to save the business. But where to start? Everything seemed so uncertain. Anna was not the sort of person to give up easily. She and her team worked tirelessly, determined to keep the school operating. They brainstormed and came up with a plan. They invested in purchasing large screens and made a bold announcement inviting to take classes online for those who were scared to come to them physically. That crucial decision helped Anna save her business from a staggering loss of 10 million rubles.[1] Moreover, by spending 200,000 rubles for the team's training,[2] she provided a smooth and quick transition to online teaching. Within two weeks, all her teachers had learned to work online, and were equipped with the necessary skills to operate online platforms and electronic textbooks. Anna's efforts paid off. Her students rallied around her, and many continued their studies online. Anna's school weathered the storm and emerged even more robust. The first month of the pandemic caused some losses, but the second month increased cash flow. Half of the staff decided to continue working remotely even after the centers reopened physically in September 2020. Anna sensed a gradual shift to online practices, and her business adapted accordingly. Even though investing in online teaching was challenging, it was a game-changer and ultimately saved her business.

Managing the turbulence: the Russia–Ukraine war

In February 2022, Anna was caught off guard by the outbreak of war between Ukraine and Russia, which significantly impacted the social life of her country. She felt devastated and decided to leave for Turkey, hoping to escape the tension and turmoil that had enveloped society. However, after three weeks, Anna returned to Moscow and was stunned by the sudden increase in demand for English classes among Russian citizens. People were looking for new ways to cope with the uncertainty and upheaval caused by the war. Anna realized that was an opportunity to capitalize on the newfound interest in learning English. So, she created new courses and modified the existing ones to satisfy the growing demand. Her efforts paid off, as the revenue from her classes tripled within a few weeks. But the real surprise came when the sale of the *Advanced Interview Techniques* course reached an unusual figure – 150 recipients per month.

Anna was thrilled with the success and felt grateful for the opportunity to make a difference to people's lives during time of uncertainty and change. She continued to improve her school courses to meet the ever-changing needs of her students, being confident that her efforts would help them succeed in a rapidly evolving world.

The second wave of turbulence: Russian mobilization

As the tension between Russia and Ukraine escalated, the Russian government declared a partial mobilization in September 2022, signaling the onset of the war. This development shocked the Russian citizens, who hoped for a quick resolution to the conflict. Many had migrated to different countries in March, but others followed them in massive waves after the governmental announcement. Amidst this chaos, Anna suggested that her clients freeze the language packages they bought, thus alleviating their situation in times of turbulence. However, her customers refused to do that and preferred to face the problem bravely. It was a time of great uncertainty as people struggled to grasp the reality of the war. Yet, amidst the confusion and chaos, there were signs of hope and determination as the Russians tried to stay strong in the face of adversity.

> We are again facing a period of instability and a lack of support. Although people are trying to preserve their "normal faces," everyone understands the consequences are coming. We are helpless, defenceless in the face of the black swans that threaten to swoop down and destroy everything we have meticulously built!

Moving to Kazakhstan

As the mobilization process escalated, many Russian men decided to leave their homes for neighboring countries, such as Kazakhstan. Upon arriving in Kazakhstan, Anna and her husband saw the potential for business and entrepreneurship. They were impressed by the rapid growth of the economy and the supportive environment for small businesses. After carefully considering different options, Anna's family settled in Kazakhstan permanently. It was a conscious choice, despite the uncertainty and challenges that loomed ahead. But Anna and her husband were determined to build a new life in their new home. They saw it as an opportunity to start from scratch, to create something new and exciting.

> As I arrived in Kazakhstan, the assistant who met me casually recounted her recent trip to Barcelona, and I was left speechless. It had been so long since I had heard anyone talk about travel, about seeing the world beyond their borders. The war in Ukraine had thrown everything into chaos, and my home country had become much darker and more uncertain. But in Kazakhstan, people seemed to be living in a different context. Looking around me, I realized there was so much I still had to learn about this place. I had to open myself up to new experiences, people, and a new way of life. It was a daunting prospect, but I knew I had to embrace it if I was going to make a life for myself here. And so, with a mixture of hope and uncertainty, I began my journey into the unknown, eager to discover all that Kazakhstan had to offer.

Anna made a bold move and joined the 999 Business Club of Entrepreneurs in Kazakhstan. Eager to immerse herself in the local business community, she wasted no time organizing a series of events to unite like-minded individuals. She saw potential in the local market and opened her legal entity in Kazakhstan. With a keen eye for talent, she hired two employees who could test all potential customers, not just those in Kazakhstan.

> I was struck by the infectious energy of the people I met in Kazakhstan. They were open-minded, terrestrial, and educated. Moreover, they speak three languages fluently – Kazakh, Russian, and English. This starkly contrasted with what I had experienced in Russia, where only 7 percent of the population knew foreign languages. In Kazakhstan, people easily switch between languages, demonstrating impressive linguistic skills.
> Moreover, Astana sets off a palpable energy of money and innovation presence; people here are determined to succeed. However, I also noticed that what a consumer wants is only sometimes apparent. While some are willing to pay a premium price for something flashy and pretentious, others prefer to spend as little as possible. Professionalism is only sometimes valued unless it is appropriately packed.

Anna planned to collaborate with local professionals to develop a promotional strategy. Online training was not widespread in Kazakhstan; offline courses were more prevalent. Anna felt that working remotely was more effective, allowing her to observe business dynamics objectively without any contextual influence.

Re-emerging in Kazakhstan

Upon arriving in Kazakhstan, Anna quickly built a local business network and joined various clubs. At first, she reached out to potential business partners sending them promotion letters. But soon, she started receiving invitations to attend different business events. Anna was surprised to learn that such activities in Kazakhstan were often organized primarily for women entrepreneurs.

> At a recent business event, I had the opportunity to network with 60 female entrepreneurs from different industries, such as cosmetology, design, languages, medicine, and education. I also attended a business breakfast exclusively for male entrepreneurs with a different atmosphere. It used an outdated format of business where the focus was on belittling others to motivate development. In contrast, women's business events were fueled with the energy to create rather than dominate others.

Anna also noticed that Kazakh women entrepreneurs are well-equipped to combine business and family life organically, without special training. Traditionally, women in Kazakhstan are expected to care for their families, so integrating work and family life is second nature to them.

Remote management of the business in Russia amidst the changing entrepreneurial landscape

After moving to Kazakhstan, Anna continued to oversee her Russian school remotely. She kept on holding Zoom meetings with her employees, who got used to that. Successfully settled in the new country, she occasionally traveled to Moscow to conduct face-to-face team meetings. The school's corporate client network rapidly expanded in Russia. Moreover, now it includes exclusively Russian companies, thus highlighting the need for language proficiency, particularly in Chinese.

> When I received a letter from Iran, I didn't know how to react, whether I should laugh or cry. It offered training for top managers on how to function in an outcast mode and navigate tricky situations. The sender highlighted their ten-year experience in the field. But, on the other hand, I got the point that almost all international companies now refuse to work with us, the Russians.

Anna pointed out that TikTok was one of their last international partners to depart from the local market. However, such withdrawal of international representations benefited Anna's business. For example, her testing department enhanced its performance after IELTS and Cambridge English-language testing providers suspended operations in Russia. Consequently, Anna's school became a hub for an increasing number of Russian companies in certifying their employees. That demonstrated that Russian entrepreneurs responded to international sanctions by building their resilient ecosystem.

> Entrepreneurial minds and skills are ingrained in Russian people, and they can find solutions to any problem quickly. In the past, Russia has successfully rebranded and reopened many world-famous trademarks under new names and with new logos. While, on the one hand, I respect and feel proud of such efforts, on the other hand, sanctions do not benefit ordinary people. Unfortunately, some entrepreneurs gave up despite their resilience.

Anna suggested that, notwithstanding the present disagreement with Putin's war policies, patriotism in Russia experienced a resurgence, and people became proud of themselves for their ability to confront the West. Sensing that sentiment, Anna noted that 'individuals must adapt to their environment to avoid suffering; failing to do so may be destructive in the long run.' She emphasized the importance of engaging in intercultural communication to understand Russia's current state of affairs better.

Future plans
Anna's customers have been affected by the recent political climate in Russia. Some have become unmotivated to learn foreign languages due to the fear of an "iron curtain" descending again. Others are actively enhancing their English skills and planning to move abroad. This has resulted in a significant surge in the sale of online language courses.

> Maintaining team spirit was of utmost importance to us. In February, when everything happened, I became aware of a mission: my school and I had a responsibility to help people cope with the psychological turmoil. They were feeling depressed and had a negative outlook. On the evening of February 24, when I arrived at my Business English lesson, I noticed the students were all sitting with tears [in their eyes].

When Anna and her business partner launched TED-style public talks shortly after the invasion, it turned out that many invited speakers refused to travel to Moscow, so they had to move an upcoming conference to Istanbul. That quick understanding of the situation and adapting to it confirmed Anna's belief that being a woman was an advantage; she could sense the right way of doing business and, therefore, was unstoppable.

Concluding her story, Anna shared an assurance that an international online school could allow her to live and work anywhere. Anna said that the longer she stayed away from Russia, the less likely she was to return.

Looking from the outside, you wonder if you want to return. But, despite this, Russia will always hold a special place in my heart since it is my homeland, where my family, life savings, and friends are.

4.2 Olga's Narrative

Olga owns the English Language Gamification company, which has been organizing large-scale conferences for English teachers from the non-governmental sector in Russia since 2013. In 2021, her company organized the biggest in the post-Soviet territory Central Asia Conference and brought together teachers from language schools in Kazakhstan and Uzbekistan. Another field of the company activity is the development of educational games that teachers can use in their English classes. The company also provides training programs on how to use those games effectively, what types of games exist, and how they can help students in the educational process.

Before launching the company, Olga had experience of managing her own language school in the Moscow suburbs. However, her professional career started at a federal unit where she worked as a methodologist and a lecturer at the Moscow University of Physics and Technology. Born in Novosibirsk, Olga moved to North Kazakhstan, Rudny City, at six with her parents. After completing her secondary education there, she returned to Novosibirsk and graduated from Novosibirsk University. Her husband, an ethnic Kazakh from Kazakhstan, studied in Moscow, where they met, and Olga moved there. They settled in Moscow and started to work together. But on March 3, 2022, they returned to Kazakhstan shortly after the war broke out. Olga hoped that she would regain Kazakhstani citizenship, but it was not an easy task because she left the Republic of Kazakhstan when it was a part of the U.S.S.R. and carried with her the old Soviet passport. However, everything has changed, and it looked like the citizenship procedure would drag on indefinitely. Therefore, when Olga's husband received a job offer from Cyprus at the end of March, they moved there in May.

Managing the turbulence I: COVID-19 as a preparatory stage for further ordeals

Olga knows what it means to manage her business remotely. She has significant experience in that and considers it customary.

> Our team started working remotely much earlier than all those turbulent times began. We worked online even before COVID-19. We have six permanent employees located in different places, and we rarely meet face-to-face, only when launching our events. Thus, my Marketing Director lives in Batumi, and my Chief Methodologist, responsible for online teaching, lives in Novosibirsk; our web designer is in Paris. Therefore, we are accustomed to working remotely and have never had a problem working online.

Olga is convinced that she and her company led the transition of English Language Teaching in Russian into online mode. On March 19, 2020, they organized the first conference on how to shift to remote education and how to keep working there. Moreover, by June 2020, Olga's company hosted 35 free and paid events for teachers and language school leaders on how to shift quickly to online teaching and manage life there.

Olga recalls that time as happy and blissful, notwithstanding the challenging and busy schedule from 8a.m. until midnight. For example, she and the whole team had no day off from March to the end of May 2020. Everyone worked hard but also earned good money. In those days, the main focus was switching regular activity, teaching students of different age groups, gaming, practicing language skills, into postnormal reality. That experience proved to be quite helpful when the next tsunami wave was about to drown Olga's business and more.

Managing the turbulence II: the Russia–Ukraine war

When Russia started its invasion of Ukraine, Olga was about to leave for a business trip to Volgograd. She planned to attend a training session on game-based interactive learning but could not go by plane on February 25, 2022 due to the airport closure. Therefore, she opted to travel by train. While on her way to Volgograd, Olga thought over her necessary actions. Her first idea was about capitalizing on what her company was doing the best. Event organizing!

> Getting sporadic Internet access, I organized a conference called The ELT Unites People. Very quickly, 16 [people] speaking from around the world responded to my invitation to support Russian teachers. Moreover, 800 people registered for the event. And finally, we had a full-day conference on February 26.

The event was spontaneous and attracted many volunteers, those who were ready to moderate, conduct sessions, and supervise technically. Olga felt satisfied with the result because her first impulse was to support English language teachers. After all, they were her company clients; also, to preserve the excellent reputation of Russian English Language professionals in the global community. However, things proved to be more complex and complicated.

> Another reason I left the country was an unpleasant discovery that made me shudder. Finally, I got out of the bubble that made me think that all people around believe alike. But when you start getting comments that some readers are making screenshots of your posts and threatening you to send them to authorized bodies, you realize there is little fun in it.

Such comments from Russian teachers were unpleasant, to say the least. It was Olga's sad revelation that the bubble of those, who were with her and like-minded, was tiny. People hold different, sometimes highly opposite opinions in the 40,000 community of Russian teachers that Olga supervised. Therefore, Olga and her teammates quickly removed "No war" slogans from their avatars to avoid provocation.

> I'm lucky. Our team is small, but we share the same spirit regarding the conflict and do not have an internal division (unlike my husband's company). Nevertheless, I must be cautious about expressing my views on social networks and saying certain things to maintain peace. Because different people have different opinions, skipping burning issues discussions is much better.

After fleeing the country, Olga thought she would regain her freedom of expression. But after careful consideration, she dropped that itching desire, for she is responsible for that half of her team that stays in Russian and can be directly affected by – and even arrested for – her posts.

Despite all the political turmoil, Olga had to keep the business operating. In March, they conducted a big import substitution event where different professionals shared their experience, substituting traditional and well-known global tools with local Russian ones. They taught teachers many new skills, such as working on platforms similar to Zoom and using the Yandex Disk instead of Google Drive. Also, they published several articles on the same topics. Those events were critical support for Olga's customers because most of them are freelance teachers and have no other means to keep working effectively.

No discouragement tainted Olga's feelings. On the contrary, she was sure that every problem had a solution.

> We have always had Russian contractors who have helped us with different professional platforms. Zoom is still there, and I keep coming for our offline events. In November 2022, I attended our big conference but skipped the one in June in St.

Peterburg. However, the team did an excellent, superb job! Then the idea struck me out that finally I am free! I don't need to meddle in their work and have to let them bear their responsibilities. Moreover, they do that job even better than I do!

It was a delightful discovery because Olga characterizes herself as bossy, and delegating duties to others has always been problematic for her. But now, the situation itself pushed her to change her management style.

Establishing a new business network in Cyprus

After moving with her husband to Cyprus, Olga continued to run her business remotely, trying to establish a business community in her new location. However, things turned out to be complicated. Olga only got one registration for the first networking event, and only one person attended it. So, she concluded that the Russian strategy she applied to 40,000 English-language teachers serving a 147 million population required profound reshaping. The scale matters.

Due to Cyprus's political stand, the country is a part of the European Union, but culturally, it is a part of the Middle East. Therefore, Olga started to seek new business contacts from that region. Despite her difficulties, Olga feels that the business environment in Cyprus is supportive. It welcomes Russians and Ukrainians who are affectionate and supportive of one another. However, Olga recognized the stressfulness of her relocation.

> Cyprus is a Russian-speaking place. Almost everyone speaks Russian here! So you can easily find Russian-speaking partners and join Russian-speaking groups. However, for my specific business, it's not good. I have to switch to an English-speaking Cypriot community, families where one spouse is a Cypriot and the other is a foreigner. And in this case, things are more complicated. Only after nine months of interacting with them, I've gradually started to understand their mentality and way of thinking.

Olga generally describes her involvement in the international business community in Cyprus as a positive experience. It helps her to start thinking globally and get out of her bubble.

Turbulence is a new reality

As the world mobilized in response to the chaos of the pandemic and the war, Olga's company experienced a heavy blow. Sales dropped to zero, and the team were paralyzed with fear and stress. Yet, before international sanctions, Olga's company was a market leader, with partnerships and sponsors from the likes of the Cambridge, Macmillan, and Montessori- Pierson publishing houses. But now, they all were gone. So, the company had to restructure, find new partners and sponsors, and ultimately change how they worked to stay afloat.

Radical changes were initiated by the fact that renowned international speakers, methodologists, and authors of different English-language manuals were gone and not returning. As a result, Olga and her company stayed on their own, struggling to survive:

> The turbulence is our new reality, whether inside or outside Russia. We can't escape that it. Event preparation has been a hectic thing always. Thus, COVID-19 initiated a pile of checklists and working provisions for events in case of their cancelling due to a pandemic. Now, we face the same bureaucratic routine of writing the same protocols but initiated by the event cancellation due to martial law.

Of course, bureaucratic paperwork affected many of Olga's customers. However, while it was lower than before COVID-19, the quantity was growing. Moreover, the online component marked the financial indicators even higher than before the pandemic. Though the current turbulent situation has left Olga's company the only player in their market, she hopes that, after a while, the new organization can emerge and compete with her agency, thus healing the business atmosphere that needs healthy competition.

Future plans
Olga is convinced that keeping all "eggs in one basket" is not wise, and people are still determining how the situation will turn out in Russia. Her company keeps operating there but also looks for opportunities in other countries. It has always been a cherished dream – to launch a business outside, but it needed a great trigger – like the current war situation – to start acting on that dream. For example, the Middle East, which has close ties with Cyprus and hosts many people from Lebanon, looks like a potential and up-and-coming partner for Olga. She also seriously considers reshaping the company's activities. Games that have always been their leading sphere might give way to something new. For example, the Online Teaching Skills course could probably bring a new focus to Olga's business.

> I have interviewed teachers from different countries and realized they have the same problems as ours. Therefore, our developed products can benefit them and bring us income.

5.   DISCUSSION

This study centers on two women entrepreneurs from Russia who made the difficult decision to leave their homeland and start anew in different countries with varying political, cultural, and geographic landscapes. The primary objective of our research was to explore how these migrant women entrepreneurs exhibited adaptability and agility in navigating their businesses during times of postnormal crises. For this purpose, we delved into the narratives of Anna and Olga, whose cases complemented each other, offering unique perspectives and insights that helped us complete the overall picture. Through careful analysis, we have gained a deeper understanding of the challenges and opportunities in their entrepreneurial journeys, especially during tumultuous times. By examining the ways in which Anna and Olga overcame obstacles and adapted their business strategies, we uncovered valuable lessons that could inform and inspire other migrant entrepreneurs facing similar challenges. Our study highlights the importance of agility, resourcefulness, and a willingness to learn from experiences to thrive in uncertain and ever-changing environments. Ultimately, the stories of these two women illustrate the power of entrepreneurship to transform lives and create positive change, even in the face of adversity.

5.1   The Internal and External Drivers of Agility

In this section, drawing on the works of Sharifi and Zhang (2001) and Bessant et al. (2001), we discuss the drivers that influenced agility development for Anna and Olga. Both entrepreneurs faced significant external turbulence that impacted their businesses. First, the COVID-19 pandemic forced them to pivot their businesses online and upskill their teams with new techniques, while later, the Ukraine–Russia war broke out and disrupted the "new normal" routine that they had begun to form. Along the way, these two major waves created additional ripples, which align with Walter's (2021, pp. 357–358) examples of external agility drivers. The external agility drivers further included political pressure in the form of Western sanctions and political and economic turbulence in Russia. This resulted in Anna and Olga needing to adapt and find new business partners, with Anna searching for new partners in Kazakhstan and Olga seeking them out in Cyprus and worldwide.

The second type of driver that influenced Anna's and Olga's agility development was the expansion of their product range and the launching of extra-business activities. Specifically, they created TED-like talks and organized anti-war conferences to unite people around a common cause. These actions helped them not only diversify their offerings but also build a loyal customer base that was aligned with their values. With changing customers' needs, the entrepreneurs, particularly Anna, had to focus on courses that were of little demand during peaceful times.

The development of agility in both entrepreneurs was strongly influenced by social changes. When a society is divided into those who support war and those who oppose military action, it inevitably affects leadership, making leaders more adaptable in their efforts and more careful in what they say if their company is to survive. This factor is a double-edged sword, demonstrating its postnormal nature both externally and internally. Anna and Olga had to make decisions for themselves regarding their personal and public stance on the war, which further complicated their already challenging leadership positions. Their responsibilities and duties to their employees, students, families, and friends only added to the complexity of this driver. In short, social changes played a critical role in the development of agility for both Anna and Olga, and this factor acted as a dual-role driver, both internally and externally.

In both narratives, we noticed several factors that drove internal agility (Walter, 2021). Firstly, there were workforce expectations, which had shifted in the wake of the COVID-19 pandemic. Both entrepreneurs mentioned that their staff members preferred to work remotely, even after the quarantine measures were lifted. Secondly, they were engaged in continuous improvement strategies, enabling their businesses to offer new courses and training opportunities for their employees, thereby empowering them with new skills and knowledge. Thirdly, their management styles evolved to become more trusting and less controlling. Fourthly, organizational structures became more dissolved as both entrepreneurs moved to remote locations or foreign countries.

However, it is important to note that, in the case of Anna and Olga, competitive strategy was an area that required special attention; it accounted for the corresponding cultural context. Inayatullah (2015) highlights culture's critical role in developing transformative agile strategies. Although Anna and Olga recognize similarities between Kazakhstani/Cypriot and Russian cultures, they had to adjust due to critical differences. For example, Anna discovered that personal contacts and face-to-face communication are essential to Kazakh people, and high-quality products must be specially packaged. Olga faced a complex cultural situation in Cyprus, as it is part of Europe geopolitically, but culturally, it is close to the Middle East.

5.2   The Role of Feminine Capital

Anna and Olga's success in navigating a challenging business environment can be attributed to their possession and utilization of feminine capital. Feminine capital refers to the unique qualities, experiences, and skills that women bring to entrepreneurship, including empathy, intuition, resilience, collaboration, and adaptability (Brush et al., 2009). Women, particularly those who are mothers, possess a wealth of feminine capital that enables them to excel in the face of adversity and change. Anna and Olga leveraged their feminine capital to respond quickly and effectively to their industry's uncertainty, dynamic customer demands, and frequent environmental changes. They regarded their female perspective as a privilege and an added skill that gave them a competitive advantage.

Anna's emotional intelligence, her ability to understand and manage her emotions, helped her connect with her customers and employees. She was empathetic toward her customers' needs, which helped her provide them with a personalized experience. Similarly, she supported her employees and created a positive work environment, resulting in high employee satisfaction. Collaboration is another feminine skill that Anna used to her advantage. She understood the importance of collaboration and worked closely with her network of business owners and industry experts to learn about the local market. She also collaborated with her employees to develop and improve new services. This collaborative approach helped her build strong relationships and gain valuable insights into the industry.

By embracing their feminine qualities and experiences, Anna and Olga were able to build a successful business that thrived in a dynamic business environment. The concept of feminine capital aligns with the entrepreneurial agility literature, which emphasizes the importance of adaptability and competitiveness in changing circumstances (Hatzijordanou et al., 2019; Meinhardt et al., 2018). Anna's and Olga's agility proved a valuable asset that enabled them to seize business opportunities and differentiate themselves in a rapidly evolving industry. They recognized that agility was a desirable trait and a critical strategy for achieving success in a dynamic business environment.

5.3   Agility Leading to Improved Business Performance

Anna's and Olga's experiences further demonstrate the positive correlation between business performance and agility (Inman et al., 2011; Vickery et al., 2010). Anna's business demonstrated agility by responding to customers' demands with the introduction of discussion clubs, language courses, and kids' courses. She successfully launched online teaching during external social and health demands, provided professional preparatory courses, and kept offline language club meetings for customers' psychological needs. Olga's business agility was evident during the quarantine period, as she had to start teaching others to work online and develop courses on how to keep financial inflows for English teachers amidst social-political chaos. She also had to build a new network in a foreign country to maintain business operations. Both Anna and Olga showed agility by identifying new opportunities and adjusting their businesses to the changing social-political context, responding to various crises by changing their practices. For example, Anna modified and rebuilt her business structure, making the company international and opening a subsidiary in Kazakhstan. This is similar to the agility strategy described by Meinhardt et al. (2018) as a differentiation strategy in a dynamic business environment.

Moreover, both Anna and Olga managed to stay financially afloat and even improve their business performance through their agility. Their experiences provide real-world examples of how businesses can adapt and succeed in challenging circumstances.

Our research findings support the notion that agility is the outcome of a combination of both internal and external factors, as posited by Sharifi and Zhang (2001) and Bessant et al. (2001). However, it is crucial to note that in times of postnormal crises characterized by the 4Ss (speed, scope, scale, and simultaneity) and 3Cs (complexity, chaos, and contradictions), agility should be viewed as a multifaceted factor that cannot be separated into discrete internal or external drivers. Rather, agility should be perceived as a complex construct encompassing various dimensions, including political, social, moral, financial, personal, and public factors. In complex times, agility is akin to the intricate and contradictory identities that Anna and Olga describe in their narratives. They are women, entrepreneurs, leaders, Russians, mothers, decision-makers, wives, business partners, and citizens of their country, all at the same time. They are opposed to war, yet they must continue operating within its context, as they bear the responsibility of ensuring the well-being of their employees and families. This moral dimension of agility has not been extensively discussed in the business literature and represents a unique contribution to our research findings.

6. CONCLUSION

This study has presented two narratives highlighting the importance of recognizing the multifaceted nature of agility, particularly during times of crisis. Anna's and Olga's experiences exemplify the intricacies of agility and emphasize the need to consider various dimensions when navigating complex and uncertain situations, including the moral aspect. The study's findings shed light on how migrant women entrepreneurs employ agility strategies to deal with various types of business crises.

We contribute to the existing literature by outlining the agility strategies employed by these entrepreneurs when faced with crises related to (re)starting, recovering, exiting, and surviving. Moreover, the study underscores how psychological agility shapes the effectiveness of these strategies. Our findings reveal that despite having different upbringings and migration trajectories, Anna's and Olga's agility strategies were similar in most crisis situations. Overall, the study provides a new perspective on agility strategies employed by a unique group of entrepreneurs and contributes to the literature by highlighting the importance of acknowledging the complexity of agility, particularly during times of crisis. The study's insights can inform the development of policies and programs that support migrant women entrepreneurs in dealing with crises.

NOTES

1. 10 million rubles equals 110,000 euros at the exchange rate of the Central Bank of the Russian Federation as of November 2020.
2. 200,000 rubles equals 2,200 euros at the exchange rate of the Central Bank of the Russian Federation as of November 2020.

REFERENCES

Ahlbäck, K., Fahrbach, C., Murarka, M., & Salo, O. (2017). How to create an agile organization. *McKinsey & Company*. https:// www .mckinsey .com/ business -functions/organization/our-insights/how-to-create-an-agile-organization. Accessed 13 April 2023.

Ashrafi, A., Ravasan, A. Z., Trkman, P., & Afshari, S. (2019). The role of business analytics capabilities in bolstering firms' agility and performance. *International Journal of Information Management*, *47*, 1–15.

Audretsch, D. B., Momtaz, P. P., Motuzenko, H., & Vismara, S. (2023). War and entrepreneurship: A synthetic control study of the Russia–Ukraine conflict. CESifo Working Paper No. 10466. Available at: https:// ssrn .com/ abstract = 4470386 or http://dx.doi.org/10.2139/ssrn.4470386.

Bauman, Z., & Mauro, E. (2016). *Babel*. Polity, Oxford.

Bessant, J., Francis, D., Meredith, S., Kaplinsky, R., & Brown, S. (2000). Developing manufacturing agility in SMEs. *International Journal of Manufacturing Technology and Management*, *2*(1–7), 730–756. https://doi.org/10.1504/ijmtm.2000.001374.

Bessant, J., Francis, D., Meredith, S., Kaplinsky, R., & Brown, S. (2001). Developing manufacturing agility in SMEs. *International Journal of Manufacturing Technology and Management*, *2*(1–7), 28–54. https://doi.org/10.1504/ijmtm.2000.001374.

Bodlaj, M., & Čater, B. (2019). The impact of environmental turbulence on the perceived importance of innovation and innovativeness in SMEs. *Journal of Small Business Management*, *57*(S2), 417–435. https://doi.org/10.1111/jsbm.12482.

Brown, J. L., & Agnew, N. M. (1982) Corporate agility. *Business Horizons*, *25*(2), 29–33. https://doi.org/10.1016/0007–6813(82)90101-x.

Brush, C. G., de Bruin, A., & Welter, F. (2009). A gender-aware framework for women's entrepreneurship. *International Journal of Gender and Entrepreneurship*, *1*(1), 8–24. https://doi.org/10.1108/17566260910942318.

Coombs, W. T. (1995). Choosing the right words: The development of guidelines for the selection of the 'appropriate' crisis-response strategies. *Management Communication Quarterly*, *8*(4), 447–476. https://doi.org/10.1177/0893318995008004003.

Coombs, W. T. (2007). Protecting organization reputations during a crisis: The development and application of Situational Crisis Communication Theory. *Corporate Reputation Review*, *10*, 163–176. https://doi.org/10.1057/palgrave.crr.1550049.

De Smet, A., & Aghina, W. (2015). The keys to organizational agility. *McKinsey & Company*. https:// www .mckinsey .com/ business -functions/ organization/ our -insights/the-keys-to-organizational-agility. Accessed 13 April 2023.

Doern, R., Williams, N., & Vorley, T. (2019). Special issue on entrepreneurship and crises: Business as usual? An introduction and review of the literature. *Entrepreneurship & Regional Development*, *31*(5–6), 400–412. https://doi.org/10.1080/08985626.2018.1541590.

Ghannad, N., & Andersson, S. (2012). The influence of the entrepreneur's background on the behaviour and development of born globals' internationalisation processes. *International Journal of Entrepreneurship and Small Business*, *15*(2), 136–153.

Glenn, M. (2009). *Organizational Agility: How Business Can Survive and Thrive In Turbulent Times.* Economist Intelligence Unit.

Harari, Y. N. (2020). Every crisis is also an opportunity. *The UNESCO Courier*, *2*, 48–53.

Hatzijordanou, N., Bohn, N., & Terzidis, O. (2019). A systematic literature review on competitor analysis: Status quo and start-up specifics. *Management Review Quarterly*, *69*(4), 415–458. https://doi.org/10.1007/s11301–019–00158–5.

Inayatullah, S. (2015). Ensuring culture does not eat strategy for breakfast: What works in futures studies. *World Future Review*, *7*(4), 351–361.

Inman, R. A., Sale, R. S., Green, K. W., & Whitten, D. (2011). Agile manufacturing: Relation to JIT, operational performance and firm performance. *Journal of Operations Management*, *29*(4), 343–355. https://doi.org/10.1016/j.jom.2010.06.001.

Jones, C., Serra del Pino, J., & Mayo, L. (2021). The perfect postnormal storm: COVID-19 chronicles (2020 edition). *World Futures Review*, *13*(2), 71–85. https://doi.org/10.1177/19467567211027345.

Khurana, I., Dutta, D. K., & Singh Ghura, A. (2022). SMEs and digital transformation during a crisis: The emergence of resilience as a second-order dynamic capability in an entrepreneurial ecosystem. *Journal of Business Research*, *150*, 623–641. https://doi.org/10.1016/j.jbusres.2022.06.048.

Kwong, C. C., Cheung, C. W., Manzoor, H., & Rashid, M. U. (2019). Entrepreneurship through bricolage: A study of displaced entrepreneurs at times of war and conflict. *Entrepreneurship & Regional Development*, *31*(5–6), 435–455.

Lee, Y., Kim, J., Mah, S., & Karr, A. (2023). Entrepreneurship in times of crisis: A comprehensive review with future directions. *Entrepreneurship Research Journal*. https://doi.org/10.1515/erj-2022–0366.

Liu, H.-M., & Yang, H.-F. (2019). Managing network resource and organizational capabilities to create competitive advantage for SMEs in a volatile environment. *Journal of Small Business Management*, *57*(S2), 155–171. https://doi.org/10.1111/jsbm.12449.

Meinhardt, R., Junge, S., & Weiss, M. (2018). The organizational environment with its measures, antecedents, and consequences: A review and research agenda. *Management Review Quarterly*, *68*, 195–235. https://doi.org/10.1007/s11301–018–0137–7.

Mitroff, I. I., Pauchant, T. C., & Shrivastava, P. (1988). The structure of man-made organizational crises: Conceptual and empirical issues in the development of a general theory of crisis management. *Technological Forecasting and Social Change*, *33*(2), 83–107. https://doi.org/10.1016/0040–1625(88)90075–3.

Sardar, Z. (2010). Welcome to postnormal times. *Futures*, *42*, 435–444. https://doi.org/10.1016/j.futures.2009.11.028.

Sardar, Z. (2019). *The Postnormal Times Reader.* International Institute of Islamic Thought.

Shariatmadari, D. (2022). A year of 'permacrisis.' *Collins Dictionary.* 1 November. Language Lovers Blog. https://blog.collinsdictionary.com/language-lovers/a-year-of-permacrisis/.

Sharifi, H., & Zhang, Z. (2001). Agile manufacturing in practice—application of a methodology. *International Journal of Operations & Production Management, 21*(5–6), 772–794. https://doi.org/10.1108/01443570110390462.

Taylor, S. E., & Brown, J. D. (1988). Illusion and well-being: A social psychological perspective on mental health. *Psychological Bulletin, 103*(2), 193–210. https://doi.org/10.1037/0033–2909.103.2.193.

Teece, D. J., Peteraf, M., & Leih, S. (2016). Dynamic capabilities and organizational agility: Risk, uncertainty, and strategy in the innovation economy. *Californian Management Review, 58*(4), 13–35. https://doi.org/10.1525/cmr.2016.58.4.13.

Vickery, S. K., Droge, C., Setia, P., & Sambamurthy, V. (2010). Supply chain information technologies and organisational initiatives: Complementary versus independent effects on agility and firm performance. *International Journal of Production Research, 48*(23), 7025–7042. https://doi.org/10.1080/00207540903348353.

Vinodh, S., Aravindraj, S., Pushkar, B., & Kishore, S. (2012). Estimation of reliability and validity of agility constructs using structural equation modelling. *International Journal of Production Research, 50*(23), 6737–6745. https://doi.org/10.1080/00207543.2011.623246.

Vinodh, S., Devadasan, S. R., Vasudeva, R. B., & Ravichand, K. (2010a). Agility index measurement using multi-grade fuzzy approach integrated in a 20 criteria agile model. *International Journal of Production Research, 48*(23), 7159–7176. https://doi.org/10.1080/00207540903354419.

Vinodh, S., Sundararaj, G., Devadasan, S. R., Kuttalingam, D., & Rajanayagam, D. (2010b). Amalgamation of mass customisation and agile manufacturing concepts: The theory and implementation study in an electronics switches manufacturing company. *International Journal of Production Research, 48*(7), 2141–2164. https://doi.org/10.1080/00207540802456257.

Walter, A.-T. (2021). Organizational agility: Ill-defined and somewhat confusing? A systematic literature review and conceptualization. *Management Review Quarterly, 71*, 343–391. https://doi.org/10.1007/s11301–020–00186–6.

Wang, Z., Pan, S. L., Ouyang, T. H., & Chou, T. C. (2014). Achieving IT-enabled enterprise agility in China: An IT organizational identity perspective. *IEEE Transactions on Engineering Management, 61*(1), 182–195. https://doi.org/10.1109/tem.2013.2259494.

2. Italian women entrepreneurs during the Covid-19 pandemic: striving for a collective response through female employer and business membership organizations

Luisa De Vita and Elisa Errico

INTRODUCTION

The Covid-19 pandemic was the first large-scale crisis the world experienced since the beginning of the twenty-first century. Liñán and Jaén (2020) described the economic consequences of Covid-19 as worse than those of previous crises because of the co-presence of a demand-side, supply-side, and financial-side crisis. The unpredictable nature of this crisis caused a disruption to global and local value chains, with varying levels of inequality across different regions, leading companies to develop different strategies for cost-cutting. The International Labour Organization and International Organisation of Employers (ILO and IOE, 2020) reported that the increase in business costs throughout the Covid-19 pandemic caused a drop in the number of memberships for employer and business membership organizations (EBMOs), especially among small and medium-sized enterprises (SMEs). The role of these organizations is crucial in providing support and services to help SMEs, which are most affected by the crisis. This negative trend also affected Italian EBMOs (Bergamante et al., 2020; Fanfani et al., 2021). However, building on the well-established tradition of social dialogue with Italian EBMOs, their influence on policymaking in times of crisis appears to be crucial. Stemming from the political relevance of Italian EBMOs, this chapter first investigates the specific characteristics of these organizations. The aim is to analyse how Italian female EBMOs responded to the Covid-19 pandemic, namely what supporting actions they put in place to address their members' needs. This entails considering whether female EBMOs provided adaptation strategies to meet their members' new expectations during the Covid-19 pandemic. The value of this study lies in its novelty. Scholars point out the scarcity of research on employers' associations (Bergamante et al., 2020), especially on those with a gender perspective, as well on the behaviours of these organizations in the face of external shocks such as a pandemic.

Female entrepreneurship represents a consistent, albeit still minor, part of the Italian productive fabric, accounting for approximately 22 per cent (Unioncamere, 2022). Before the onset of the Covid-19 pandemic, Italy experienced an exponential growth and strengthening of women's business networks across various sectors, alongside a marked increase in female activities. The formal acknowledgement of Italian female EBMOs in industrial relations is noteworthy since these organizations can influence the political agenda as well as the allocation of additional resources to firms. Furthermore, each female professional organization connects to a larger organization that is specific to the sector and size of the company. The capacity of these associations to confront gender-related issues caused by the Covid-19 pandemic and to answer to the new expectations of their associates was essential for the robustness of the Italian economy.

To provide context for our research, the next section of the chapter outlines the features and current trends related to female entrepreneurship in Italy. We look at the effects of the pandemic on Italian women entrepreneurs to comprehend the issues faced by Italian female EBMOs. Next, we explore the structural and relational elements that the academic literature attributes to women's professional networks and we outline how these form expectations and actions of female EBMOs during the Covid-19 pandemic. We also discuss our research method and present our empirical findings. Finally, we draw conclusions, suggesting future research pathways and policy recommendations.

FEMALE ENTREPRENEURSHIP AND EBMOs IN ITALY

Data from the last Unioncamere Report on Women's Entrepreneurship (2022) show a steady increase in female-led enterprises in Italy, accounting for approximately 22 per cent of the entrepreneurial sector. However, women still own smaller businesses: 96.7 per cent of these are micro (0–9 employees), 3.1 per cent are small (10–49 employees), and 0.3 per cent are medium/large (50 employees and above). The birth rate of Italian women-led businesses was negatively affected by the pandemic. Prior to Covid-19, new women-led businesses were the fastest growing entrepreneur category (+4.2 per cent over the period 2014–19), and although the rate of women-led business fell continuously throughout 2020, the rate is beginning to rise again, albeit slightly. About 84,000 women's businesses were started between January and December 2021, and despite the difficulties related to Covid-19, women's businesses are now growing faster than men's businesses. It should also be noted that, following the Covid-19 outbreak, many women established new start-ups. Although they are still concentrated in the service sector, female entrepreneurs were also prominent in typically male-dominated industries (i.e. high-tech products or services). While these are positive signs of recovery, women's businesses have been more exposed than men's because of the Covid-19 pandemic. Women entrepreneurs experienced an unprecedented financial crisis, exacerbating existing inequalities in Italy. Traditional gender gaps in Italy include difficulties sourcing credit, juggling family and professional life, and lower digital and financial know-how (Mari et al., 2016).

Brush et al. (2009) suggest that statistical discrimination disadvantages women entrepreneurs in accessing financial resources. The Covid-19 pandemic caused business angels, banks, and investment funds to increase sex-segregated networks, reinforcing this phenomenon. However, financial issues are not the only contributor to the professional isolation of women entrepreneurs (Sharafizad and Coetzer, 2016); the prevalence of small-scale businesses – where women often serve as both employer and employee – also plays a role. The pandemic intensified this related sense of professional and personal detachment because of safety protocols. In such uncertain conditions getting help from those outside the company, through the exploitation of personal and professional relationships, was fundamental to moving female businesses forward.

Scholars have debated the relationship between enterprise characteristics and employers' propensity for associationism. Some (Perulli and Catino, 1997) have argued that "market weakness" is the main reason that entrepreneurs view employers' organizations as "the first choice" to defend their business interests and hence decide to become members. Firms' characteristics (i.e. concentration of their businesses in the service sector, smaller size, and increased care responsibilities) could be linked to female employers' increased propensity to rely on these associations during the Covid-19 pandemic. In contrast, a study by Bergamante et al. (2020) suggests that companies with characteristics typically attributed to women's enterprises (i.e. small size, concentrated in the service sector) could be less likely to join business associations due to the scarcity of internal resources (i.e. finance and time). Italy's long-standing tradition of industrial relations and the institutional relevance of female EBMOs at national level seem to support the first argument: women entrepreneurs attach importance to these business networks, especially during turbulent times.

FEMALE PROFESSIONAL NETWORKS: STRUCTURAL AND RELATIONAL FEATURES

In recent decades, alongside the increase in female entrepreneurship, there has been an increase in the participation and creation of formal and institutionalized cross-sector female networks (Vinnicombe et al., 2004). Evidence from Italy shows an increase in female associations, along with a remarkable capability of female entrepreneurs to create professional and personal networks.

When we talk about networks, we are referring to a configuration of concrete personal relationships, whose functions and actions depend on their structural and relational dimension (Granovetter, 1973). The former relates to the quantity and configuration of impersonal relationships within the network, while the latter relates to the quality of personal relationships between members (Nahapiet and Ghoshal, 1998). These two aspects shape the network model and influence members' expectations. These could also change over time due to internal (e.g. employer's professional needs) or external factors (e.g. the Covid-19 pandemic).

Regarding structural gender-based differences in networking, some scholars (Renzulli et al., 2000; Dawson et al., 2011) affirm that, compared to their male counterparts, female networks are more homogeneous, more informal in membership (i.e. friends and family members), and restricted. Empirical research by Vinnicombe et al. (2004) shows that female professional networks are highly structured with different international partnerships and regional centres. The first assumption of "structural weakness" has been related to different explanations. Academics connect this characteristic to the gender homogeneity of female networks (Renzulli et al., 2000) and to the feeling of inadequacy or unease when engaging in male-dominated networks (Greguletz et al., 2019). According to Vinnicombe and Colwill (1995) and Greguletz et al. (2019), women are less inclined to use social relationships for utilitarian reasons, and this hinders their professional networking opportunities. The exploitation of network ties for women entrepreneurs depends on their personal traits, the entrepreneurial environment, managerial and organizational aspects, and the business time horizon (Paoloni and Lombardi, 2017). They also suffer from an extrinsic barrier related to gender structural segregation in getting involved in less effective professional networks. This phenomenon is relevant in male-dominated careers in which gender-based social prejudices affect women (Van den Brink and Benshop, 2014). Thus, to overcome this lack of recognition and to foster professional legitimacy, women entrepreneurs tend to search for female business partners or ties. However, Burt (1995) highlights the risks of having a network composition that is too homogeneous – the structural dimension of a network must be homogeneous enough to guarantee collective identification but "open" to the outside to gain access to non-redundant information. Changing the configuration of networks over time, by having formal and informal relationships with different actors is crucial to avoid segregation and stagnation of the networks themselves (Burt, 2017; Renzulli et al., 2000).

With regard to relational aspects, Nahapiet and Ghoshal (1998, 244) define relational embeddedness in a network as "the personal relationships that people have developed with each other through a history of interactions". Paoloni (2011) suggests that various factors shape the relational aspects of female professional networking. Regarding gender homogeneity in formal and informal female networks, a homophile mechanism concurs with choosing and creating strong professional and personal ties between women entrepreneurs. This is linked to the formation of long-term and trusting connections with individuals who have similar traits or interests (Ibarra, 1992) or those who are structurally closer (Kossinets and Watts, 2009), often through personal or informal contacts (Renzulli et al., 2000; Dawson et al., 2011). The nature of female ties has been described as a mix of informal and formal relations with specific demanding functions; there is a gender preference in establishing strong informal ties that do not occur when networking is task-oriented or technical (Cromie and Birley, 1992; Ibarra, 1992). Women's expectations of female networks entail a greater emotional intensity, since they relate these relationships not only to professional reasons but to social support and friendships (Vinnicombe et al., 2004). Thus, female networking patterns are based on a mix of instrumental and expressive reasons in terms of choosing which professional networks to join (Durbin, 2011). They are driven by the need to increase their business and professional opportunities through access to task-oriented resources (i.e. information and experience) (Dawson et al., 2011). However, compared to men, they see professional networks as learning environments rather than a space to do business (Moran, 2005; Vinnicombe et al., 2004). Alongside these motivations, they search for a feeling of interpersonal closeness and psycho-social support (Vinnicombe et al., 2004) to feel less isolated professionally and personally.

Research by Klyver et al. (2018) explores the timing of supportive action for women entrepreneurs and finds that their age and firm stage require different support. Paoloni (2011) affirms that, especially in the start-up phase, women entrepreneurs benefit more from the relational aspects of these professional networks because of their need to be encouraged in a new professional experience. During all stages of women-owned firms, however, these networks can act as a comfort-zone where they can share their concerns and their ideas without feeling judged (Sharafizad and Coetzer, 2016). Moreover, the intensity and stability over time of network interactions favour the building of a trustworthy environment and collective identification (Nahapiet and Ghoshal, 1998). Trust-building mechanisms encourage the adoption of cooperative and emphatic behaviour that facilitates the sharing of valuable resources without fear of opportunistic behaviours in an entrepreneurial competitive context (Uzzi, 1997; Sharafizad and Coetzer, 2016). These mechanisms promote a regular and active engagement within the network by developing mutual understanding through shared languages, codes, narratives, attitudes, and values that foster their collective identification and commitment (Nahapiet and Ghoshal, 1998). These enable the building of a strong collective identity which, in turn, increases the actual representativeness of female professional networks in the public domain.

These structural and relational aspects of women entrepreneurs' professional networks will help contextualize our research findings. We discuss these in depth in the following sections.

METHODOLOGY

The employer associations' landscape in Italy is populated by a range of different actors who represent the diversity of businesses. Since Italian female enterprises are mostly SMEs, we involved only female EBMOs dedicated to smaller businesses. In selecting the associations, we relied on two criteria: first, political relevance at national level, and second, representativeness of women's entrepreneurship. Indeed, the inclusion of EBMOs in the decision-making processes can be considered as a proxy of the degree of their structuring and formal recognition in industrial relations. In the first part of our study, we explored the most interesting Italian associations via a desk analysis to get an idea of the characteristics of these organizations, as well as how they reacted to the Covid-19 crisis, to determine whether and how they could support female business owners. We selected three that fulfilled the criteria of national relevance in industrial relations and having a specific organizational unit dedicated to women's entrepreneurship. In each association, female entrepreneurs registered directly with the association's female dedicated branch while also enjoying all the benefits of membership in the same national association.

The first organization we chose was the CNA "Confederazione Nazionale dell'Artigianato e della Piccola e Media Impresa", which has been representing and protecting the interests of craft enterprises, SMEs, and all forms of self-employment for over 60 years. CNA represents about 623,000 members. The second association was the API, "Associazioni Piccole e Medie Industrie". Founded in 1946, API has about 2,000 industries operating in all areas of production. The third was Confcommercio, "Confederazione Generale Italiana delle Imprese, delle Attività Professionali e del Lavoro Autonomo", which has over 700,000 enterprises concentrated in the trade, tourism, services, culture, and transportation sectors. We focused on the specific units dedicated to women's businesses within these three EBMOs: CNA Impresa Donna; APID Imprenditorialità Donna, and Confcommercio Terziario Donna. A summary of the main attributes of these Italian female EBMOs is provided in Table 2.1.

To explore the characteristics and supportive actions of these organizations during the Covid-19 pandemic, we adopted a qualitative approach. We conducted in-depth interviews involving the heads and executive board members of the three associations; this allowed us to identify the features and supportive

Table 2.1   *Summary of the main attributes of the female EBMOs included in the study*

Female EBMO	Affiliation	Structure of the affiliation organization	No. female members	No. interviews	Interviewee role
CNA Impresa Donna	CNA	19 regional groups 95 local headquarters 45 professional groups aggregated in 10 national groups 17 collective agreements 5 interest groups (including female entrepreneurs)	61,000	1	national head
Terziario Donna	Confcommercio	21 regional groups 85 local headquarters 5 sectoral groups 103 national trade associations 2 interest groups (including female entrepreneurs)	250,000	1	national head
APID	API	63 local headquarters 13 national trade unions 1 national trade association 2 interest groups (including female entrepreneurs) 13 bilateral institutions	350	2	executive board members

Source: Author.

actions of Italian female EBMOs through the perspective of the "privileged witnesses". Our "insiders" have first-hand information and are directly involved in political negotiation roundtables. The aim was to delve into the interviewees' points of view by soliciting in-depth responses (Della Porta, 2014) by adopting a "[…] flexible and non-standardized interrogation structure" (Corbetta, 1999, 405) for our interviews. The flexibility afforded by this approach allowed us to address the topic by adapting our interview questions to match the interviewees' roles and their specific context.

We conducted four interviews remotely via online platforms, each lasting between 50 and 80 minutes, and recorded them with the consent of participants. A consent form guaranteed complete anonymity. The authors conducted and transcribed the interviews. The first part of the interviews dealt with comprehending the features of female EBMOs and their relationship with other female associations or other stakeholders. The second part dealt with their supportive actions before and during the Covid-19 pandemic.

We analysed our qualitative data according to the themes covered in the interview tracks and derived from our literature review. We then created a semantic analysis grid. Thus, we proceeded from our general dimensions to detailed aspects, comparing different points of view on the same dimensions to capture the complexity and variety of actors' perspectives. Our findings reflect the interviewees' points of view through a selection of direct quotes taken from the interview transcripts. The outcome is an interweaving of the research team's analysis with the empirical exemplification represented by the "voice" of the interviewees.

FINDINGS

Our research question focused on the characteristics and supportive actions of Italian female EBMOs during the Covid-19 pandemic. The characteristics of each organization shape the expectations of its members and, therefore, its supportive actions. As the literature demonstrates, the two relevant dimensions for determining the characteristics of each female EBMOs are structural and relational. Indeed, these organizations include a mix of professional and expressive needs of members (Durbin, 2011) depending on their expectations at the time (Klyver et al., 2018). Following this distinction, female EBMOs provide at least two types of supportive actions: technical-instrumental and emotional-psychological support. Among the technical-instrumental support there are actions related to representing the specific interests of female entrepreneurs in industrial relations, namely lobbying and advocacy actions. Besides these, female EBMOs also provide informational and practical support to members regarding bureaucratic procedures, professional training, and business networking. These supportive practices are supplemented with emotional-psychological support for members both from a professional and personal standpoint. These organizations are described primarily as informal-friendly environments offering listening and mutual support between female entrepreneurs. To increase female personal and professional self-confidence in the business sector, they organize specific training activities for members. Alongside these, female EBMOs also engage with social projects outside their professional sphere to raise awareness and generate positive impact on women's issues (e.g. gender-based diseases, social inequalities). We present our interview findings below, following these two thematic categories, and discuss them in the subsequent section. Below we report, through the voices of the interviewees, on the main supports received before and after the Covid-19 pandemic.

The interviews showed that these organizations perceived themselves as the principal in charge of detecting and assessing difficulties faced by female entrepreneurs compared to male entrepreneurs. They provided gender-specific institutional representation in entrepreneurship and offered support tools to members.

> The organization addresses the difficulties and opportunities for female entrepreneurship. Our role is to identify whether there are any difficulties that a female entrepreneur, as a woman, has differently from a man in the same sector. When it is possible, to provide her with adequate tools to overcome these difficulties and to exploit all the potential opportunities. [CNA Impresa Donna]

In addition, heads of female EBMOs claimed to have a representative role for women entrepreneurs, promoting their specific interests and business vision that are not equally protected and expressed at confederal level.[1] The added value of these organizations is, in their words, that of enhancing a complementary or alternative vision to the traditional one of entrepreneurship, through a gender lens.

> It is incorrect to say that the women's association represents us more. It is just that until now; we have always been underrepresented. The male point of view was very much supported. The need to express the female point of view was necessary because before, there was only the male perspective. To establish networks between women's enterprises is fundamental in representing what their firms need, besides the male-prevailing point of view. [...] We definitely have a way of doing business which differs from the male ones. [APID Torino]

In the interviews, respondents also emphasized the increased importance of a reference actor in charge of the representation and lobbying of the specific difficulties that women enterprises experienced during the pandemic. They also reported an increase in their membership rates with the attraction of new entrants, and a reinforcement of the participation of their historical female members.

> There was a stronger attachment (to the association), certainly the usefulness of representative organizations in this period was clearer. [...] when you are in the routine and everything is fine, you do not realize it. [CNA Impresa Donna]

The interviewees felt responsible for informing the government about the specific issues and requests of female entrepreneurs, promoting dialogue between social partners. Female EBMOs' research offices and other national or international partners empirically validated evidence provided to the public decision-maker. All interviewees expressed that they had undertaken lobbying activities to make the government aware of the gender disadvantage for female entrepreneurs during periods of forced closure. Taking into consideration their smaller company size and specific industries, as well as their personal caring tasks, women experienced gender-related issues in managing their businesses during the Covid-19 pandemic. In this frame, Italian female EBMOs' lobbying and advocacy practices resulted in government approval for at least two important measures: a fund dedicated to start-ups and existing women's enterprises, and corporate and public procurement's gender equality certification.[2] Respondents reported that these actions were a step forward for gender equality in the business start-up context. To reinforce these achievements, they exerted cultural pressure to reverse gender biases in entrepreneurship.

> There is no female and male way of doing business. To do business, you must make a profit. The rules of doing business, however, are not the same from a gender perspective, so we start at a disadvantage. Women do not have the same conditions of access to credit. One of the association's main objectives is that to have equal opportunities, we must create equal starting conditions. [Confcommercio Terziario Donna]

Informational support addressed the need for female entrepreneurs to access clear information in a situation of ever-changing government regulations both from a sanitary perspective (e.g. timing of forced shutdowns, opening regulations, healthiness of workplace and individual protection disposals for staff) and a financial perspective (e.g. bonus, funds, subsidies for businesses, new trends related to market opportunities and technical help in getting access to such economic resources during the pandemic).

> [...] for firms at such an uncertain historical moment, when it was essential to have clear information [...], the association became a point of reference. [APID Torino] Being part of a team in times of crisis, compared to when everything is going well, is crucial. [APID Torino]

An example reported by one interviewee highlighted the vital support of Italian female EBMOs in assisting members to get access to funds dedicated to upskilling and training their employees, and to better manage the organizational changes that the crisis prompted.

> I have just completed an in-company financed training for which I had the support of the association. [...] This allowed us to continue operating comfortably without

having to invest our own money in this activity. This psychological opportunity came thanks to the association. [APID Torino]

In addition to the initiatives supporting access to public training funds that were in place before the pandemic, interviewees affirmed that female EBMOs also organized workshops, webinars, online and face-to-face classes and events dedicated to the training needs of female employers. These ranged from financial to digital, to the enhancement of personal skills (e.g. public speaking, networking). Respondents agreed women are less likely to use networking skills for utilitarian reasons compared to their male counterparts, and that they need to learn how to better exploit the potential of their relationships. Such training activities provide both technical-instrumental and emotional-psychological support for female entrepreneurs. Italian female EBMOs adapted their supportive activities during the Covid-19 pandemic; the motivation was twofold – new requests from members, and financial constraints. For example the lack of sponsors increased the remoting of supportive activities to avoid organizational costs when physical presence was not essential. Regarding the content of training activities, respondents highlighted that the demands of female entrepreneurs shifted from "hard" business-related competencies to the improvement of personal skills, particularly with regard to controlling emotional self-regulation and on how to optimize choices under future conditions of constant risk and unpredictability.

The training demands of female entrepreneurs after the pandemic were related to learning how to manage uncertainty [...]. One of the first things they need is the tools to manage emotionality in emergencies and optimize choices. [CNA Impresa Donna]

We have identified the need to do training on how to manage emotionality or public speaking [...]. We have always had a focus on all those issues that go beyond the business sphere, that concern soft skills rather than hard skills. Some topics are more demanded by the female gender. [APID Torino]

Female EBMOs, even before the Covid-19 pandemic, organized initiatives to boost female entrepreneurs' professional self-confidence through the enhancement of soft skills related to interaction, which, in the opinion of respondents, were less developed than their male counterparts. These organizations not only considered networking within the business sector but also established ties with other partners, both at local and international level, with initiatives that more broadly embraced the female entrepreneur landscape. Here, local actors played a key role as facilitators for the onboarding and retention of women entrepreneurs within these organizations through constant and direct relationships with them. Another interesting element that emerged is that even if each female EBMO was involved in building networks at different levels for their members, according to three of the respondents, there were few shared initiatives among the different associations due to competitive dynamics.

> We do not have any particular activities that we perform with other associations. […] We pretend, but there is competition. [Confcommercio Terziario Donna]

One interviewee reported some attempts to collaborate on joint initiatives between different female EBMOs:

> I would say that there is a good relationship [between different organizations] even if the last few years have not been favourable except at some bargaining tables where we get together, when possible, on shared points. [CNA Impresa Donna]

The emotional-psychological support acquired pivotal importance during the Covid-19 pandemic. All respondents agreed that women entrepreneurs would be more likely than their male counterparts to refer to female EBMOs, besides professional consultancy, for personal help.

> The female entrepreneur is more likely to demand this kind of support. They definitely found answers during the Covid-19 pandemic, but above all, someone they could rely on and get emotional support from. [CNA Impresa Donna]

> The association provides women entrepreneurs with a place of exchange where networking creates opportunities for growth and technical advice, but also offers psychological support that creates personal links beyond the professional sphere. [APID Torino]

These organizations wanted to provide a safe space for female entrepreneurs to discuss their emotions, support each other, and share ideas and solutions in group brainstorming sessions during the Covid-19 pandemic. Some respondents reported that their organization also organized fun activities to reduce pressures and reinforce cohesion between members.

> Every Friday at one o'clock we met on Zoom and brainstormed for two hours about projects to do together. We experienced an incredible moment of cohesion that meant even in isolation at home, we could feel united. […] We did online gymnastics sessions together in our homes. These are things that united us so much and helped us not to go crazy during the pandemic. [Apid Torino]

A strong sense of member identification and involvement was evident in respondents' narratives, motivating them to respond proactively to crises together. A strong desire to pursue common goals alongside the positive beliefs associated with the value of associationism emerged as levers prompting member participation. Participants agreed that being structurally involved in an EBMOs was not in itself a "lifeline" for member firms because their value depended primarily on active member participation. Strong ties and high-intensity interactions among members tend to foster a more effective collective reaction, especially during times of difficulty, as our findings for this Italian case demonstrated.

DISCUSSION

This chapter aimed to address a gap in the literature on Italian female professional associations by exploring their specific characteristics and types of supportive actions before and during a particular turbulent era – the Covid-19 pandemic. In this section we discuss our findings in the context of the relevant literature.

We found that most of the practices of women's EBMOs changed according to members' new needs, with those relating to "emotional-psychological support" increasing. Consistent with Vinnicombe et al. (2004), respondents agreed that female EBMOs are a precious resource for women entrepreneurs. Our findings also appear to reflect those of Cromie and Birley (1992), Durbin (2011), Paoloni (2011), and Vinnicombe et al. (2004), who found that motivations for networking among female entrepreneurs are both instrumental and expressive, and that women attribute major value to the latter aspect.

Regarding the structural dimension of female EBMOs, these organizations are homogeneous in terms of their members' gender, but they have relationships with heterogeneous external partners, including institutional, private, non-profit actors at different local, national, international levels. Thus, our study confirms prior work by Cromie and Birley (1992) and Vinnicombe et al. (2004) who discovered sophisticated structures and heterogeneous relationships among female professional networks. However, our findings differ from those of Renzulli et al. (2000) and Dawson et al. (2011) since we cannot state that Italian female networks are more informal in their partner selection (given that they are all professional and entrepreneurs), nor can we claim that these networks are restricted. In our case, however, this might be explained by the fact that Italian female EBMOs are part of a bigger professional or industry confederation. Consistent with Dawson et al. (2011) and Vinnicombe et al. (2004), female EBMOs' structures help members accomplish technical and instrumental activities, especially those connected to professional networking, problem solving, and knowledge sharing. During the Covid-19 pandemic, Italian female EBMOs focused on giving informational support to entrepreneurs on new regulations and new business opportunities, assisting members with bureaucratic aspects. They also increased their efforts to lobby and advocate for public institutions to highlight the specific difficulties women entrepreneurs were facing during Covid-19 and gain gendered policy tools to support them. The effectiveness of these actions convinced decision-makers to adopt important positive actions (i.e. funds for female-owned firms, gender certification for companies, and in the new public procurement code[3]).

Regarding the relational dimension of Italian female EBMOs, our interviews revealed that they benefit from a strong cohesion among members that seems to impact the opportunity to pursue certain actions, especially those related to psychological-emotional support for women. These findings agree with previous literature (Paoloni, 2011; Vinnicombe et al., 2004): women attribute more value to this type of support compared to men. The strong and high-intensity ties, both formal and informal, characterized Italian female professional networks and allowed them to tailor supportive actions to the specific needs of their members during the Covid-19 pandemic. Furthermore, relationships' stability over time fed positive beliefs on the value of associationism, stimulating emotional and professional commitment of members in responding collectively to the Covid-19 crisis (Nahapiet and Ghoshal, 1998). According to respondents, they reached this level of commitment because of an interpersonal closeness by sharing the common everyday entrepreneurial and personal experiences that they perceive as different compared to their male counterparts. Thus, these findings align with previous academic research by Ibarra (1992) and Nahapiet and Ghoshal (1998). In contrast to Vinnicombe et al. (2004) and Greguletz et al. (2019), the need to institutionalize and engage in these EBMOs does not seem to come from a sense of exclusion from male-dominated networks but from the urgency to propose a more inclusive or alternative gender-related narrative in entrepreneurship. Among Italian female EBMOs, a strong sense of identification and engagement from members motivated them to participate in activities. In contrast to findings from the ILO and IOE (2020), Italian female EBMOs registered an increase in female membership levels, with no defections from historical members. These findings align with Perulli and Catino (1997) who found that female entrepreneurs related greater vulnerability to the need to receive more support compared to normal times.

In performing their supportive activities before and during the Covid-19 pandemic, Italian female EBMOs adopted an empathetic approach to women entrepreneurs' expectations. An example of this was found in the shift in the content of workshops, courses, seminars, and mentoring activities from a more didactic approach to strengthening personal skills, such as managing uncertainty. This finding aligns with Dawson et al. (2011) and Vinnicombe et al. (2004) whose studies affirm that, compared to men, women entrepreneurs consider a professional network as a learning environment where they expect to gain useful skills for their careers. A major challenge in these training activities was the effort to re-conceptualize activities that were previously held in person; this was a forced choice not only due to Covid-19's sanitary regulations but also because of EBMOs' reduced or withdrawn financial resources. The limited financial budgets related to travel costs to take part in events and non-essential organizational costs for organizing events which could be conducted remotely, as reported by ILO and IOE (2020). In addition, they increased activities such as informal online knowledge and experience-sharing moments and collective brainstorming, which also supports the creation of a learning environment. As reflected in the interviews, this helped them receive and share suggestions for innovating and managing their businesses to better overcome the crisis. Italian female EBMOs also organized recreational activities to help reduce the feeling of isolation and negative stress (e.g. online gym sessions or virtual coffee breaks) experienced by their members.

In conclusion, our findings show that Italian female professional networks are neither structurally weaker nor less effective. Rather, they demonstrated an ability to adapt their practices promptly to members' needs during the pandemic, diversifying or strengthening their previous activities. At such a critical time for women's businesses, they exerted political pressure to secure government approval for positive gender equality actions. All these practices fit the guidelines for effective employers' organizations for women entrepreneurs by the ILO (2014). Figure 2.1 summarizes the main emerging evidence on the characteristics and collective response of female EBMOs before and after the Covid-19 pandemic.

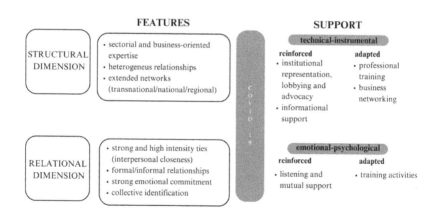

Source: Author.

Figure 2.1   Summary of the characteristics and supporting actions of Italian female EBMOs in addressing Covid-19

Despite the effective, albeit "isolated", activism of each female EBMO, there was a lack of collaboration on joint initiatives, which prevented them from increasing their political bargaining power and achieving further goals for their women entrepreneur members. The reason for this may lie in the competitive dynamics concerning the membership, and the representativeness and power of each organization. Finally, with regard to the effectiveness of these professional networks, it should be remembered that membership of female EBMOs is voluntary, which may suggest such organizations involve only those entrepreneurs who are already aware of the value of associationism. Thus, female EBMOs should explore other mechanisms to increase women entrepreneurs' participation in these networks.

CONCLUSIONS

This chapter contributes to exploring the characteristics and the collective response of Italian female EBMOs to support women entrepreneurs before and during the Covid-19 pandemic. These organizations proved valuable and effective professional networks, capable of adapting their practices to fulfil the expectations of their members during the crisis. Our research demonstrates that gender-specific structural and relational characteristics were deeply reflected in the behaviour of Italian female EBMOs both before and during the Covid-19 pandemic. To manage the emergency phase, EBMOs intensified their technical-instrumental support, especially through lobbying and advocacy. Moreover, these valuable practices had positive results in tackling gender inequalities in entrepreneurship. They provided professional and personal networking activities to help members exploit new business opportunities. To reduce uncertainty about new sanitary regulations and to ensure access to female-dedicated funds or market opportunities, EBMOs introduced new technical support services. This also required changing the content and delivery method of some of their training and mentoring activities. They also provided emotional-psychological support through informal activities to reduce both professional and personal isolation, stimulating positive attitudes among the women entrepreneurs to help them deal with the Covid-19 pandemic.

Regarding the limitations of this study, our research did not consider all Italian women's business associations (i.e. informal organizations) since we selected only the most relevant to our study. Expanding the study to a broader sample of organizations could constitute a pathway for future research. Furthermore, exploring the presence and features of female EBMOs in other countries might be useful to identify possible synergies, build collaboration at the transnational level, and compare strengths and weaknesses to help improve effectiveness. Another trajectory for future research could focus on the motivations for the "isolated" activism of each Italian female EBMO and the potential mechanisms to overcome it.

For policymakers, our study emphasizes the need for the public sector to implement initiatives aimed at strengthening dialogue between the different organizations representing women entrepreneurs at both national and local levels. Such initiatives could also promote the achievement of common goals for female enterprises as well as greater activation of local networks that are less active. In contexts such as Italy, characterized by deep territorial asymmetries, these initiatives could be extremely fruitful for southern territories. These regions have historically suffered from a lack of resources and infrastructure which, when added to female unemployment rates and fewer care services, risk the crystallization of gender inequalities in entrepreneurship. Therefore, greater activation of female EBMOs in these territories, alongside stronger interactions with local public authorities and private actors, could contribute to increased rates of women entrepreneurs while promoting socio-economic development at territorial and national level.

NOTES

1. In Italy, female EBMOs are part of broader confederations aggregated according to sector, economic activity, size class or territories of firms. The absence of these organizations as interest groups which represent the specific demands of women as a minority, would not give sufficient voice to them in industrial relations.
2. The fund is intended for new or established businesses where ownership or management is at least 60 per cent women and provides access to grants and subsidized financing. Gender certification (UNI/PdR 125:2022) provides tax benefits on social insurance contributions, concessional granting of state aid and co-financing for certified enterprises, and scoring facilities in public procurement (legislative decree no. 36/2023).
3. The Italian legislative decree no. 36/2023 introduced a bonus in the allocation of public procurement contracts for companies with policies favouring gender equality.

REFERENCES

Bergamante F., Morocco M., & Polli C. (2020). L'associazionismo datoriale in Italia: trasformazione o declino? Un'analisi sulle imprese. *Stato e mercato*, 120(3). https://doi.org/10.1425/99823.

Brush, C. G., De Bruin, A., & Welter, F. (2009). A gender-aware framework for women's entrepreneurship. *International Journal of Gender and Entrepreneurship*, 1(1), 8–24.

Burt, R. S. (1995). *Structural Holes: The Social Structure of Competition*. Harvard University Press.

Burt, R. S. (2017). Structural holes versus network closure as social capital. In N. Lin, K. S. Cook, & R. S. Burt (Eds.), *Social Capital: Theory and Research*, 31–56. De Gruyter.

Corbetta P. (1999). *Metodologia e Tecniche Della Ricerca sociale*. Il Mulino.

Cromie, S., & Birley S. (1992). Networking by female business owners in Northern Ireland. *Journal of Business Venturing*, 7(3), 237–251.

Dawson, C., Fuller-Love, N., Sinnott, E., & O'Gorman, B. (2011). Entrepreneurs' perceptions of business networks: Does gender matter? *The International Journal of Entrepreneurship and Innovation*, 12(4), 271–281. https://doi.org/10.5367/ijei .2011.0047.

Della Porta, D. (2014). *L'intervista Qualitativa. Gius*. Laterza & Figli Spa.

Durbin, S. (2011). Creating knowledge through networks: A gender perspective. *Gender, Work & Organization*, 18(1), 90–112.

Fanfani, B., Lucifora, C., & Vigani, D. (2021). *Employer Association in Italy: Trends and Economic Outcomes* (No. def109). Università Cattolica del Sacro Cuore, Dipartimenti e Istituti di Scienze Economiche (DISCE).

Granovetter, M. S. (1973). The strength of weak ties. *American Journal of Sociology*, 78(6), 1360–1380.

Greguletz, E., Diehl, M.-R., & Kreutzer, K. (2019). Why women build less effective networks than men: The role of structural exclusion and personal hesitation. *Human Relations*, 72(7), 1234–1261. https://doi.org/10.1177/0018726718804303.

Ibarra, H. (1992). Homophily and differential returns: Sex differences in network structure and access in an advertising firm. *Administrative Science Quarterly*, 37(3), 422–447.

ILO (2014). Women employer association capacity building guide. Available at www .oitcinterfor.org/sites/default/files/wea_guide.pdf (last accessed November 2022).

ILO and IOE (2020). A global survey of employer and business membership organizations: Inside impacts and responses to Covid-19. International Labor Office, Geneva. Available at https://www.ilo.org (last accessed November 2022).

Klyver, K., Honig, B., & Steffens, P. (2018). Social support timing and persistence in nascent entrepreneurship: Exploring when instrumental and emotional support is most effective. *Small Business Economics*, 51(3), 709–734.

Kossinets, G., & Watts, D. J. (2009). Origins of homophily in an evolving social network. *American Journal of Sociology*, 115(2), 405–450.

Liñán, F., & Jaén, I. (2020), The Covid-19 pandemic and entrepreneurship: Some reflections. *International Journal of Emerging Markets*. https://doi.org/10.1108/ IJOEM-05-2020-0491.

Mari, M., Poggesi, S., & De Vita, L. (2016). Family embeddedness and business performance: Evidence from women-owned firms. *Management Decision*, 54(2), 476–500.

Moran, P. (2005). Structural vs. relational embeddedness: Social capital and managerial performance. *Strategic Management Journal*, 26(12), 1129–1151.

Nahapiet, J., & Ghoshal, S. (1998). Social capital, intellectual capital, and the organizational advantage. *The Academy of Management Review*, 23(2), 242–266. https:// doi.org/10.2307/259373.

Paoloni, P. (2011). *La dimensione relazionale delle imprese femminili*. FrancoAngeli.

Paoloni, P., & Lombardi, R. (2017). Exploring the connection between relational capital and female entrepreneurs. *African Journal of Business Management*, 11(24), 740–750.

Perulli, P., & Catino, M. (1997). Le organizzazioni di rappresentanza imprenditoriale: verso uno sperimentalismo istituzionale. *Stato e mercato*, 2, 217–248. https://doi .org/10.1425/394.

Renzulli, L. A., Aldrich, H., & Moody, J. (2000). Family matters: Gender, networks, and entrepreneurial outcomes. *Social Forces*, 79(2), 523–546.

Sharafizad, J., & Coetzer, A. (2016). Women business owners' start-up motivations and network content. *Journal of Small Business and Enterprise Development*, 23(2), 590–610. https://doi.org/10.1108/JSBED-07–2015–0085.

Unioncamere, Centro Studi Tagliacarne, & Si.Camera (2022). V Rapporto Unioncamere sull'imprenditoria femminile. http:// www .unioncamere .gov .it/ osservatori -economici/ imprenditoria -femminile/ rapporto -nazionale -imprenditoria -femminile (last accessed November 2022).

Uzzi, B. (1997). Social structure and competition in interfirm networks: The paradox of embeddedness. *Administrative Science Quarterly*, 42, 35–67.

Van den Brink, M., & Benschop, Y. (2014). Gender in academic networking: The role of gatekeepers in professorial recruitment. *Journal of Management Studies*, 51, 460–492.

Vinnicombe, S., & Colwill, N. (1995) *The Essence of Women in Management*. Prentice Hall.

Vinnicombe, S., Singh, V., & Kumra, S. (2004). *Making Good Connections: Best Practice for Women's Corporate Networks*. Cranfield University School of Management and Opportunity Now.

3. Challenges facing Bangladeshi female entrepreneurs in the Brick Lane area of East London, UK: turbulent times from 2019 to 2023

Spinder Dhaliwal and Richard George

INTRODUCTION

According to the London Chamber of Commerce and Industry's report: *Ethnic Diversity in Business: Removing Barriers Impeding Business Success* (2022), the increase in the number of Asian businesses has been a key feature of the small business population in the United Kingdom over the last decade (LCC&I, 2022). Less evident has been the role of female Asian entrepreneurs. Businesses led by people from ethnic minority backgrounds, particularly Black and Asian people, reflect the complex and evolving history of ethnic diversity in the UK. Initially setting up in geographical locations and sectors where they originally settled, Black and Asian people are now running businesses in diverse sectors and various locations (MSDUK, 2021).

Set in the context of the Brick Lane area in East London, this research focuses on the often-neglected issue of the contribution of Asian women to entrepreneurship in the UK and the issues they face when setting up and running a small business as well as the challenges they faced during the COVID-19 pandemic years. London is one of the most ethnically diverse cities in the world (Gov.uk, 2023). Despite this, access to finance and procurement opportunities by people from ethnic minority backgrounds is unsatisfactory. Black and Asian businesses struggle to access funding and procurement opportunities. Indeed, between 2009 and 2019, all-ethnic teams received an average of 1.7 per cent of venture capital investments. This concerning phenomenon suggests that not only are Black and Asian people facing hurdles in setting up and running businesses, but they also face challenges in accessing additional support which compounds rather than alleviates their problems (LCC&I, 2022).

Brick Lane, E1 is located in the ward of Spitalfields and Banglatown in the borough of Tower Hamlets in East London. According to the 2021 British Census, the largest ethnic groups in the area are Black, Asian and Multi-Ethnic (BAME) groups (61 per cent), comprising mostly of Bangladeshi residents (35 per cent) (ONS, 2021). The ward had a gender split of 54 per cent male and 46 per cent female (Warren, 2022). The borough of Tower Hamlets has the highest number of Muslim residents in the country (38 per cent), compared with 5 per cent in England and 13 per cent in London (Warren, 2022), with a population density of 15,695 persons per km^2 (the population density in England was 434 persons per km^2 and in London it was 5,598 per km^2) (ONS, 2021). According to the 2021 British Census, Tower Hamlets possesses a median age of 30, making it the youngest borough in England and Wales (ONS, 2021). Many businesses in Tower Hamlets are small to medium enterprises (SMEs), accounting for almost 90 per cent of all businesses in the borough (Tower Hamlets, 2023). Brick Lane itself has a strong tourism 'pull' with its boutique shops (mainly vintage clothing), the development of the Truman Brewery site, bookshops, and various other artisanal shops. Its restaurants are the centre of excellence for Bangladeshi cuisine.

The challenges Bangladeshi women in East London face include difficulties setting up their enterprises. The start-up phase is problematic and challenging for all, but the added lack of support from community and social norms dictating that they are homemakers first provide extra challenges. They face the issues of stereotyping, particularly if they go into a business beyond the type perceived as 'female'. The issues of motherhood and juggling both family and business responsibilities are pertinent, as is the social recognition they lack as businesswomen working in a male-dominated sphere. Some of the Bangladeshi women may struggle with language and so any formal support is problematic for them. Finally, growing and developing the business is a major issue. They often lack business skill know-how and have limited professional networks from which they can get advice. They have limited experience in marketing and branding and see themselves as entrepreneurs.

The COVID-19 pandemic has left a trail of destruction for many small businesses and has also had a severe impact on these women who have already depleted resources. There is an awareness of the challenges faced by ethnic minority businesses at government level, and there is some action to support them. The British Business Bank's (2020) *Alone Together* report found that access to finance is a major barrier for ethnic minority entrepreneurs. Since its launch (2012) the *Start-Up Loans* programme has issued around 20 per cent of its loans to Black, Asian, and ethnic-minority business. The government is also delivering actions set out in the *Inclusive Britain* report (Theyworkforyou, 2022), which aims to support ethnic minority entrepreneurs. Ministers regularly engage with ethnic minority business leaders and networks to better understand the issues facing them.

The last few years have been particularly turbulent, mainly impacted by an economic downturn caused partly by COVID-19 and other macro-economic factors such as the 2022/24 war in Ukraine and rising fuel costs (ONS, 2023). At a micro level, a number of businesses in the Brick Lane area have moved away from traditional sectors (for example, textile) towards the creative industries (fashion, arts and crafts, music, and digital media) (BOP, 2017). In addition, shifts towards technology businesses in the area mean that if some businesses do not change, they will struggle to survive: the same is true of start-up businesses.

Bangladeshi female entrepreneurs trying to start up and run businesses in this area currently face a multitude of complex challenges. There is a paucity of research on female entrepreneurs in the Black, Asian and minority-ethnic group (BAME) categorisation. This study attempts to add to the body of knowledge in this field.

This research examines several issues relating to Bangladeshi female entrepreneurship. We look at three stages of the challenges facing small Asian women businesses, namely, as start-ups, during 2020–2023, and currently.

LITERATURE REVIEW

Female Entrepreneurship

Asian women in the UK have been perceived as silent contributors for many decades (Dhaliwal, 1998). These women are often pivotal to businesses, but because they come from a patriarchal society, many still tend to play a supporting role despite the emergence of many among them successfully heading up their own businesses (Dhaliwal, 1998). These new ventures are often supported by their husbands/sons/fathers in terms of financial advice and other support. Volery (2007) refers to the cultural values and norms shared by South Asians in perceiving self-employment as a means for their livelihoods. Despite the many challenges they face, Asian women in business in the UK have historically displayed remarkable resilience, and their survival and robustness in a difficult economic environment is now recognised.

The Asian business community has been noted for its contribution to the UK economy as a successful immigrant group, despite the challenges, both social and economic, they have had to face (Dhaliwal & Gray, 2008). Cultural characteristics contributing to the success of the first generation include thrift, hard work, and a reliance on family labour (Razin, 2002; Waldinger, McEvoy & Aldrich, 1990). These traits gave Asian entrepreneurial endeavours some competitive edge over other businesses, but cultural factors have also served to restrict growth by creating excessive reliance on the local ethnic community as a market (Basu & Goswami, 1999; Ram, 1994). Asians have been pushed into setting up their own businesses due to the difficulties of finding suitable employment and the lack of opportunities (Brah, 2011; Sharafizad & Coetzer, 2016). Asian female entrepreneurs, however, do not enjoy the same access to resources and thus have a reduced chance of business success (Dhaliwal, 2000; Khan, 2021). Training and education can help empower these women, and female autonomy grows with time and experience (Khan, 2021).

Female entrepreneurship is essential to the expansion of firms and the economy (Said & Enslin, 2020), with several studies demonstrating its positive effects on fighting poverty and marginalisation in society (Deng et al., 2021; Lock & Lawton-Smith, 2016). Female entrepreneurs play an important role in local and global economies (Hechavarría et al., 2018; Hughes & Jennings, 2020; Jamali, 2009; McClelland et al., 2005). However, women have a disadvantaged status in society, and this is amplified for South Asian women who often defer to their husbands, fathers, or brothers rather than take credit for their own entrepreneurial attributes and success (Dhaliwal, 1998). Further, societal and institutional norms play a key role in determining entrepreneurial behaviour (Shane & Venkataraman, 2000). According to Alsos, Carter and Ljunggren (2014), there has been a paucity of research into household business decisions. There are many factors that play a part in this. Educational level is a strong factor (Amoako-Kwakye, 2012) and impacts on pursuing self-employment, the types of businesses women enter, and their level of self-confidence. Education also influences the choice of becoming self-employed (Calvo & Wellisz, 1980). Higher levels of education may also generate better outside options (i.e. more lucrative wage employment under better working conditions) and thus decrease the likelihood of entrepreneurship as the preferred choice (van der Sluis, van Praag & Vijverberg, 2008: 798). Empirical findings confirm this indeterminate effect of education level on advancement in the entrepreneurial process (Dilli & Westerhuis, 2018).

Asian female entrepreneurs are a heterogeneous group with considerable variation in terms of educational achievement, family influences and support, types of business, and aspirations for growth (Franzke et al., 2022). There is no 'one-size-fits-all' solution for promoting them. However, ethnic minority women are now being recognised as an increasingly important entrepreneurial minority; although they were previously excluded from academic literature (Dhaliwal, 2000; Jones & Ram, 2010). In order to understand this complex minority, we need to look at their entrepreneurial background, characteristics, and social and cultural background (Li et al., 2021). Female entrepreneurs are being recognised as key to the formation, operation and expansion of businesses (Acs et al., 2011; Said & Enslin, 2020). They have made a significant contribution to job creation and innovation (Hechavarria et al., 2019).

Several studies have highlighted the resilience and adaptability of women entrepreneurs during the recent COVID-19 pandemic. Many women managed to capitalise on the constraints imposed by the pandemic and successfully transition their businesses to the digital sphere (Afshan, Shahid & Tunio, 2021; Mustafa & Treanor, 2022). One study conducted by Althalathini, Al-Dajani and Apostolopoulos (2021) shed light on how female entrepreneurs not only overcame patriarchal expectations but also made significant social and economic contributions to their families and society. However, it is important to acknowledge that despite their remarkable adaptability, some female entrepreneurs faced additional challenges that further emphasised their subordination. Balancing the responsibilities of both caring for their families and catering to their customers' needs created an extra layer of duty for these women (Afshan et al., 2021; Mustafa & Treanor, 2022).

Moreover, the COVID-19 pandemic-induced economic downturn not only decreased market opportunities for women entrepreneurs but also had severe repercussions on their mental and financial well-being. Unfortunately, the heightened stress and vulnerability left many women susceptible to physical and sexual violence from their domestic partners (Roesch et al., 2020).

Issues Facing Bangladeshi Women Entrepreneurs

The literature on ethnic minority businesswomen has largely focused on their backgrounds, entrepreneurial motivations such as push and pull factors, and influences (Basu, 1998; Brush, Carter & Gatewood, 2004; Chaganti & Greene, 2000; Clark & Drinkwater, 2000; Raimi et al., 2023). Push and pull factors also play a large role. Some South Asians have tended to enjoy the freedom their business gives them and the propensity to get rewards for their work, while others see it as a route to survival due to poor market and job prospects. There are generational issues too; the first generation sought self-employment as a necessity and the younger generation is embracing higher growth potential sectors such as information communication technology (ICT) or business services rather than more traditional retail occupations (Dhaliwal & Gray, 2008; Ram & Jones, 2008).

Many of the current issues faced by Bangladeshi women in East London are similar to those of all small businesses, namely: access to finance, dealing with the aftermath of the COVID-19 pandemic, marketing, branding, and growing the business. However, additionally, Bangladeshi women face issues of stereotyping, juggling motherhood and family responsibilities with the business, culture and religion, lack of business skills and know-how, limited business networks and a difficult and uncertain economy. They also struggle with social recognition and status as businesswomen, and some struggle with language. Sobhan's (2022) study – which looked at female entrepreneurs in

Bangladesh – found that, due to the women's status and reliance on men, they confront many obstacles that limit their financial capability and their ability to deal directly with financial institutions. The same constraints appear to be true of Bangladeshi female entrepreneurs in East London.

Women often rely on personal financial savings and bootstrapping as they are reluctant to go to formal institutions for support.[1] Mitra and Rauf (2011) looked at Pakistani females and found that they often opt for low value, low-growth businesses so that they can be a 'good' mother and a 'responsible' wife. The female role in many Asian societies, and in Bangladeshi society in particular, strongly associates women with family, children, and homemaking (Achtenhagen & Welter, 2003). These women constantly strive to progress but are faced with enormous challenges and an unhelpful attitude from society, thus presenting them with enormous obstacles (Henry & Kennedy, 2003). Any perception of inferiority to their male counterparts will impact both their attitude and potential as entrepreneurs (Achtenhagen & Welter, 2003).

A study by Karim et al. (2022) found that female entrepreneurs in Bangladesh face various social, cultural and institutional barriers and challenges. This present study hypothesises that this is equally true of Bangladeshi female entrepreneurs in Brick Lane. There is still a paucity of research on Asian female entrepreneurs (Dhaliwal, 2000; Jones & Ram, 2010; Khan, 2021). Studies to date have included looking at their background (Chaganti & Greene 2000; Evans, 1989), their influences (Brush, Carter & Gatewood, 2004), and their entrepreneurial experiences (Levie, 2007).

This study looks at the challenges Bangladeshi women entrepreneurs face during the start-up phase, the turbulence of the past few years which were dominated by the COVID-19 pandemic, and the current challenges they face in light of the economic downturn. There is a dearth of research into Asian women entrepreneurs, in particular research into the socio-economic challenges. This study attempts to fill this gap by exploring the challenges facing Bangladeshi female entrepreneurs in East London, UK.

METHODOLOGY

We conducted qualitative interviews with six Bangladeshi women entrepreneurs in the Brick Lane area of East London (UK). Issues explored included the background of their business; business type; age of business; facilitating and hindering factors at start-up stage; and the particular barriers that confront them as Asian business women. In addition, the research aimed to find out whether cultural and religious factors influenced the women when setting up their business. Further, the study aimed to establish the challenges they faced when they started their business as well as those they face currently.

Women operating in a community group develop new ways of working from a social constructivism perspective. With this in mind, this research comes from a social constructive perspective. Social constructionism is a theory in sociology, social ontology, and communication theory which proposes that certain ideas about physical reality arise from collaborative consensus, instead of pure observation of said reality. The theory centres on the notion that meanings are developed in coordination with others rather than separately by cach individual (Leeds-Hurwitz, 2009). This approach captures the complex entrepreneurial journeys and challenges of these women who operate within a close-knit community.

Social constructivism is a learning approach based on the ability of learners to construct their knowledge. The knowledge that the learner constructs is based on their experiences from interactions. Social constructivism proposes that learning is fostered through social interactions and the assistance of others, often within a group setting. Soviet psychologist Lev Vygotsky (1896–1934) is credited with developing the theory of social constructivism. Central to this concept is the notion that knowledge does not simply mirror an objective reality; rather, it arises from the mind's process of selecting, interpreting, and reconstructing experiences. Consequently, knowledge is seen as an outcome of the interplay between subjective factors and environmental influences. This is particularly important for the group of women in this study who have started and developed their businesses in a complex environment.

Kvale defined the qualitative research interview as one whose purpose is to gather descriptions of the lifeworld of the interviewee with respect to inter-pretation of the meaning of the described phenomena (1983: 174). Interviews were conducted by telephone. The advantages of this technique are that inter-views can be conducted more rapidly and at a lower cost than either personal interviews or postal surveys (Opdenakker, 2006). Telephone interviews also made it easier to gain access to the study participants. Another advantage of telephone interviewing is that the interviewer can interview people who are not otherwise easily accessible (Opdenakker, 2006). As was the case in this research study, researchers asked to speak to interviewees by name or to those who have the desired characteristics.

Telephone interviews increase flexibility but are also researcher biased. The way in which the interviewer asks questions, or their tone of voice used, may discourage respondents from answering certain questions (Aaker et al., 2020: 195). Thus, one of the limitations of asynchronous communication of place by telephone is the reduction of social cues (Opdenakker, 2006). The interviewer does not see the respondent, so body language cannot be used as a source of additional data. Nevertheless, social cues such as voice control and intonation are available (Chapple, 1999).

A number of difficulties were encountered with the women in the sample. Several non-respondents appeared reluctant to come forward and participate in the study. This may have been due to issues of trust and disclosure (namely: talking about their business enterprise). A great deal of effort was made to contact this hard-to-reach group. Due to the cultural sensitivities of the group, direct contact proved problematic and so access to the community of Muslim women was gained through contacts and referrals from colleagues of one of the authors who was a key member of the Bangladeshi business community and well networked. This led to a snowballing approach. The women felt more comfortable once the mutual friend was introduced to the researchers and the purpose and importance of the research was explained. Some women were initially concerned about the purpose of our study until they were assured of its confidentiality and understood that their names would not be disclosed so they could not be identified. Interviews were conducted in English. These women were chosen as a sample of respondents (interviewees) as their experiences are deemed representative of other Bangladeshi women in small businesses in the Brick Lane vicinity.

We believed that telephone interview rather than a questionnaire was the best way to seek a complete, in-depth and fuller picture of the interviewees' lives. As researchers, we felt we could be reasonably objective as we are not from the community. For most of the participants, this was their first opportunity to discuss their professional and personal lives without their husbands being present. One or two of the respondents had difficulty understanding one of the questions ('whether they receive social and societal recognition'). Besides being of Bangladeshi origin, the other prerequisite for the research was that interviewees had to be small business owners or entrepreneurs. No specific type of business was stipulated.

FINDINGS

Background of the Respondents

The women in our sample differed in terms of business sector, business size, their academic levels and business experiences. This was an eclectic group of mainly micro businesses run by Bangladeshi women that included health care, a consulting business, an accountancy firm, a driving school, a textile business, and a care home. Some of the interviewees employ workers, while others work alone. Qualifications ranged from Higher National Diploma (HND) to National Vocational Qualification (NVQ) and one of the women had graduated with a degree. All of the interviewees are of Bangladeshi origin and currently run their own businesses from within the Brick Lane area. The most established business was set up six years ago whilst the newest business is two years old.

Challenges in Setting up the Business

The biggest obstacle one of the interviewees faced was 'stereotyping'. She felt she did not receive the status that should have been afforded to her for running a business: "I was not respected as a business woman." She found that the start-up phase was a steep learning curve for her: "I lacked practical knowledge and felt insecure." Her lack of concrete and basic business skills such as writing, filling in forms, and communicating with people outside of the Bangladeshi community proved problematic. She was very conscious that as a Bangladeshi woman entering self-employment, she was joining the realm of a largely male-dominated sphere. The family were supportive of her decision to become self-employed and because hers was a textile business it was seen as being 'feminine'.

Another woman stressed that the business domain she experienced was very male- dominated. As a professional woman setting up an accountancy practice, she found that the other firms in the area were mostly run by men, for men: "I wasn't even given an opportunity to show what I could do." She faced several difficulties in marketing herself to the Brick Lane/Whitechapel community and felt that many doors were closed and that people, mostly men, were not willing to have a female accountant whom they did not perceive was as good as their male counterparts.

One respondent who started up a consultancy business struggled with juggling her roles: "there were not enough hours in the day." She had a young family and was torn between family responsibilities and commitments to the wider family and her business ambitions.

Another respondent set up a driving school and she, too, was juggling motherhood with work. She faced sexism from the male-dominated customer base and struggled to survive in the early phase of the business. Another woman in the care sector was more concerned with her limited business acumen. In particular, she felt that she struggled with technology and so much of the business needed her to be information technology (IT) savvy.

All the women said that they struggled with marketing themselves effectively and writing business communications. In fact, one of the women's struggles with the English language proved to be a liability.

Gender Bias

More than half of the interviewees had felt some kind of bias for being Bangladeshi women in business in the Brick Lane community. They felt they had to fight the stereotype of being "just mothers and wives". They also felt that the community was to blame for its attitudes to the role and expectations of women. One woman felt that it was not just from her personal contacts in the community but entering the male-dominated financial sector and trying to prove that she was competent as a qualified accountant. Another interviewee stated that she found male colleagues and other driving instructors expressed shock and surprise when she set up her own school: "some men were clearly shocked and couldn't respect me as a business woman." All the interviewees felt that the men did not take them seriously: "I was so frustrated trying to prove myself." This was a cause of distress for the women entrepreneurs and hampered their business progress.

BACKGROUND AND INFLUENCES

Religion/Culture

In terms of the specific roles religion or culture played, whilst the two are different, they were often spoken about as the same. The general consensus amongst the women was that they were made to feel that "women should stay at home". For example, one interviewee was repeatedly told that running an accountancy firm is "not the norm for women", so she felt ostracised. She felt culturally bound and constrained. Others found it both a positive and negative experience. For example, one interviewee revealed that "although women are not meant to set up their own businesses", she felt that her religion, Islam, gave her the strength and courage to move forward. Another interviewee said that "women were pushing the boundaries in a male-dominated sector" and that was frowned upon by a large part of the community. However, she was proud that she had more female customers wanting to learn to drive and, thus, she played a role in empowering them. She continued: "For a practising Muslim woman who prays five times a day, it is easier to do this when you are self-employed." She also felt that she was a role model for younger Muslim women in the Brick Lane community who aspired to be entrepreneurs.

The respondent from the care sector said that she felt encouraged by her religion in that she was helping the more vulnerable in society and so doing what her faith encouraged. She found this rewarding and felt that being in the care sector was more likely to be accepted and respected in the Brick Lane community as it was perceived to be a 'feminine' role.

Family

The amount of support, both tacit and practical, from family differed greatly amongst the women. Some said their families were supportive, but others said that they were supportive now but had not been in the early stages of the business: "initially I had a lot of resistance", commented one interviewee. Others admitted that there had been clashes with the family. The majority of interviewees did, however, credit their families with offering them support, which included financial support, encouragement, and advice.

Over time, the women did receive some measure of support from their families, but this was only after they had had to fight hard to start the business and prove that it had potential. One woman said, "I really appreciated the advice I received from my family, they pooled together to buy equipment for me." Financial and emotional support were the most welcome resources. Sharing information and helping them find customers were mentioned, as was being encouraged to develop the business. This trust and support boosted them within their community. The support and help, when received, came from various members of the family, including siblings, parents, and spouses. This was specifically so once the businesses flourished, and family members were able to acknowledge that the enterprises were becoming successful and bearing fruit.

Experiences of Entrepreneurship

All the interviewees struggled with growing their businesses. Two of the interviewees stated that they employ staff. Taking on people to help was a big step forward for two of the interviewees. "It has been a huge benefit having staff to help with the business as it has meant that I can focus more on managing the company as well as looking to increase business and get more clients", claimed one of the interviewees. One entrepreneur employs five carers in a care home: "recruiting and finding good carers is a big problem." Another has administrative help as well as another accountant in her accountancy practice. The women struggled with growth: "I didn't understand the legal aspects", stated one of the entrepreneurs. "I found it hard going from a home business to a fully fledged professional one", said another. Learning about the legal side of the business, human resource practices, health and safety, and other essential bureaucratic necessities, was a steep learning curve for several of the interviewees.

Recent Challenges

When asked about the main challenge they faced in 2020–2023, nearly all the interviewees said COVID-19. The pandemic caused issues with travel and utilities, further hampered by an uncertain economy: "I was so worried I had lost everything." Working from home and a reduction in income had a serious negative impact on their businesses. These factors led to financial challenges faced in terms of dealing with rising costs, lower incomes from customers, and the uncertainty and insecurity of the economy. Several of the interviewees stated that they had struggled with recruitment and funding during the economic downturn.

The interviewee who owns the driving school stated that the COVID-19 pandemic had a major negative impact on her business: "every day it got worse, petrol prices were going up and I could barely afford to keep going." She added that the recent economic downturn had not helped and the rise in petrol prices has resulted in extremely high costs that she was unable to pass on to her customers who were already struggling with a smaller disposable income.

Current Challenges

The main challenge faced by one of the respondents who owns a small manufacturing textiles business was access to finance and the finance needed to grow the business from being based at home to a fully fledged professional business. Locating premises and dealing with the red tape that goes with that was also found to be problematic. Employing people and adhering to legal aspects and efficient human resource protocols was stated as an additional challenge. Another interviewee mentioned that the lack of knowledge regarding the legal aspects of the business was an issue: "I lacked legal training and did not know where to go for help"; she also cited promoting and growing the business as a major hurdle: "I did not have a clue about expanding the business, there was so much to learn and cope with, I struggled." Rising fuel costs was also a major challenge for the care home owner who found that utility costs were "eating into my profits quite substantially". She also had a lot of difficulty finding and recruiting carers. Even some of the positive aspects of the business, such as dealing with increasing daily orders, created problems in respect of meeting this growing demand.

All the interviewees stated that they felt it was important to be recognised as business- women and entrepreneurs. They worked hard, had many challenges, and wanted the community to recognise their efforts. Most of them enjoyed the prestige of being a businesswoman and self-employed. They were proud of motivating others, particularly being role models for younger Muslim women. One of the interviewees felt she had achieved some measure of recognition, "but it has taken me three-and-a-half years!" Succeeding and running a business against the odds in a community that did not see this as the 'done thing' is an immense source of pride. Another interviewee felt that her business recognition was more a result of a presence on social media rather than the Brick Lane community.

Several of the women belong to formal business trade organisations and this has helped them network and market themselves more effectively. Most interviewees had not approached the local authority for help other than one of the interviewees who is a member of Spitalfields' Small Business Association located in Whitechapel.

CONCLUSION

Our study reveals a picture of intelligent and creative women who are resilient in the face of challenging circumstances. They were determined to survive during the COVID-19 crisis and, more importantly, wanted their businesses to be at the cutting edge so that not only would they survive the crisis but they would also emerge much stronger beyond it. This research adds to the growing body of literature on women in business and is relevant for practitioners, academics, and policy makers. It adds to the paucity of literature on ethnic minority women, particularly Asian women in the UK. It also sheds light on and gives a voice to Bangladeshi female entrepreneurs in the Brick Lane area of London, UK. Findings should inform policymakers enabling resources to be accessible to this group of women.

There are distinct issues pertinent to this group of women who will, in future years, prove to be an important part of an entrepreneurial minority. They are role models for their community and particularly for other Bangladeshi and Asian women. The turbulent economy continues to bring more challenges, so their continued resilience is needed in the face of the economic downturn and the still prominent after-effects of the COVID-19 pandemic.

This research is not without its limitations. While our qualitative approach allowed us to gain deep insights, our sample size was small. Future research should include a larger sample and a mixed methods approach to capture the micro and macro picture. This study provides a greater understanding of Bangladeshi female entrepreneurs and the community and business world in which they aspire to flourish. Future research could explore other minority communities in which women entrepreneurs operate.

NOTE

1.   Bootstrapping—defined as "highly creative ways of acquiring the use of resources without borrowing money or raising equity financing from traditional sources" (Freear et al., 1995: 102).

REFERENCES

Aaker, D., Kumar, V., Leone, R. & Day, G. (2020). *Marketing Research*, 13th edn. New York: John Wiley & Sons.

Achtenhagen, L. & Welter, F. (2003). Female entrepreneurship in Germany: Context, development and its reflection in German media. In J. Butler (Ed.), *New Perspectives on Women Entrepreneurs* (pp. 77–100). Greenwich, CT: Information Age Publishing.

Acs, Z. J., Bardasi, E., Estrin, S. & Svejnar, J. (2011). Introduction to special issue of small business economics on female entrepreneurship in developed and developing economies. *Small Business Economics*, 37(4), 393–396.

Afshan, G., Shahid, S. & Tunio, M. (2021). Learning experiences of women entrepreneurs amidst COVID-19. *International Journal of Gender and Entrepreneurship*, 13(2), 162–186.

Alsos, G. A., Carter, S. & Ljunggren, E. (2014). Kinship and business: How entrepreneurial households facilitate business growth. *Entrepreneurship & Regional Development*, 26(1–2), 97–122.

Althalathini, D., Al-Dajani, H. & Apostolopoulos, N. (2021). The impact of Islamic feminism in empowering women's entrepreneurship in conflict zones: Evidence from Afghanistan, Iraq and Palestine. *Journal of Business Ethics*, 178(1), 1–17.

Amoako-Kwakye, F. (2012). Background characteristics and determinants of performance of women's business operations in Agona and Asikuma-Odoben-Brakwa districts, Ghana. *Journal of Management Policy and Practice*, 13(3), 129–148.

Basu, A. (1998). An exploration of entrepreneurial activity among Asian small businesses in Britain. *Small Business Economics*, 10, 313–326.

Basu, A. & Goswami, A. (1999). South Asian entrepreneurship in Great Britain: Factors influencing growth. *International Journal of Entrepreneurial Behavior & Research*, 5(5), 251–275.

BOP (2017). *The East London Fashion Cluster.* BOP Consulting. Available at https://www.fashion-district.co.uk/wp-content/uploads/2018/09/East-London-Fashion-Cluster-Draft-and-Strategy-Plan.pdf (accessed 4 August 2023).

Brah, A. (2011). Cartographies of diaspora: Contesting identities. In M. Eagleton (Ed.), *Feminist Literary Theory: A Reader* (pp. 391–392). London: Wiley-Blackwell.

British Business Bank (2020). *Alone Together*. Available at https://www.british-business-bank.co.uk/about/research-and-publications/alone-together-entrepreneurship-diversity-uk (accessed 12 July 2023).

Brush, C., Carter, N. & Gatewood, E. (2004). Women entrepreneurs, growth, and implications for the classroom. *2004 Coleman Foundation White Paper Series for the United States Association for Small Business and Entrepreneurship: Entrepreneurship in a Diverse World*, 47–91.

Calvo, G. & Wellisz, S. (1980). Technology, entrepreneurs, and firm size. *The Quarterly Journal of Economics*, 95(4), 663–677.

Chaganti, R. & Greene, P. (2000). Who are migrant entrepreneurs? A study of entrepreneurs' migrant involvement and business characteristics. *Journal of Small Business Management*, 40, 126–143.

Chapple, A. (1999). The use of telephone interviewing for qualitative research. *Nurse Researcher*, 3(Spring), 85–96.

Clark, K. & Drinkwater, S. (2000). Pushed out or pulled in? Self-employment among ethnic minorities in England and Wales. *Labour Economics*, 7(5), 603–628.

Deng, W., Liang, Q., Li, J. & Wang, W. (2021). Science mapping: A bibliometric analysis of female entrepreneurship studies. *Gender in Management*, 36(1), 61–86.

Dhaliwal, S. (1998). Silent contributors: Asian female entrepreneurs and women in business. *Women's Studies International Forum*, 21(5), 463–474.

Dhaliwal, S. (2000). Entrepreneurship–a learning process: The experiences of Asian female entrepreneurs and women in business. *Education and Training*, 42(8), 445–453.

Dhaliwal, S. & Gray, D. (2008). The Asian business sector and the dynamics of change: A story of growth, diversity and success in the UK. *Equal Opportunities International*, 27(3), 221–236.

Dilli, S. & Westerhuis, G. (2018). How institutions and gender differences in education shape entrepreneurial activity: A cross-national perspective. *Small Business Economics*, 51, 371–392.

Evans, M. (1989). Immigrant entrepreneurship: Effects of ethnic market size and isolated labor pool. *American Sociological Review*, 54(6), 9509–9562.

Franzke, S., Wu, J., Froese, F. & Chen, Z. (2022). Female entrepreneurship in Asia: A critical review and future directions. *Asian Business Management*, 21, 343–372.

Freear, J., Sohl, J. & Wetzel, W. (1995). Angels: Personal investors in the venture capital market. *Entrepreneurship & Regional Development*, 7(1), 85–94.

Gov.uk (2023). Regional ethnic diversity. Available at https:// www .ethnicity -facts -figures .service .gov .uk/ uk -population -by -ethnicity/ national -and -regional -populations/regional-ethnic-diversity/latest (accessed 12 May 2023).

Hechavarría, D., Terjesen, S., Stenholm, P., Brännback, M. & Lång, S. (2018). More than words: Do gendered linguistic structures widen the gender gap in entrepreneurial activity? *Entrepreneurship: Theory and Practice*, 42(5), 797–817.

Hechavarria, D., Bullough, A., Brush, C. & Edelman, L. (2019) High-growth women's entrepreneurship: Fuelling social and economic development. *Journal of Small Business Management*, 57(1), 5–13.

Henry, C. & Kennedy, S. (2003). In search of a new Celtic tiger. In J. E. Butler (Ed.), *New Perspectives on Women Entrepreneurs* (pp. 203–224). Greenwich, CT: Information Age Publishing.

Hughes, K. & Jennings, J. (2020). A legacy of attention to embeddedness in gendered institutions: Reflections on a key contribution of women's entrepreneurship research. *International Journal of Gender and Entrepreneurship*, 12(1), 53–76.

Jamali, D. (2009). Constraints and opportunities facing women entrepreneurs in developing countries. *Gender in Management: An International Journal*, 24(4), 232–251.

Jones, T. & Ram, M. (2010). Review article: Ethnic variations on the small firm labour process. *International Small Business Journal: Researching Entrepreneurship*, 28(2), 163–173.

Karim, S., Kwong, C., Shrivastava, M. & Tamvada, J. (2022). My mother-in-law does not like it: Resources, social norms, and entrepreneurial intentions of women in an emerging economy. *Small Business Economics*, 60, 409–443.

Khan, A. (2021). Entrepreneurship among Pakistani women in the United Kingdom: Exploring hindrances and opportunities. PhD thesis, University of Gloucestershire.

Kvale, S. (1983). The qualitative research interview. *Journal of Phenomenological Psychology*, 14(1–2), 171–196.

Leeds-Hurwitz, W. (2009). Social construction of reality. In S. Littlejohn & K. Foss (Eds.), *Encyclopaedia of Communication Theory.* Thousand Oaks, CA: Sage.

Levie, J. (2007). Immigration, in-migration, ethnicity and entrepreneurship in the United Kingdom. *Small Business Economics*, 28(2), 143–169.

Li, Y., Wu, J., Zhang, D. & Ling, L. (2021). Gendered institutions and female entrepreneurship: A fuzzy-set QCA approach. *Gender in Management*, 36(1), 87–107.

Lock, R. & Lawton-Smith, H. (2016). The impact of female entrepreneurship on economic growth in Kenya. *International Journal of Gender and Entrepreneurship*, 8(1), 90–96.

LCC&I [London Chamber of Commerce and Industry] (2022). *Ethnic Diversity in Business: Removing Barriers Impeding Business Success*. London: LCC&I.

McClelland, E., Swail, J., Bell, J. & Ibbotson, P. (2005). Following the pathway of female entrepreneurs: A six-country investigation. *International Journal of Entrepreneurial Behavior and Research*, 11(2), 84–107.

Mitra, J. & Rauf, A. (2011). Role of personal networks in the growth of entrepreneurial ventures of ethnic minority female entrepreneurs. *SSRN Electronic Journal* (23 August). University of Essex CER Working Paper No. 5.

MSDUK (2021). Minority businesses matter. Available at https://www.minoritybusinessesmatter.org/# (accessed 26 June 2023).

Mustafa, M. & Treanor, L. (2022) Gender and entrepreneurship in the New Era: New perspectives on the role of gender and entrepreneurial activity. *Entrepreneurship Research Journal*. Available at https://www.degruyter.com/document/doi/10.1515/erj-2022–0228/html (accessed 2 September 2023).

ONS [Office for National Statistics] (2021). *Census 2021*. London: ONS. Available at https://www.ons.gov.uk/census.

ONS [Office for National Statistics] (2023). *GDP in History: How the COVID-19 Pandemic Shocked the UK Economy*. London: ONS. Available at https:// www .ons .gov .uk/ economy/ gros sdomesticp roductgdp/ articles/ gd pandevents inhistoryh owthecovid 19pandemic shockedthe ukeconomy/ 2022–05–24 (accessed 12 June 2023).

Opdenakker, R. (2006). Advantages and disadvantages of four interview techniques in qualitative research. *Forum: Qualitative Social Research*, 7(4), 11–20.

Raimi, L., Panait, M., Gigauri, I. & Apostu, S. (2023). Thematic review of motivational factors, types of uncertainty, and entrepreneurship strategies of transitional entrepreneurship among ethnic minorities, immigrants, and women entrepreneurs. *Journal of Risk Financial Management*, 16(83). https://doi.org/10.3390/jrfm16020083.

Ram, M. (1994). Unravelling social networks in ethnic minority firms. *International Small Business Journal*, 12(3), 42–53.

Ram, M. & Jones, T. (2008). Ethnic-minority businesses in the UK: A review of research and policy developments. *Environment and Planning: Government and Policy*, 26(2), 352–374.

Razin, E. (2002). The economic context, embeddedness and immigrant entrepreneurs. *International Journal of Entrepreneurial Behaviour & Research*, 8(1/2), 162–167.

Roesch, E., Amin, A., Gupta, J. & García-Moreno, C. (2020). Violence against women during COVID-19 pandemic restrictions. *British Medical Journal*, 369. https:// doi .org/10.1136/bmj.m1712.

Said, I. & Enslin, C. (2020). Lived experiences of females with entrepreneurship in Sudan: Networking, social expectations, and family support. *Sage Open*, 10(4). https://doi.org/10.1177/2158244020963131.

Shane, S. & Venkataraman, S. (2000). The promise of entrepreneurship as a field of research. *The Academy of Management Review*. Available at https://about.jstor.org/terms (accessed 23 May 2023).

Sharafizad, J. & Coetzer, A. (2016). Women business owners' start-up motivations and network content. *Journal of Small Business and Enterprise Development*, 23(2), 590–610.

Sobhan, N. (2022). Examining the impact of formal and informal institutions: A mixed-method study of female entrepreneurs in Bangladesh. PhD thesis, University of West Scotland (UWS).

Theyworkforyou (2022). New businesses: Ethnic groups. Available at https://www.theyworkforyou.com/wrans/?id=2022–11–15.87715.h (accessed 26 June 2023).

Tower Hamlets (2023). Draft Tower Hamlets priority needs. Available at https://democracy.towerhamlets.gov.uk/mgConvert2PDF.aspx?ID=215062.

van der Sluis, J., van Praag, M. & Vijverberg, W. (2008). Education and entrepreneurship selection and performance: A review of the empirical literature. *Journal of Economic Surveys*, 22(5), 795–841.

Volery, T. (2007). Ethnic entrepreneurship: A theoretical framework. In L.-P. Dana (Ed.), *Handbook of Research on Ethnic Minority Entrepreneurship* (pp. 30–41). Cheltenham: Edward Elgar Publishing.

Waldinger, R., McEvoy, D. & Aldrich, H. (1990). Spatial dimensions of opportunity structures. In R. Waldinger, H. Aldrich & R. Ward (Eds.), *Ethnic Entrepreneurs: Immigrant Business in Industrial Societies* (pp. 106–130). London: Sage.

Warren, T. (2022). *Review of Whitechapel and Spitalfields Business Growth Potential and Opportunities*. No publisher.

4. Addressing crises through entrepreneurial resilience: migrant women entrepreneurs in the United Arab Emirates

Nadeera Ranabahu and Maryam Fozia

1. INTRODUCTION

To ensure the survival or growth of their ventures, entrepreneurs often have to manage or respond to crises in the marketplace or in their businesses. A crisis is defined as "a sudden and unexpected event that threatens to disrupt an organisation's operations and poses both a financial and a reputational threat" (Coombs, 2007, p. 165). It can "harm stakeholders physically, emotionally and/or financially" (Coombs, 2007, p. 165). While the definition of crisis has evolved over time, it captures events that are considered low probability, unexpected or unpredictable (i.e. a crisis as an event) and everyday occurrences that may occur over time to threaten a business's viability or function (i.e. crisis as a process) (Doern et al., 2019; Williams et al., 2017). Recently, due to the COVID-19 outbreak, the word crisis has become linked with the global pandemic. However, a crisis can be internal or external, intentional or unintentional, violent or non-violent, major or minor, technical or economic in nature, and people-, social-, or organisational-centric. A crisis may occur as the result of a rumour, an intentional act, an accident, scandal, war, social unrest, political upheaval, economic recession, or technological turbulence (Coombs, 1995, 2007; Doern et al., 2019; Mitroff et al., 1988). Therefore, in this chapter we focus on crises beyond the COVID-19 pandemic to address our core research question: How do migrant women entrepreneurs start and navigate their businesses during periods of crisis and develop entrepreneurial resilience?

Any of the above-mentioned types of crises may affect a business's reputation (Coombs, 2007) and shape its performance, innovativeness, agility, adaptability, and resourcefulness (Bodlaj & Čater, 2019; Liu & Yang, 2019). In recent years, entrepreneurs have had to deal with the effects of the COVID-19 pandemic. Some have successfully adjusted to the changing situation by quickly pivoting their businesses, going virtual, changing their marketing strategies, and capitalising on new and emerging opportunities (Khurana et al., 2022). The effects of the COVID-19 pandemic have been catastrophic for some businesses. As a result of global lockdowns, many have experienced financial difficulties, disruptions in their supply chains, and freeze-hiring due to a lack of demand. Some businesses have even gone bankrupt (Donthu & Gustafsson, 2020). In addition, entrepreneurs have had to manage challenging internal situations resulting from errors, scandals, shocks, or disruptions to routines. If unmanaged situations such as these can quickly escalate into crisis (Vogus & Sutcliffe, 2007). In order to survive and operate businesses in times of crises, entrepreneurs require resilience strategies such as relying on networks or accessing external resources and information (Liu & Yang, 2019).

Different groups of entrepreneurs employ different types of resilience strategies to deal with business crises (Bodlaj & Čater, 2019; de Vries & Hamilton, 2021; Doern, 2021; Khurana et al., 2022). For example, entrepreneurs who live under the continual threat of a natural disaster often prepare themselves by learning from a previous experience(s) of recovering from a disaster, reflecting on the venture's needs in case they have to re-build their business, and searching and enacting new ideas (Muñoz et al., 2019). In contrast, a family business dealing with an internal crisis may reconfigure their existing family social capital to improve the business's chance of survival (Hadjielias et al., 2022). Gaining an understanding of how different groups of entrepreneurs in various situations build their resilience may help shape the development of theory, policy, and practice.

This study provides insights into migrant women entrepreneurs living in the Middle East, a rarely studied group of entrepreneurs. In particular, it investigates how they develop resilience when starting and operating their businesses during times of crisis. Aligning with the definition of crisis provided above, we study resilience strategies in multiple crisis situations, beyond those represented by the COVID-19 pandemic. This chapter makes two key contributions. First, it contributes to a growing body of literature on entrepreneurial resilience during times of crisis by outlining how different crises shape and reshape migrant women's entrepreneurial endeavours and their resilience strategies. Second, it identifies how migrant women entrepreneurs use both home and host country resources and structures to develop their resilience.

The remainder of this chapter provides a review of literature on entrepreneurial resilience, identifying strategies migrants use in business start-up and day-to-day operations. The chapter then explains the study's context and methods, before presenting detailed case narratives of two migrant women who operate/ed businesses in the United Arab Emirates (UAE). Finally, the chapter discusses the findings, outlines implications for future research, and concludes with a summary.

2.   LITERATURE REVIEW

2.1   Entrepreneurial Resilience

Entrepreneurs aim to manage crises by "bringing the organisation back to normal functioning" (i.e. crisis management) or maintaining "reliable" functions of a business throughout the disruption (i.e. resilience) (Doern et al., 2019, p. 403). Our focus here is resilience, defined as, "the process by which an actor (i.e., individual, organisation, or community) builds and uses its capability endowments to interact with the environment in a way that positively adjusts and maintains functioning prior to, during, and following adversity" (Williams et al., 2017, p. 742). We use this definition to frame our study as it combines elements associated with psychological and organisational resilience in explaining entrepreneurial resilience. Furthermore, in small business situations the business and the business owner cannot be separated; hence, it makes sense to use both psychological and organisational resilience in combination to explain entrepreneurial resilience.

Psychological resilience refers both to the exposure to adversity and how entrepreneurs "respond to this adversity through affective, cognitive, and behavioural mechanisms" (Hoegl & Hartmann, 2021). An entrepreneur's personal characteristics and attributes (such as their self-efficacy, learning and development, personal experiences in overcoming trauma, a growth mindset, beliefs and values, and coping strategies) contribute to the development of psychological resilience (Hartmann et al., 2022). In addition, a person's financial or resource position, cognitive capabilities (i.e. having a clear vision, or sense of purpose), and behavioural capabilities (i.e. ability to manage social connections and regulate emotions) strengthen their psychological resilience. Contextual factors such as environmental dynamism, availability of resources, and social networks further shape and influence the development of entrepreneurial resilience (Hartmann et al., 2022).

Organisational resilience is defined as the "maintenance of positive adjustment under challenging conditions" in such a way that the "organisation emerges from those conditions strengthened and more resourceful" (Vogus & Sutcliffe, 2007, p. 3418). It is particularly important because if organisations do not cope with less severe continuous disruptions and challenging conditions, these disruptions and challenges may accumulate and escalate into severe organisational crises (Haase & Eberl, 2019; Vogus & Sutcliffe, 2007). Organisational resilience includes employing strategies of adaptability and flexibility, developing capabilities to cope with change (Ayala & Manzano, 2014; Hartmann et al., 2022; Kantur & Iseri-Say, 2015; Vogus & Sutcliffe, 2007), or in the case of start-ups, routinising tasks to manage uncertainty

(Haase & Eberl, 2019). These strategies shape how an organisation anticipates, prevents, mitigates, or adjusts to crises (Williams et al., 2017).

Entrepreneurs combine, and sometimes separate, psychological and organisational resilience strategies to manage business functions (de Vries & Hamilton, 2021). In extreme crisis events such as natural disasters, entrepreneurial resilience helps an individual to recover, survive, or exit from a business (de Vries & Hamilton, 2016, 2021). The entrepreneurial resilience strategies used during COVID-19 seem to be different, perhaps due to the long-term nature of the pandemic and the introduction of legally enforceable lockdowns and physical distancing measures. For example, during COVID-19, entrepreneurs relied on psychological resilience capabilities to manage expectations and regulate emotions as stress and feelings of negativity (Doern, 2021). Furthermore, entrepreneurs adjusted to the unfolding pandemic by employing organisational resilience strategies as closing their non-essential businesses to avoid the physical risks, monitoring financial, human, and physical damages to ascertain losses and detect risks, mobilising resources from their networks, and changing their business processes (Doern, 2021). Hence, entrepreneurial resilience, resulting from a combination of elements of psychological and organisational resilience, is essential for maintaining reliable functions of a business throughout a disruption.

2.2   Resilience among Migrant Women Entrepreneurs

Among migrant groups, the literature often discusses entrepreneurial resilience among forced migrants/refugees (Yeshi et al., 2022). This focus is not surprising given that refugees have to overcome extreme hardships or trauma when settling in a new country (de Vries et al., 2021; Yeshi et al., 2022). Among refugee women, entrepreneurship is perceived as a way to overcome restrictions associated with mobility and earn money to meet their children's needs (Abuhussein, 2022). The women use their social capital to navigate financial and administrative hurdles in host country policies (Alexandre et al., 2019). In addition, when starting or expanding their businesses, the refugees frequently draw on their ethnic networks and family members for psychological support (Zehra & Usmani, 2021). In this context, women's limited business experiences lead them to learn and rely on their family and immediate social network (Abuhussein, 2022). Organisational resilience strategies such as adaptability, flexibility, and resourcefulness (Ayala & Manzano, 2014) are evident among those women whose journeys were forced and who start and operate businesses (Huq & Venugopal, 2021; Ranabahu et al., 2021). As Yeshi et al. (2022) note, refugee entrepreneurs' resilience is not a static status, but rather an "interrelated, dynamic process influenced by factors at individual, relational, and institutional levels" (p. 6).

As crises create insecurities, women (whether they are migrants or not), rely on family members, business mentors, and networks, to enhance their level of entrepreneurial resilience (Kogut & Mejri, 2022). However, beyond forced migrants, entrepreneurial resilience strategies are rarely discussed among other types of migrant women (i.e. skilled migrants, business migrants, and temporary migrants). When starting and operating their businesses, migrants also face change, confusion, and hardships due to political, economic, social, and cultural situations in the host countries (Osaghae & Cooney, 2020; Tengeh, 2016). These situations can be sources of crises. Any false or risky step in response to these situations can undo their businesses (Naman & Slevin, 1993). Such situations may also leave migrant women entrepreneurs feeling both psychologically and physically exhausted, such as in the case of the COVID-19 pandemic (Abuhussein, 2022). However, the literature rarely discusses migrant women entrepreneurs' resilience and, in particular, the ways in which they develop psychological resilience and use organisational resilience strategies. This chapter addresses this research gap and explores how migrant women entrepreneurs start and navigate their businesses during periods of crisis.

3.   THE BUSINESS CONTEXT: THE UNITED ARAB EMIRATES (UAE)

Geographically, the UAE is situated in the Middle East. The country shares borders on the west and the south with Saudi Arabia, and to the east and north-west with Oman (Britannica, 2022). The UAE is the result of joining together seven emirates (called Trucial states) back in the nineteenth century (GMI, 2022). The discovery of oil in the region in the 1950s led to the UAE's economic and social development. At that time, the local population was only 70,000. As a result of growing opportunities, the country became a destination for migrant labour (GMI, 2022). Currently, 89 per cent of the UAE's population are migrants, with the highest number of migrants coming from India, followed by Pakistan, and Bangladesh (Migration Policy Institute, 2022). This labour migration process is facilitated by the UAE's *Kafala* (sponsorship) programme. The *Kafala* system operates in a similar manner to other countries in the Middle East, such as in the Kingdom of Saudi Arabia, where an individual, a placement agency, or a company/institution in the host country (known as *Kafeels*), sponsors migrants for employment for a set period (Fozia & Ranabahu, 2022).

Although primarily an oil-based country, the UAE is focused on economic diversification (Haouas & Heshmati, 2014). Aligning with this, the UAE's national strategy of Fifty Economic Plan concentrates on enhancing entrepreneurship through promoting small and medium enterprises and creating a culture of entrepreneurship (Ministry of Economy: UAE, 2020). The country thus encourages migrant entrepreneurship, as evident in its business policies and regulations which allow foreign ownership of businesses in the UAE, issue golden visas for entrepreneurs, and have established specialised free zones (Ministry of Economy: UAE, 2020). In recent years, the UAE has taken steps to improve access to entrepreneurial finance, post-school entrepreneurial education, research and development relating to infrastructure, and have introduced business-friendly government policies (Global Entrepreneurship Monitor; GEM, 2023). As a result of these activities, the UAE was ranked 1st in the world in the latest National Entrepreneurship Context Index (GEM, 2023).

However, diversification of the UAE's economy may make the country vulnerable to external shocks outside of its control (Haouas & Heshmati, 2014). During the 2008 global financial crisis, the sharp decline in the price of oil, heavy losses on equity investments, and reductions in the number of construction and real estate projects led to a slowdown of the country's economy (Sharma, 2010). During this period, the profitability levels of financial institutions also declined, affecting their ability and readiness to extend credit facilities (Haouas & Heshmati, 2014). Many expatriate/migrant communities also lost jobs during the financial crisis (Sharma, 2010).

More recently, the COVID-19 pandemic impacted both oil and service industries (e.g. tourism, events, and conferences) in the UAE (Aburumman, 2020; Mansoori et al., 2021). Global lockdowns led to the cancellations of events, lack of supply, and a reduction in profits, resulting in the closure of companies and job losses (Aburumman, 2020; Mansoori et al., 2021). As a result of the pandemic, construction costs have skyrocketed and many ongoing projects have been delayed or cancelled (Mansoori et al., 2021). While the government has provided assistance to small and medium businesses, only some survived the initial, global periods of lockdown (Mansoori et al., 2021). Although total entrepreneurship activity slowed down at the onset of the pandemic, there are signs in the UAE that entrepreneurial activity is increasing once again (GEM, 2023). The GEM (2023) data reveal an upward trend in the establishment of international businesses, with new and existing customers from both local and overseas markets, and job creation by such businesses.

3.1   Women Entrepreneurs in the UAE

In relation to women's empowerment, the UAE ranked 26th out of 162 in the Gender Inequality Index in 2018. Approximately 78.8 per cent of adult women living in the country have acquired a minimum of secondary education compared to 65.7 per cent of men in the same age range (Al Khayyal et al., 2021). Despite the UAE's establishment of female empowerment initiatives, women's participation in the area of entrepreneurship remains lower compared to countries with a similar gross domestic product (Al Khayyal et al., 2021). Tlaiss (2014) suggests that cultural and contextual factors may explain the low rates of female entrepreneurship in the UAE. For example, Kemp and Zhao (2016) studied the cultural orientation of Emirati women (local women in the UAE) using Hofstede's (2001) cultural dimensions. Emirati women had a high rating on collectivism, a fact which reflects the important role that relationships and family have on an individual's decisions (Forstenlechner & Baruch, 2013). In addition, in this context, females (both children and adults) are expected to be less assertive, indicating what Hofstede refers to as a high masculinity society (Littrell & Bertsch, 2013). Due to the dominance of masculine cultural values in the UAE, families reject women's entrepreneurial tendencies as running a business is perceived as a male job (Tlaiss, 2014). The gender stereotypes associated with women's work negatively affect the business start-up process (Sandhu et al., 2021). In contrast, UAE's collectivist cultural norms shape social network formation and inform individual decision-making (Bastian et al., 2023). This norm helps women to acquire resources and maintain their well-being and entrepreneurial self-efficacy (Bastian et al., 2023). To enhance entrepreneurial activities among Emirati women, Matroushi et al. (2018) and Sandhu et al. (2021) recommend conducting education programmes, skill development sessions, training, and seminars, and encouraging involvement in the activities of innovation/incubation centres.

4.   METHOD

Aligning with the constructivist epistemology that uses qualitative method, namely interviews, to study how women entrepreneurs construct their lives and businesses (Ahl, 2006), we used a narrative inquiry technique (Larty & Hamilton, 2011) to answer our core research question: How do migrant women entrepreneurs start and navigate their businesses during periods of crisis and develop entrepreneurial resilience?

In one of our current projects, we have been exploring how migrant entrepreneurs in the Middle East start and navigate their businesses during periods of crisis. We have obtained ethical clearance from the Human Research Ethics Committee at the University of Canterbury in New Zealand to conduct this project. From this project, we selected two migrant women entrepreneurs based in the UAE. Both women (Anna and Hina[1]) migrated to the UAE from two different countries: Anna from the USA (United States of America) and Hina from India. Both established businesses to address particular needs in the Middle Eastern market. However, they had polar opposite ways of viewing the UAE entrepreneurial context which shaped their entrepreneurial resilience strategies. As Eisenhardt and Graebner (2007) note, polar type cases in which researchers study extreme cases (e.g. very high- or very low-performing cases), are needed to observe contrasting patterns in the data. Studying Anna's and Hina's contrasting views highlights nuances which may not be identified from the data collected using other sampling techniques.

One of the authors of this chapter is based in the Middle East. She identified the two women using her network. She contacted them, provided information about the study, obtained their consent according to ethical guidelines, and conducted interviews via Zoom/telephone. During the interviews, she elicited their individual stories by asking about their upbringing, migration, business start-up and development, and the opportunities and challenges they faced along the way. Hence, the narratives contain first-person descriptions of each woman's life and business events (Larty & Hamilton, 2011). While a semi-structured interview guide was used to direct the process, the interviewer listened to their stories and allowed the questions and dialogue to flow naturally (Larty & Hamilton, 2011). The interviewees willingly shared their stories as they saw this as an opportunity share their journeys. The interviews were conducted in English language as both Hina and Anna were proficient in English. On several occasions, however, Hina (from India) used a mix of Hindi and Urdu words or phrases. The interviewer was able to understand these terms and phrases due to her fluency in both Hindi and Urdu languages. The interviews lasted for around 60–90 minutes. They were recorded with the participants' consent, and verbatim scripts were developed from the recordings.

We used NVivo to arrange the data and explore the narratives in detail. During our initial analysis of the transcripts, we found that Hina considered the host country to be an easy place to conduct business:

> The rules and regulations they have in Dubai are very easy going. I've got the advantage of being a woman in the construction line [of business] too. Here they respect women a lot, there is no doubt about it. […]. If I was in India or in any other country, it would not have been such an easy journey.

In contrast, Anna found it difficult to conduct business in the UAE:

> I don't know if they do it on purpose, but they make it so difficult. I don't feel supported. […] I'm a woman so they didn't treat me with […], this high regard of a business owner.

This was one of the primary reasons Anna left the UAE and returned to the USA, her home country. From there, she has continued to operate her business in the UAE. We analysed the data by taking into account these polar opposites in relation to their home country, education and upbringing, motivation for migration, and the women's individual views on the entrepreneurial context. In the analysis, we also investigated the different crises that each woman had encountered, the elements which developed their psychological and organi-sational resilience, and situational or home/host country factors that shaped their resilience strategies. Hence, the analysis provides a different perspective on the theory building process in relation to entrepreneurial resilience during crises. We then explain the analysis by linking it with the existing literature, discuss the implications, and outline our contributions.

5.   FINDINGS: NARRATIVES OF MIGRANT WOMEN ENTREPRENEURS

5.1   Anna's Narrative

Anna's business start-up and expansion to the UAE
Anna came from a small town in the USA and had a very sheltered upbringing. She had limited exposure outside of her hometown: she explained that when she went to the university, she was "kind of blown away". After her mother passed away, Anna dropped out of university to help her father. Her father was an engineer and had started a few businesses. Anna thinks that assisting her father's businesses influenced her entrepreneurial self-efficacy:

> He was an engineer but he also had started a couple of small businesses and […], his message always was, you can do anything you want. You just have to decide and work hard but you can, you can do anything, and I never felt really held back because of that.

In the USA, Anna's first business was creating silk screen posters. She progressed to owning a print shop. She owned the print shop for seven years before selling the company to an employee. She then went to work in a high-tech company related to publishing and ended up starting a business in the same industry:

> I ended up starting a company, when that company folded because of mismanage-ment, I started a company and picked up the work. I built a company, starting in my basement and moving into a building right in the neighbourhood.

However, this venture "got bigger and bigger". She then "sold that company" and went back to employment, first in a tech research organisation, later in learning software development, and finally, in educational resource/language test development. While working at BEST,[2] a language test development organisation, the company was contracted to make Arabic language tests.

> XXXX Foundation called and they asked if we would please create Arabic tests for them, and I actually thought it was a joke because why would they call this little company halfway around the world in America to create Arabic tests.

Anna soon discovered that it was a serious business call and BEST signed a contract with XXXX foundation. This was Anna's first exposure to working with the Gulf Cooperation Countries (GCC). The tests BEST developed "started spreading throughout the GCC without any marketing effort at all, because people wanted something like that". Later, when BEST was struggling financially, she and one of the other managers at BEST offered to buy BEST's Middle Eastern subsidiary. After purchasing the subsidiary Anna registered the company in the USA. The company had a 100 per cent export perspective and focused on sales in the Arabic-speaking region.

While Anna was developing her business in the Middle East, and travelling in the region, she received another call saying that BEST, the parent company, was "going out of business". She was asked whether she would like to buy it "from the bankruptcy court". At that point in time, she did not know what to do. Their product, however, was becoming popular in the Middle East. At the same time, she was contacted by an organisation associated with Emirates schools in the UAE that wanted to develop tests in the Arabic language. They agreed to fund the project right from the initial developmental stage. The project was for two years and came with regular financing that provided much-needed funding to continue the business. Hence, she was able to buy BEST, the parent company, which she also registered in the UAE.

Adjusting to geopolitical tensions

During the venture's expansion in the region, Anna faced both internal and external crises. In response to geopolitical tensions in the region, Anna had to develop resilience. Explaining one situation, Anna mentioned that although she was based in the UAE, due to tensions between Qatar and neighbouring countries, one venture capitalist did not want to invest in her company:

> There was another uproar between Qatar and their neighbours and, when we first started, we went out to get venture capital [...] and then we had to present to one partner from the Omani company and, as soon as the word Qatar came out of my partner's mouth, he stood up, said "I don't want anything to do with you people," and walked out. [...] He was going to end up making a lot of money from it but he was so angry that we had anything to do with Qatar that he walked out.

At that time, her business website showcased all the projects they had completed in the UAE and Qatar. This event led her to reconsider what to display on her website:

> [...] That was almost a year of work to develop the business plan, the model, the investors. Our investment banker went out and got the investors to invest in this fund [...] I realised we needed to take them [neighbouring country project showcase details] off ... our website.

Hence, when expanding her business and seeking investments, Anna considered the geopolitical tensions. In addition, she employed a trustworthy local who could help her to navigate the regional tensions and political issues. This reflects use of organisational resilience strategies.

Responding to a cybercrime: an internal crisis

Anna's original business partnership, formed with one of the colleagues from BEST, still existed when she established her business in the Middle East. This partnership, however, did not work out. In her words, "he became a horrible partner." It all started with clashes in their individual value systems:

> I have certain principles in my business that are not, you know, it's a solid line and integrity is, is the most important. If you don't tell the truth, there's no reason to even be here, right, and this guy started asking me to lie to customers because he wasn't getting his job done.

This situation led Anna to confront her business partner, escalating the tensions between them:

> I actually confronted him and told him I regretted becoming his partner because he had no integrity. That was [...] probably a little bit too candid because, from that moment on, our life together was horrible and he refused to answer my emails or my calls.

Explaining the fall-out, Anna mentioned that she fired him, then changed the passwords and denied him access to the system and the source code. However, as Anna explained "within two weeks, he went in, stole one of our employee's ID, went into the learning management system".

Anna found it difficult to bounce back from this internal crisis. It took her "about six months and about 25,000 US dollars to repair the damage that he had done". The worst thing was, he still owned 41 per cent of her company.

Hence, there were tensions for the next two years. The business partners finally resolved their issues through a "friendly buyout":

> My lawyer and his lawyer negotiated a buyout and so I ended up buying his stock, and I do have one other investor, that came in and, invested some money, and got a small part of the company.

This internal crisis, caused by a business partner, led Anna to reflect upon and develop her psychological resilience by learning from her experience. At the same time, Anna used organisational resilience by changing business practices and managing partnership issues.

Managing business during COVID-19

COVID-19 and the associated lockdowns in the initial stage of the pandemic had a detrimental effect on Anna's business: she lost 32 per cent of revenue in 2020. Due to the pandemic, Anna decided to move back to the USA and realised that there she had a lot of support back in her home country.

> There's a lot of support here, from the American government, especially for small companies that do exporting, and 100 per cent of our income is from either the Middle East or the UK.

Anna revealed that her business could not have survived without the US government's support. She understood that as an expatriate she could not expect support from the host country:

> Honestly, without the support of the US government, we would not have survived. […], the US government gave me an emergency loan. […] I got two different grants to cover payroll. Everything the US government gives us is supposed to be for our US employees only and so that's fine and, I respect that, so that any revenue we have coming in, I can use to pay the off-shore employees. But you know, […] without the government support, we would not have survived and, and we didn't get any support from [the] UAE government, nor would I expect to as an ex-pat.

Ultimately, the pandemic led Anna to question the need for premises in the Middle East. Anna has now employed a manager to supervise operations in the UAE, look after her existing business, and represent her in the Middle East. These reflect organisational resilience strategies. Although she believes that her business clientele in the Middle East will continue to grow, she does not see any point in maintaining a branch office there:

> I don't know whether we will keep the branch office in Abu Dhabi after this year. There's really no reason to. All of our customers, you know, pay us directly to the US anyway so we don't really need [an] Abu Dhabi presence anymore.

As these statements reveal, Anna's focus on organisational resilience appears to be shaping her business decisions.

5.2   Hina's Narrative

Hina's business start-up in the UAE

Hina grew up in a village in India. She belonged to a political family, lived in various cities for educational purposes, moved around the country, and graduated from a prominent university in India. She got married and the couple moved to Bahrain due to her husband's employment. Hina had a very active life in India. She revealed that it was very important for her "to keep on doing something", even after migrating to another country. While she did not know anything about business start-up, she had completed a training programme on salon work during her university years. She used her prior learning and started her first business by converting the living area of her house into a salon. She employed staff for her business. However, when she had her first baby, Hina shut down her salon and began importing ready-made garments from India into Bahrain instead:

> I started working with garments. Because I used to design my own, give them in the market, got them approved, then I got them completed in India and got them delivered in Bahrain.

After just two years, Hina's husband was transferred to Qatar and she moved with him. Soon after, Hina gave birth to their second child and for the next five years she did not engage in any business activities. In 2006, the family had to move to Dubai (in the UAE). It was here that she ventured into a trading business. Hina's ability to adapt, experiment, and then change illustrates the use of both psychological and organisational resilience strategies.

Identifying opportunities during an economic recession

In 2006, Hina noticed that construction was booming in Dubai. She saw an opportunity to supply rebar (reinforcing bar), a construction material normally used to reinforce concrete. Hina's prior experience in garment trading helped her to manage the process:

> I had entered the trading line through garments in Bahrain. When we came in 2006, construction was booming. The Palm [Palm Jumeirah] and tallest tower were constructed at that time. So, we were supplying rebar to them.

Hina bought rebar from China, imported them, and sold them in the UAE. While she was initially successful, the economic recession had a detrimental effect on her business:

> We brought rebar from China and sold in UAE. In 2008, the world suffered with recession. I was also affected. […] Very bad situation.

The recession put a stop to all construction meaning Hina could not continue her rebar business as there was no demand for her product. As a result of the construction industry grinding to a halt, there was a lot of "scrap" metal stockpiled within the UAE. So, Hina pivoted her business: she began exporting scrap metal from the UAE to other countries:

> After recession all the construction stopped and everyone had a huge stock of such items as rebar, that was to be sold in scrap. So, I switched to dealing in scrap. That's from where I got this idea.

In this way, Hina was able to keep her trading business afloat. After some time, Hina noted that since the "UAE is a small country", exporting scrap metal also "had its own limits". So, as the scrap metal business began to slow down, she ventured into dismantling old or damaged ships so she could continue to export metal/scrap material. These practices show Hina's use of organisational resilience strategies:

> After scrap, I opened up a company called BBB, in which I acquired the permission for moving the scrap. Dubai to Pakistan, Dubai to India, to Dhaka to their ports. We bought ships and the cutting of ships [ship breaking] happened at the port. We had all facilities in this company.

In all her businesses, she had to learn the rules of the game: "whatever field I did business, I studied about it definitely all the time." In her construction business, she learnt about handling labour in a male-dominant industry:

> Only males are there, females are not seen. In the beginning I saw there are 100 per cent or 99.9 per cent males. In the beginning it was difficult, especially labour handling.

These learnings enhanced her self-efficacy. In the ship dismantling business, rules of the game included that she inspected ships before breaking them. She also had to take appropriate safety procedures:

> I had to go into the sea to inspect the defective ships. I had the entire team with me, going with me. […] I was the only female. Everyone was in uniform, though after using the helmet and the entire attire one can't differentiate between male and

female. But you are not on land, one of the ships takes everyone into the water, and then we had to jump into the other ship we were to inspect. There were some difficult situations no doubt.

In order to conduct these activities, Hina had to develop her emotional resilience and can-do attitude. These reflect psychological resilience and helped in managing day-to-day crises and taking responsibility in crises. As the company's managing director, although Hina had a team, she explained that the buck stopped with her:

> You have an engineer, supervisor also, but whenever there is a crisis in the company, the owner has to solve the problem. Sometimes there may be [an] accident on the site, your company cars get into trouble. And in such situations, only a managing director is called by the authorities.

Hina revealed that she experienced a heavy loss – one of the ships sunk. This unfortunate event meant that they were not able to dismantle it or obtain any scrap metal:

> I had a loss of 1.6 million Dirhams [the UAE currency]. We had bought a ship in scrap. We were unable to pull out the ship, it sunk into the sea. We tried a lot. I was upset for a week.

Managing losses required her to be emotionally resilient. Such kind of losses and business situations led Hina to her cleaning services provision. This reflects organisational the resilient strategy of pivoting business practices.

Managing business during COVID-19

The COVID-19 restrictions affected Hina's cleaning business. Her business served high-rise buildings. The company employed appropriately 38 migrant employees. When the lockdowns occurred, Hina considered her employees' well-being first, but later was forced to lay-off some of her staff.

> Salaries were given every month for five months in lockdown, best possible accommodation, etc. Whatever was best/possible, I did for my employees. But after that, if I would not have offloaded some workforce, our survival was on the brink [...] We haven't got our money back, whatever was stuck in the market. Everyone is struggling.

As Hina explained, COVID-19 created significant cash inflow problems, meaning she ultimately had to close the business; this is also an example of an organisational resilient strategy:

> In Corona situation we had to close down the company (cleaning service business) because we had huge credit stuck in the market. We had to get out of liabilities, so I cancelled many visas of my team members.

However, COVID-19 also created other opportunities. By looking at the market and the situation in the UAE, Hina identified the need for perishable items to be imported into the country:

> We thought that the country we live in, they don't have their indigenous production of food, grains, from pulses to rice, everything is imported. If ports close, does [the] UAE have enough supply to support the people living in the country? The moment this came to our mind, we started approaching India and talking around [imports into] UAE. We reached [the] conclusion that foods and vegetables will definitely work. [...] We talked to people in [the] UAE about our perishables and they were also interested because their supply chain was on the verge of breakdown.

Using contacts from her home country, Hina was able to import perishable goods from India to the UAE. She saw this transaction as benefiting both countries:

> But, by doing this, we saved those [produce] in India. Because there [in India], the situation was so bad that the goods were getting perished in mandi [granaries]. It exited from there, reached here.

Ultimately, the pandemic led Hina to realise that the most feasible business option for her was to import perishable goods. Hina explained that her current business makes sense: it can withstand crises because it provides basic human needs that are required at all times. As she explained:

> Presently I am running perishables and garments business. Corona taught me a lesson that come what may, these two things [food and clothing] will always be needed by human beings. Business can survive on these two things.

Such attitudes contributed to the development of Hina's entrepreneurial resilience.

6.   DISCUSSION

This study has focused on migrant women entrepreneurs in the Middle East and sought to answer the following research question: How do migrant women entrepreneurs start and navigate their businesses during periods of crisis and develop entrepreneurial resilience? To address this question, we analysed Anna's and Hina's narratives, two cases which we categorised as polar opposites. Drawing on Coombs' (1995, 2007) work, crises similar to those faced by Anna and Hina can be grouped in different ways. Anna faced both internal (i.e. cybercrime) and external (i.e. geopolitical tensions and COVID-19) crises. The internal crisis occurred as the result of an individual's malicious actions. In Hina's case, all of the crises (e.g. economic recession and COVID-19) she faced were external. Regardless of the source, all of the crises led her to change, pivot, exit, and change her business focus. Both Anna's and Hina's narratives highlight that all these crises affected their businesses' reputations, viability, and operations (Doern et al., 2019; Williams et al., 2017).

Our findings indicate that while Anna and Hina had opposing views about the business support provided by the host country and experienced differences in their upbringing, some of their entrepreneurial resilience strategies were similar. Aligning with entrepreneurial resilience literature which combines both psychological and organisational resilience (Williams et al., 2017), Anna and Hina employed a number of different strategies. Anna's psychological resilience was strengthened and developed by her previous business experience. Moreover, working with her family shaped her self-efficacy, learning and development, beliefs and values, and ability to cope with adversity. Hina's psychological resilience was born from her education, self-efficacy, and growth mindset (she was willing to experiment and take action). When both women experienced a loss or hardship, they reflected on the next step; in Hina's case, this step included emotional regulation. Hence, these strategies reflect elements of psychological resilience (Hartmann et al., 2022).

Both Anna and Hina used organisational resilience strategies, such as identifying new opportunities, pivoting their initial businesses, adjusting to situations, and responding to various crises by changing their practices or closing businesses. In particular, Hina pivoted, modified, and changed her direction to align with changes in the market and emerging opportunities. Such strategies are similar to organisational resilience strategies identified in the literature (e.g. Ayala & Manzano, 2014; Hartmann et al., 2022; Kantur & Iseri-Say, 2015; Vogus & Sutcliffe, 2007). Yet, our findings differ from existing literature as we show that the particular forms of organisational resilience identified here required both home and host country resource structures and networks.

Our findings also concur with the view that entrepreneurial resilience results from a combination of psychological and organisational resilience strategies. In crises, both Anna and Hina followed their own self-efficacy and behavioural attributes with organisational strategies of recover, survive, and exit. Such resilience strategies have also been identified among small business owners in natural disasters (de Vries & Hamilton, 2021). Both Anna's and Hina's narratives demonstrate that these strategies are interconnected: the women's choice of strategy/strategies ([re]start, survival, exit, and recover) depended on the type of crisis, as depicted in Figure 4.1.

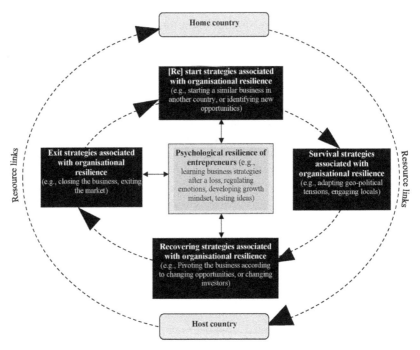

Source: Author.

Figure 4.1   Entrepreneurial resilience of migrant women entrepreneurs

As Figure 4.1 illustrates, having resource links with home and host countries, and the ability to alternate between contexts for resources, shaped these migrant women entrepreneurs' business processes. For example, Anna's and Hina's resource links with their home countries shaped how they survived the pandemic. For example, Anna moved back home and used resources and established support structures in the USA to manage her business in the UAE. She is now considering fully relocating to the USA, and running her Middle Eastern business from her home country. In contrast, Hina used contacts she had in her home country and established a trading business which supplies perishable goods to the UAE. Their polar opposite views on whether the host context is conducive to business shaped their entrepreneurial resilience strategies. Hence, these findings illustrate that entrepreneurial resilience among migrant women is dynamic and evolves as a result of their interactions with home and host countries. It is also shaped by geopolitical tensions, cultural differences, and/or the crises they face. The women's resilience is also affected by their perceptions of the host country's business environment and available support.

6.1   Implications and Future Research

Our findings highlight the ways that migrant women entrepreneurs employ resilience strategies in dealing with different types of business crises. We contribute to the extant literature by outlining resilience strategies related to (re)start, recovery, exit, and survival and how these strategies are shaped by an entrepreneur's psychological resilience attributes. We also show how women combine both psychological and organisational resilience strategies. Our two narratives show that although the women entrepreneurs' upbringings and their migration trajectories to the Middle East were different, their resilience strategies were similar in most crisis situations. However, the entrepreneurs' experiences in their home countries influence how they view the host country's support systems. This viewpoint also determines how they use home country-based resources in different crises. Therefore, our findings contribute to literature by illustrating the resilience strategies of a novel group of entrepreneurs and by providing a new perspective.

This study is not without its limitations. As we used polar cases (two cases), these findings may not be generalisable to other migrant women entrepreneurs. Future studies could collect data from a larger sample and see whether findings from these polar cases are applicable to other migrant women entrepreneurs in the UAE. In addition, we only focused on women in the UAE. Even within the Middle East, there are contextual differences; thus, studying resilience strategies during crises among migrant women in other Gulf countries may provide more insights. Another future area of research is the resource links between home and host countries and how these resource links contribute to the development of entrepreneurial resilience. Such a study would require the use of theories such as the resource-based view, entrepreneurial ecosystems, or social capital theory.

7.   CONCLUSION

This chapter sought out to explore how migrant women entrepreneurs start and navigate their businesses during periods of crisis and develop entrepreneurial resilience. We explained that migrant women faced periods of crises: geopolitical tensions, economic recession and, recently, the COVID-19 pandemic. We also explained a malicious act of an individual as an internal crisis and how one of the migrant woman entrepreneur dealt with that. We employed entrepreneurial resilience, the combination of psychological and organisational resilience, to study how women managed crises in their business. We highlighted the entrepreneurial resilience strategies that migrant women use to overcome different types of crises and illustrated how they combine psychological and organizational resilience strategies. Based on the findings we conclude that migrant women sharpen their psychological resilience by learning business strategies after a loss, regulating emotions, developing growth mindset, and testing their ideas. They combine these with organisational resilience strategies of (re)start, survive, recover, or exit businesses in dealing with different crises. In addition, we conclude that development of entrepreneurial resilience is dynamic; in our case, having resource links to both home and host countries facilitated migrant women's entrepreneurial resilience. Hence, we contribute by illustrating the links between psychological and organisational resilience of migrant women and how home and host country resource links shape their entrepreneurial resilience. These findings could be used to further strengthen entrepreneurial resilience theories and enhance policy and practice.

NOTES

1.   'Anna' and 'Hina' are pseudonyms.
2.   All organisation names are pseudonyms.

REFERENCES

Abuhussein, T. (2022). The impact of COVID-19 on refugee women's entrepreneurship in Jordan. *Journal of Enterprising Communities: People and Places in the Global Economy* (ahead-of-print). https://doi.org/10.1108/JEC-12–2021–0176.

Aburumman, A. A. (2020). COVID-19 impact and survival strategy in business tourism market: The example of the UAE MICE industry. *Humanities and Social Sciences Communications*, 7(1), 1–11. https://doi.org/10.1057/s41599–020–00630–8.

Ahl, H. (2006). Why research on women entrepreneurs needs new directions. *Entrepreneurship Theory and Practice*, 30(5), 595–621. https://doi.org/10.1111/j.1540-6520.2006.00138.x.

Al Khayyal, A. O., Alshurideh, M., Al Kurdi, B., & Salloum, S. A. (2021). Women empowerment in UAE: A systematic review. In Hassanien, A. E. et al. (Eds.), *Proceedings of the International Conference on Advanced Intelligent Systems and Informatics 2020* (pp. 742–755). Springer International Publishing.

Alexandre, L., Salloum, C., & Alalam, A. (2019). An investigation of migrant entrepreneurs: The case of Syrian refugees in Lebanon. *International Journal of Entrepreneurial Behavior & Research*, 25(5), 1147–1164. https://doi.org/10.1108/IJEBR-03–2018–0171.

Ayala, J. C., & Manzano, G. (2014). The resilience of the entrepreneur: Influence on the success of the business. A longitudinal analysis, *Journal of Economic Psychology*, 42(3), 126–135. https://doi.org/10.1016/j.joep.2014.02.004.

Bastian, B. L., Wood, B. P., & Ng, P. Y. (2023). The role of strong ties in empowering women entrepreneurs in collectivist contexts. *International Journal of Gender and Entrepreneurship*, *15*(1), 122–146. https://doi.org/10.1108/IJGE-10–2021–0171.

Bodlaj, M., & Čater, B. (2019). The impact of environmental turbulence on the perceived importance of innovation and innovativeness in SMEs. *Journal of Small Business Management*, *57*(S2), 417–435. https://doi.org/10.1111/jsbm.12482.

Britannica (2022). Land of the United Arab Emirates. https://www.britannica.com/place/United-Arab-Emirates/Land.

Coombs, W. T. (1995). Choosing the right words: The development of guidelines for the selection of the "appropriate" crisis-response strategies. *Management Communication Quarterly*, *8*(4), 447–476. https://doi.org/10.1177/0893318995008004003.

Coombs, W. T. (2007). Protecting organization reputations during a crisis: The development and application of Situational Crisis Communication Theory. *Corporate Reputation Review*, *10*, 163–176. https://doi.org/10.1057/palgrave.crr.1550049.

de Vries, H. P., & Hamilton, R. T. (2021). Small businesses and the Christchurch earthquakes: A longitudinal study of individual and organizational resilience. *International Journal of Disaster Risk Reduction*, *56*. http://dx.doi.org/10.1016/j.ijdrr.2021.102125.

de Vries, H. P., & Hamilton, R. T. (2016). Why stay? The resilience of small firms in Christchurch and their owners. In Hall, C. M., Malinen, S., Vosslamber, R., & Wordsworth, R. (Eds.), *Business and Post-disaster Management: Business, Organisational and Consumer Resilience and the Christchurch Earthquakes* (pp. 23–34). New York: Routledge. http://dx.doi.org/10.4324/9781315640211.

de Vries, H. P., Ranabahu, N., & Basharati, Z. (2021). From taking flight to putting down roots: A narrative perspective of the entrepreneurial journey of a refugee. In Cooney, T. (Ed.), *Palgrave Handbook on Minority Entrepreneurship* (pp. 365–389). Basingstoke: Palgrave. http://dx.doi.org/10.1007/978–3-030–66603–3_17.

Doern, R. (2021). Knocked down but not out and fighting to go the distance: Small business responses to an unfolding crisis in the initial impact period. *Journal of Business Venturing Insights*, *15*, e00221. https://doi.org/10.1016/j.jbvi.2020.e00221.

Doern, R., Williams, N., & Vorley, T. (2019). Special issue on entrepreneurship and crises: Business as usual? An introduction and review of the literature. *Entrepreneurship & Regional Development*, *31*(5–6), 400–412. https://doi.org/10.1080/08985626.2018.1541590.

Donthu, N., & Gustafsson, A. (2020). Effects of COVID-19 on business and research. *Journal of Business Research*, *117*, 284–289. https://doi.org/10.1016/j.jbusres.2020.06.008.

Eisenhardt, K. M., & Graebner, M. E. (2007). Theory building from cases: Opportunities and challenges. *The Academy of Management Journal*, *50*(1), 25–32. http://www.jstor.org/stable/20159839.

Forstenlechner, I., & Baruch, Y. (2013). Contemporary career concepts and their fit for the Arabian Gulf context: A sector level analysis of psychological contract breach. *Career Development International*, *18*(6), 629–648. https://doi.org/10.1108/CDI-07–2013–0084.

Fozia, M., & Ranabahu, N. (2022). A disadvantage to an advantage? Immigrant entrepreneurs' use of effectuation in business start-up and development in the Kingdom of Saudi Arabia. In Dana, L-P., Khachlouf, N., Maâlaoui, A., & Ratten, V. (Eds.), *Disadvantaged Minorities in Business* (1st edn) (pp. 153–176). Cham: Springer International Publishing.

GEM [Global Entrepreneurship Monitor] (2023). *Global Entrepreneurship Monitor 2022/2023 Global Report: Adapting to a "New Normal"*. London: GEM.

GMI [Global Media Insight] (2022). United Arab Emirates population statistics (2022). https://www.globalmediainsight.com/blog/uae-population-statistics/#demographics.

Haase, A., & Eberl, P. (2019). The challenges of routinizing for building resilient startups. *Journal of Small Business Management, 57*(S2), 579–597. https://doi.org/10.1111/jsbm.12511.

Hadjielias, E., Hughes, M., & Scholes, L. (2022). External crises and family social capital reconfiguration: Insights from the European debt crisis and the Covid-19 pandemic. *Family Business Review, 35*(3), 275–305. https:// doi .org/ 10 .1177/ 08944865221113136.

Haouas, I., & Heshmati, A. (2014). Can the UAE avoid the oil curse by economic diversification? *IZA DP No. 8003* [discussion paper series]. https:// www.iza.org/ publications/dp/8003/can-the-uae-avoid-the-oil-curse-by-economic-diversification.

Hartmann, S., Backmann, J., Newman, A., Brykman, K. M., & Pidduck, R. J. (2022). Psychological resilience of entrepreneurs: A review and agenda for future research. *Journal of Small Business Management, 60*(5), 1041–1079. https://doi.org/10.1080/00472778.2021.2024216.

Hoegl, M., & Hartmann, S. (2021). Bouncing back, if not beyond: Challenges for research on resilience. *Asian Business & Management, 20*(4), 456–464. https://doi.org/10.1057/s41291–020–00133-z.

Hofstede, G. (2001). *Culture's Consequences: Comparing Values, Behaviors, Institutions and Organizations across Nations* (2nd edn). Thousand Oaks, CA: Sage Publications.

Huq, A., & Venugopal, V. (2021). DIY entrepreneurship? Self-reliance for women refugees in Australia. *International Migration, 59*(1), 126–142. https:// doi .org/ 10 .1111/imig.12727.

Kantur, D., & Iseri-Say, A., (2015). Measuring organizational resilience: A scale development. *Journal of Business Economics and Finance, 4*(3), 456–472. https:// dergipark.org.tr/en/pub/jbef/issue/32406/360419.

Kemp, L. J., & Zhao, F. (2016). Influences of cultural orientations on Emirati women's careers. *Personnel Review, 45*(5), 988–1009. http://dx.doi.org/10.1108/PR -08–2014–0187.

Khurana, I., Dutta, D. K., & Singh Ghura, A. (2022). SMEs and digital transformation during a crisis: The emergence of resilience as a second-order dynamic capability in an entrepreneurial ecosystem. *Journal of Business Research, 150*, 623–641. https:// doi.org/10.1016/j.jbusres.2022.06.048.

Kogut, C. S., & Mejri, K. (2022). Female entrepreneurship in emerging markets: Challenges of running a business in turbulent contexts and times. *International Journal of Gender and Entrepreneurship, 14*(1), 95–116. https://doi.org/10.1108/ IJGE-03–2021–0052.

Larty, J., & Hamilton, E. (2011). Structural approaches to narrative analysis in entre-preneurship research: Exemplars from two researchers. *International Small Business Journal, 29*(3), 220–237. https://doi.org/10.1177/0266242611401796.

Littrell, R. F. & Bertsch, A. (2013). UN millennium development goals and gender equality in employment in the Middle East. *Foresight, 15*(4), 249–263. https:// doi .org/10.1108/fs-04–2012–0024.

Liu, H.-M., & Yang, H.-F. (2019). Managing network resource and organizational capabilities to create competitive advantage for SMEs in a volatile environment.

Journal of Small Business Management, *57*(S2), 155–171. https://doi.org/10.1111/jsbm.12449.

Mansoori, H., Alsaud, A. B., & Yas, H. (2021). The impact of Covid-19 on increasing the cost of labor and project price in the United Arab Emirates. *International Journal of Pharmaceutical Research*, *13*(1), 5069–5076.

Matroushi, H. A., Jabeen, F., & All, S. A. (2018). Prioritising the factors promoting innovation in Emirati female-owned SMEs: AHP approach. *International Journal of Entrepreneurship and Innovation Management*, *22*(3), 220–250. https://doi.org/10.1504/IJEIM.2018.10012588.

Migration Policy Institute (2022). United Arab Emirates. https://www.migrationpolicy.org/article/labor-migration-united-arab-emirates-challenges-and-responses.

Ministry of Economy: United Arab Emirates (2020). The national entrepreneurship agenda. https://www.moec.gov.ae/en/entrepreneurs-and-smes.

Mitroff, I. I., Pauchant, T. C., & Shrivastava, P. (1988). The structure of man-made organizational crises: Conceptual and empirical issues in the development of a general theory of crisis management. *Technological Forecasting and Social Change*, *33*(2), 83–107. https://doi.org/10.1016/0040–1625(88)90075–3.

Muñoz, P., Kimmitt, J., Kibler, E., & Farny, S. (2019). Living on the slopes: Entrepreneurial preparedness in a context under continuous threat. *Entrepreneurship and Regional Development*, *31*(5–6), 413–434. https://doi.org/10.1080/08985626.2018.1541591.

Naman, J. L., & Slevin, D. P. (1993). Entrepreneurship and the concept of fit: A model and empirical tests. *Strategic Management Journal*, *14*(2), 137–153. https://doi.org/10.1002/smj.4250140205.

Osaghae, O. G., & Cooney, T. M. (2020). Exploring the relationship between immigrant enclave theory and transnational diaspora entrepreneurial opportunity formation. *Journal of Ethnic and Migration Studies*, *46*(10), 2086–2105. https://doi.org/10.1080/1369183X.2018.1560001.

Ranabahu, N., de Vries, H. P., & Basharati, Z. (2021). The economic integration of women refugee entrepreneurs in New Zealand. In McAdam, M., & Cunningham, J. A. (Eds.), *Women and Global Entrepreneurship: Contextualising Everyday Experiences* (pp. 64–80). New York: Routledge.

Sandhu, M. A., Farooq, O., Khalid, S., & Farooq, M. (2021). Benchmarking entrepreneurial intentions of women in the United Arab Emirates. *Benchmarking: An International Journal*, *28*(9), 2771–2785. https:// doi .org/ 10 .1108/ BIJ -09–2020–0497.

Sharma, S. D. (2010). The Arab world amidst the global financial crisis of 2008–2009. *Contemporary Arab Affairs*, *3*(1), 38–52. https:// doi .org/ 10 .1080/ 17550910903541835.

Tengeh, R. K. (2016). Entrepreneurial resilience: The case of Somali grocery shop owners in a South African township. *Problems and Perspectives in Management*, *14*(4), 203–211. https://doi.org/10.21511/ppm.14(4–1).2016.09.

Tlaiss, H. A. (2014). Women's entrepreneurship, barriers and culture: Insights from the United Arab Emirates. *The Journal of Entrepreneurship*, *23*(2), 289–320. https://doi.org/10.1177/0971355714535307.

Vogus, T. J., & Sutcliffe, K. M. (2007). Organizational resilience: Towards a theory and research agenda. Paper presented at the 2007 IEEE International Conference on Systems, Man and Cybernetics, Montreal, Canada. https://doi.org/10.1109/ICSMC.2007.4414160.

Williams, T. A., Gruber, D. A., Sutcliffe, K. M., Shepherd, D. A., & Zhao, E. Y. (2017). Organizational response to adversity: Fusing crisis management and resilience research streams. *The Academy of Management Annals, 11*(2), 733–769. https://doi .org/10.5465/annals.2015.0134.

Yeshi, T., Harima, A., & Freiling, J. (2022). Resilience on an emotional rollercoaster: Refugee entrepreneurship under adversity. *European Management Journal, 42*(2). https://doi.org/10.1016/j.emj.2022.12.009.

Zehra, K., & Usmani, S. (2021). Not without family: Refugee family entrepreneurship and economic integration process. *Journal of Enterprising Communities, 17*(1). https://doi.org/10.1108/JEC-03–2020–0044.

5. Women home-based entrepreneurs in Iran: navigating a turbulent era

Parisa Nakhaei, Nelia Hyndman-Rizk and Saskia de Klerk

INTRODUCTION

Iran has experienced national and international challenges for almost four decades that have influenced its political, economic, social, and legal systems. The establishment of the Islamic Republic in 1979 was one of the most significant political events in Iran (Arjomand, 1988). Along with the intersectional, variable, and ongoing effects of the Islamic revolution, other political and economic events, including the Iran–Iraq war and the imposition of international sanctions since 2006, have dynamically influenced the structure of the labour market and the entrepreneurial ecosystem. Such events have specifically influenced the motivations and constraints on women's entrepreneurial activities. According to Crenshaw (1990), race, gender, and other systems intersect and shape the experience of individuals. As such, women's experiences, opportunities, and challenges in entrepreneurship in Iran have not been determined by gender alone. Rather, they have also been influenced by the broader social, political, and economic systems and circumstances that intersect and intertwine with each other over time.

Although women constitute half of Iran's population (49.88 per cent in 2021), female labour force participation in Iran is low, at just 14 per cent (The World Bank, 2022). This low female labour force participation rate is embedded in the legal system, which does not facilitate women's presence in public spaces. After the Islamic revolution, the Iranian government's hegemony influenced Iran's socio-political and economic systems and the structure of female labour force participation, controlling and limiting women's access to resources in the labour market (Hoominfar & Zanganeh, 2021). The state's policies after the 1979 revolution, regarding women's access to public spaces, imposed gender segregation, inhibited or reversed family laws, and introduced a women's dress code, all of which challenged women's participation in social and economic activities (Hoodfar & Sadr, 2010; Shahrokni, 2020). Since self-employment makes up a quarter of female labour market participation in Iran, self-employment may be one strategy to navigate women's barriers to finding employment.

This chapter asks the critical question: What are the barriers to and challenges facing women's home-based businesses in Iran? To address this question, the authors present a qualitative, comparative case study of women home-based entrepreneurs in the informal economy. The chapter focuses on Iran's garment and food industries, due to its significant share of female labour force participation. This study fills a gap in knowledge regarding the informal economy and contributes to the international entrepreneurship literature in the Middle East. Following this introductory section, the chapter outlines its theoretical framework and methodological approach and discusses women's entrepreneurship in crisis. The second part of the chapter presents a case study on women's home-based businesses in Iran, focusing on the food and garment sectors. Finally, the chapter makes recommendations on how women's home-based businesses can be better supported in Iran.

THEORETICAL FRAMEWORK

For the purposes of this study, Bouguerra's (2015) theory of entrepreneurial process was applied and adapted. The approach integrates a gender perspective in a Middle Eastern context with women's entrepreneurial process. The framework is utilized as a tool for data collection and analysis, as it explores the motivations and obstacles women entrepreneurs face while establishing a business. The model accounts for the impact of both individual and contextual factors in the entrepreneurial domain. By utilizing an iterative process, the research data, findings, and analysis further develop Bouguerra's theoretical framework in relation to the familial context of women home-based businesses. This required the inclusion of the motherhood domain, adapted from the 5M theory (Brush et al., 2009), to consider the household context of women home-based business entrepreneurs. The 5M theory identifies market, money, management, motherhood, and meso/macro environment as factors that can either support or impede the efforts of women entrepreneurs (Brush et al., 2009). Hence, this study expands the overarching theory through the inclusion of the motherhood domain to explain comprehensively the challenges facing women's home-based entrepreneurship.

Women's Entrepreneurship in Times of Crisis

In a crisis, people, organizations, and countries change their approaches to survive, innovate, and act sustainably towards growth and development (Paoloni, 2022), while overcoming the short-term and long-term consequences of the crises (Ansell & Boin, 2019). Studying how crises influence the environment and, specifically, the business environment of society requires a consideration of the critical features of the crisis concept. Bergman-Rosamond et al. pointed out that critical features have to be included in crisis, such as: "temporality, spatiality, scale, multi-layeredness, processualism, contradictions, gender, intersectionality and social inequalities" (2022: 475).

Studies on women's entrepreneurship indicate that crises have a more significant negative impact on businesses owned by women in comparison to businesses owned by men (Adams-Prassl et al., 2020; Martinez Dy & Jayawarna, 2020; Ogundana et al., 2021). The literature shows that women generally cope with various social, economic, cultural, and individual obstacles (Costa & Pita, 2020). Women entrepreneurs face cultural and social challenges, unlike those faced by their male counterparts, such as limited access to financial resources and funds, lower levels of education and government support, heavy domestic responsibilities, a lack of business role models, and a lack of access to business networks, as well as lower social status (Fernandes & Sanfilippo, 2022; Grandy et al., 2020; Kelley et al., 2015). Although women entrepreneurs face similar challenges globally, the specific context they operate in creates unique entrepreneurial environments. This research investigates the turbulent environment women face in Iran as the underlying context for their ventures. Following the Islamic revolution in 1979, Iran experienced a turbulent socio-economic and political context that shaped the business ecosystem. In the subsequent sections of this chapter, we will discuss the context of Iran after the 1979 revolution, home-based women entrepreneurs' business experience and the unique business challenges they have faced.

The Context of Iran

The Islamic Republic of Iran, located in West Asia, has Islam as its official religion and its economy mainly depends on oil and gas production for export. Iran is the third biggest member of OPEC (Organization of Petroleum Exporting Countries, 2016). During recent decades, the most important political events the country underwent were the Islamic revolution in 1979, followed by war with Iraq (1980–1988). Furthermore, it should be noted that international sanctions against its nuclear programme have impacted Iran's economy since 2006. The changes in Iran's political, legal, and economic structures have also affected women's lives in different socio-economic dimensions. The changes made to limit women's participation in public spaces included gender segregation, restrictions on family laws, and dress codes (Hoodfar & Sadr, 2010; Shahrokni, 2020). The female labour force participation rate stands at 14 per cent in Iran, which is amongst the lowest in the Middle East (The World Bank, 2022). Despite low female labour force participation, the rate of self-employment, 38.5 per cent, is comparatively high (Statistical Center of Iran, 2022). Entrepreneurship is a strategy for women to increase their participation in the labour market. In Iran, women comprise 70 per cent of the formal home-based business applicants and 51 per cent of women's employment is in the informal economy (Esfahani & Shajari, 2012; Javadian & Addae, 2013; Modarresi et al., 2017; Hashemi & Ebrahimpour, 2016).

Iran's government has faced recent crises due to state interference, economic issues, and corruption (Saleh, 2022). Inflation, sanctions, official corruption, and unmet civic demands from women, particularly the younger generation, have contributed to the most recent revolution, which began in September 2022, sparked by the death of a young woman at the hands of morality police, which is rooted in the state's control of women's bodies through dress codes and mandatory hijab laws. This revolution, led by women with the slogan "women, life, freedom", includes demands to end corruption and discrimination against women and minorities by the current political regime, which highlights Iran's ongoing turbulent era (Esfandiari, 2022: 2).

The intersectional effects of Iran's turbulent era, and the Islamic government's national policymaking, influence Iran's entrepreneurial environment. An overview of Iran's entrepreneurial ecosystem indicators in the GEM ([Global Entrepreneurship Monitor] 2020) report indicates that Iran's entrepreneurial ecosystem is not robust, or well-suited for entrepreneurial activities. As Table 5.1 illustrates, based on GEM indicators analysing the entrepreneurial ecosystem situation, Iran's position was poor compared to the other countries (GEM, 2020). Iran's entrepreneurial ecosystem, physical infrastructure, the internal market dynamic and commercial and legal infrastructure rank the lowest (54/54). Furthermore, Iran was ranked among the bottom five countries for internal market burdens, entry regulation, and entrepreneurial education at the post-school stage. Moreover, government entrepreneurship programmes, as well as cultural and social norms, highlight the ecosystem's substantial limitations for entrepreneurship.

Some of the challenges to entrepreneurship in Iran affect the establishment of a business venture, regardless of gender. For example, some of the obstacles to business start-ups include the unfavourable rent-seeking business environment of Iran, the government's dominance over the economy, economic sanctions, business policies and protectionism (Sarfaraz, 2017). Other impediments that Iranian women entrepreneurs face include: "funding availability and accessibility; lack of planning, skilled labour, and proper management skills, lack of competitiveness, technology innovation and customer loyalty, legal and regulatory framework, and social factors" (Mensah et al., 2019: 27). An overview of women's entrepreneurship in Iran indicates various obstacles within both the contextual dimension (including environmental, cultural, and organizational factors) and the individual dimension.

Table 5.1   *Entrepreneurial ecosystem indicators; Iran's rank compared to the global average*

Entrepreneurial ecosystem indicators	Iran	Iran's rank compared to the global average
Entrepreneurial finance	3.26	48/54
Physical infrastructure	3.5	54/54
Internal market burdens or entry regulation	3.32	51/54
Internal market dynamic	3.04	54/54
Commercial and legal infrastructure	2.98	54/54
Research and development transfer	3.11	42/54
Entrepreneurial education at post-school stage	3.26	53/54
Entrepreneurial education at school stage	2.98	26/54
Government entrepreneurship programmes	3.09	50/54
Government policies: taxes and bureaucracy	3.24	39/54
Governmental policies: support and relevance	3.07	47/54
Cultural and social norms	3.01	53/54

Source: GEM (2020: 114).

Arasti's (2006) research on 105 tertiary-educated women entrepreneurs in Iran highlights the following key challenges: laws and regulations, administrative bureaucracy, obtaining licenses, financing, gender discrimination, market access, costs, recruitment, suppliers, conflicts, business partners and managing the business. Moreover, the sociocultural structure of Iran does not encourage women's entrepreneurship (Modarresi et al., 2017: 249). Arasti's (2006) research finds that cultural norms and beliefs limit women's entrepreneurship. These cultural and gender norms promote the maternal role (i.e. staying home and taking care of children) as an essential role for women (Sohrab & Karambayya, 2016). In this regard, Modarresi et al. (2016) discuss how normative beliefs in Iran emphasize the male bread-winner role and the female child-caring role in the domestic sphere. These types of gender norms, stereotypes, and the gender system are influenced by institutionalized patriarchy. Patriarchy influences the social order and legal systems in Middle Eastern countries (Joseph & Slyomovics, 2011) and limits women's interaction in the public sphere in Iran. Based on the law of personal status, women need their husbands' permission to work, and men can restrict their wives from seeking employment (Moghadam, 2004b; The World Bank, 2013; The World Bank Group, 2018). Although some Middle Eastern and North African (MENA) countries, including Iran, have experienced economic development and a transition in demography, as well as the expansion of female education, patriarchy persists in the "form of economic organization, property relations, social class and a form of stratification and segmentation" (Moghadam, 2004a: 156–157).

While the social barriers to establishing a business are gradually reducing, these barriers restrain women's access to financial resources and social networks (Moghadam, 2013), despite networks otherwise expanding access to information, money, power, and friendship relations (Sharafizad & Coetzer, 2016). Women work in some male-dominated environments, and the distrust of women's managerial skills, as well as their presence as managers, limits their employment and entrepreneurship, specifically in small towns (Modarresi et al., 2016). Furthermore, Javadian and Singh's (2012) study illustrates some negative impacts of traditional culture and gender stereotypes on starting a venture. The features of women's constructed identities influence their location in society and their opportunities and social and political rights (Vossenberg, 2013). Poor gender identity and segregation affect women's attitudes and personal and psychological perspectives towards entrepreneurship (Modarresi et al., 2016). Moreover, gender differences, through socialization processes, shape individuals' identities, which affects their behavioural characteristics. Therefore, the perception of self-efficacy may influence women's ability to exploit and access opportunities in business (Poggesi et al., 2016).

Iranian women also face internal obstacles to setting up a business, such as low self-confidence, achievement, motivation, and fear of failure. Other factors include risk aversion, weak entrepreneurial networks, low levels of knowledge and skills in business and finding an appropriate business partner (Arasti & Bahmani, 2017; Modarresi et al., 2017; Sarfaraz, 2017). In addition to cultural barriers, financial, legal, administrative, and managerial dimensions affect women's entrepreneurship in Iran. Accordingly, Sarfaraz (2017) suggests a range of factors such as familial limitations, gender stereotypes, role expectations, problems relating to the labour market environment, lack of initial capital, a high rate of interest for loans, a short period for loan repayments and providing collateral for access to loans as the key barriers for women entrepreneurs in Iran.

METHODOLOGY

The study adopted a qualitative dominant, mixed methods research design, based on a comparative case study of women's home-based businesses in the garment and food industries in the formal and informal economy in Tehran, Iran's capital. During field research from December 2017 to July 2018, 40 face-to-face semi-structured interviews were conducted with women home-based entrepreneurs through purposeful sampling and snowballing. The research utilized a convergent parallel design, combining qualitative and quantitative data collection methods in an interview format (Creswell & Clark, 2017), while the interview protocol included both closed and open questions.

The initial selection of the participants in the informal economy was conducted via social networks, including Telegram and Instagram, through which the home-based women entrepreneurs sell or advertise their products. Both apps work by accessing the internet on phones or laptops. The useage of these apps is prevalent in Iran; for example, in 2016, Telegram had at least 20 million users in Iran (*The Guardian*, 2016). Due to the widespread use of social media apps and the economic situation of Tehran, recruiting participants in the informal sector via social media apps allowed the researcher to access home-based women entrepreneurs from various socio-economic backgrounds. To this end, an online recruitment strategy (Bryman, 2012) was adopted to find potential participants.

Two types of business industries were chosen for the case study: the food industry and the garment industry. Out of the 25 interviewees, 14 were engaged in the garment industry, 10 were involved in the food industry and one was active as a self-employed entrepreneur in both industries. Regarding the age of the interviewees, the research findings indicate that the participants were in the 30 to 60+ age group. Most participants, 18 interviewees (72 per cent), were between 30 and 50 years of age, while the remainder were above 50 years of age. At the time of data collection, 15 interviewees were married. The other interviewees were single, widowed, or separated and their business income was a major source of income for their families or themselves. However, some of the married women were responsible for their family's income too. In addition to marital status, the number of children impacts the entrepreneurial process. Among the participants, 18 interviewees had between one and three children, while six of the interviewees did not have any children. In terms of education, the research findings indicate that 12 interviewees (48 per cent) held diplomas or post-high school diplomas, while 11 of the interviewees (44 per cent) had successfully completed higher education at the bachelor's or post-graduate levels. Only two of the interviewees had an education level below that of a diploma.

Data analysis involved the following protocol: firstly, the interview data was transcribed and coded thematically (Bryman, 2012), in order to identify recurring social concepts, derived through the analysis of the interviewees' interpretations of categories and, accordingly, the relationship between the categories. Secondly, the overarching theoretical framework was applied to analyse the research study, as well as develop the interview questions and identify and analyse themes, categories, and patterns. Lastly, reference was made to the existing literature, specifically in the context of Iran, to determine the themes and relationships between the categories in this study. The findings of one interview were tested against other interviews until data saturation occurred and no new findings emerged from the coding process (Bryman, 2012; Mason, 2010: 2).

FINDINGS: WOMEN'S HOME-BASED BUSINESSES IN THE INFORMAL ECONOMY IN TEHRAN

Building upon the significance of the informal economy in women's economic activities in Iran, as discussed in the context section, this chapter presents the research findings on women home-based entrepreneurs within the informal economy in Iran. Home-based businesses in the garment and food industries included various economic activities in producing and offering services. In the garment industry, the businesses included those producing and selling imported garment products. In the food industry, there were businesses producing food and training services. According to the research findings, the barriers that directly or indirectly influenced these home-based business entrepreneurs were categorised into the contextual, motherhood, and individual domains. Table 5.2 includes the main themes found in this study, and we will discuss them throughout this chapter.

Contextual Domain

According to Bouguerra's (2015) model, the contextual domain includes environmental support, organizational factors, and the effect of the cultural environment. However, based on the identified themes, the contextual domain is categorized into two main groups: organizational resources and societal-structural resources. These two main groups include themes like inflation and currency value fluctuation, economic sanctions, government import policies, intellectual property issues, social norms, financial capital issues, the rate of return on capital, marketing, censorship of social media, disadvantages of running a business at home, restrictive rules to gaining a home-based business work permit, and the shipment of imported goods, as this interview highlights:

> I told my brother that I need money and there was a man we could borrow from him. My brother told him to give me the money with his guarantee. The man said: 'This is a woman. She is going to buy a few sets of clothes, but it is not clear whether she will be able to sell them or not. I will say it is for her own sake.' Then I said: 'If I were a man, you would never have said that' [...] The people's point of view is that women are more consumers than managers. (Interviewee 1, Tehran 2018)

This study identified significant societal-structural barriers, some unique to the context of Iran. These barriers include inflation, economic sanctions, government import policies, intellectual property (IP) issues, and social norms. Each

Table 5.2   *Thematic coding*

Subject	Categories	Themes
Barriers	Contextual domain (societal-structural barriers)	Inflation and currency value fluctuation
		Economic sanctions
		Government import policies
		Intellectual property issues
		Social norms
		Financial capital issue
	Contextual domain (organizational barriers)	Slow return on capital
		Marketing
		Censorship of social media
		Disadvantages of running a business at home
		Preventing and inhibiting rules of having home-based business work permit
		Shipment of imported goods
	Motherhood domain	Husband's disapproval of women's employment
		Family responsibilities
		Lack of family support
	Individual domain	Lack of skills, certificates and professional knowledge
		Disability

Source: Author.

barrier affected home-based women entrepreneurs and their coping strategies and entrepreneurial trajectory. Regarding inflation and Iran's currency value fluctuation, at the time of the research data collection in 2018, Iran's economy was already experiencing a severe currency value fluctuation crisis and had a high inflation rate. Consequently, in this study, home-based women entrepreneurs referred to inflation as a key struggle in the country's economic situation. From the point of view of home-based women entrepreneurs, these changes negatively impacted different aspects of their businesses. Furthermore, the women mentioned the effects of the economic sanctions on their businesses. As outlined in the context section, international sanctions against the Iranian government's nuclear programme commenced in 2006 (GEM, 2020), which had an adverse effect on the value of Iran's currency, its economic stability, and the well-being of its residents (Maloney, 2015). The women reflected on how the economic sanctions affected the profit margin of their businesses, through the reduction in people's purchasing power, and the increase in the price of raw materials due to Iran's currency rate fluctuations and inflation.

Also, from the perspective of the women entrepreneurs, sanctions made access to raw materials for their products more difficult. For example, the lack of access to imported raw materials resulted in the use of lower quality local materials, which affected the quality and availability of the products for sale, was a barrier to meeting customer demand, and reduced profit margins.

Furthermore, the women expressed how government import policies in Iran were another barrier to home-based businesses. In the garment industry, for example, home-based women entrepreneurs highlighted how the Iranian government's policies facilitated the import of goods from China, which led to intense market competition, which paralysed domestic manufacturers. The tax policies were also a significant barrier for home-based women entrepreneurs. In this study, the state policy on taxation is a barrier for home-based businesses selling imported garment goods. If self-employed women wish to run a business at home, there is no work permit for their business. If they wish to have a formal business, they must apply for a commercial work permit, which means they are not allowed to operate their business in residential premises. Also, a lack of government support and organizational guarantee of intellectual property resulted in potential IP infringements.

This research also found that cultural norms and beliefs limit women's entrepreneurship in Iran. One group of social norms are gender-related, such as gender stereotypes and insecurity for women. However, other social norms beyond gender issues also negatively affected the trajectory of home-based women entrepreneurs, including the underestimation of home-based businesses and their products and, lastly, the organizational culture of the administrative system. Therefore, the adverse effect of these gender stereotypes limits the networks and resources that women entrepreneurs can access. Gender stereotypes also provide cognitive representations of their category-based traits and attributes and their normative beliefs about what is appropriate and inappropriate. Thus, they can shape the perception of women entrepreneurs towards their traits and attributes. Based on the research findings, this may reduce women's aspiration to continue as entrepreneurs. According to the research findings, social insecurity was a motivation that pushed some women into starting a home-based business, and a few home-based women entrepreneurs pointed it out that social barriers limited them in running their businesses. Sexual harassment, interaction with a masculine work environment, and security issues were also noted. In this study, some women chose self-employment or running their businesses at home to be secure from sexual harassment. Some of the women also expressed that they had limitations regarding security issues in following up their business affairs due to the time they could travel and the locations they could safely visit.

Nepotism, a sub-theme in social norms, is a cultural characteristic in the government sector of Iran and a barrier for home-based women entrepreneurs.

They reported difficulties accessing resources when contacting public and state organizations. The quote below highlights the role of one's relatives and kinship network in the distribution of resources in society. This interviewee reflects on how family connections can affect your access to trade in a market bazaar:

> Once, my sister-in-law saw the mayor of our suburb and told him what to do for marketing home-based businesses. The mayor told her to come and book a place in the daily bazaars. In the daily markets, each of the sellers is an opponent. It is not easy to compete with them. Each of them has a special place for themselves. A good place in the daily markets belongs to them, and they leave a good place for their friends and acquaintances. (Interviewee 12, Tehran 2018)

There are also organizational barriers based on the prevailing organizational practices, processes, policies, and designs of the business that mediate employment. According to the thematic findings, as outlined in Table 5.2, the organizational barriers include financial issues and the slow return on capital, marketing, censorship of social media, a lack of access to shipments, disadvantages of running a business at home, preventing and inhibiting rules for having a home-based business work permit and problems with the shipment of imported goods. Based on a comparison between women's home-based businesses in the garment and food industries, the capital issue is the most frequent barrier that women entrepreneurs experience running their businesses. Home-based entrepreneurs had limited capital to run their businesses. This often forced them to seek alternative sources of capital, including their own investments, or financial support from family or friends. They mainly started their business using home tools and appliances. Thus, it can be concluded that they had business financing issues, which limited their ability to enter capital-intensive businesses. This study found that financial issues were one of the fundamental difficulties for home-based entrepreneurs in relation to starting and running a business. In some cases, the slow return on capital, which women home-based entrepreneurs invested in their businesses, was another key barrier to business survival and growth. This was especially the case for those entrepreneurs who sold their products to dealers, suppliers, or big shops. Moreover, the difficulties caused by late payments and order variations contributed to the slow return on investment for their businesses.

The second significant barrier for home-based entrepreneurs in the garment and food industry in the informal economy was accessing markets and gaining customer trust. Although they mentioned that they had inadequate marketing skills, intense competition was one of the market difficulties for women home-based entrepreneurs. The women expressed that the large manufacturers had access to cheaper raw materials and human resources. This enabled the manufacturers to enter the market with lower-priced goods and decreased the ability of women home-based entrepreneurs to compete in the market. From the perspective of the women in the garment industry, the goods imported into Iran by both small and large importers increased competition for domestic producers, especially the home-based entrepreneurs in this study. The quote below refers to this problematic competitive environment:

> The shoe market is awful due to the import of Chinese shoes. I mean that Chinese shoes have destroyed the Iranian shoe industry. (Interviewee 21, Tehran 2018)

The inability to access a daily or permanent marketplace and unacceptable market conditions for selling some business products were further barriers.

Social media censorship was the other key challenge for home-based women entrepreneurs. The Iranian government has laws to control the use of the internet and access to information, and uses social media censorship as a matter of course (Mohajerani et al., 2015). Although some Iranians use circumventing tools to curb censorship, a state ban on access to social media, such as Telegram, has influenced different aspects of the lives of Iranian people (Kargar & McManamen, 2018), a finding supported by this study, where social media played a pivotal role in enabling a significant portion of home-based businesses to operate online. So, any interruption to their access to social media could cause problems with advertisements, accessing the market, contacting customers, and updating information.

Running a home-based business can cause several difficulties, including customer attraction, inconvenience for family members, limited space, and security. Many women face additional barriers, such as a lack of work permits and engagement in the formal economy. As a result, most home-based entrepreneurs run their businesses informally:

> I think they would prefer not to act formally because it creates a series of limitations in a series of terms and that it creates responsibility. When they are limited in their capital and on the basis of their work, they do their job at home, and they are more able to handle home chores, have their own business and have an income. Of course, it is very important what their motivation is to do that business, but they most often prefer to be limited and reach the point where they can take on responsibilities of business registration. (Interviewee 10, Tehran 2018)

From the perspective of women who run their businesses informally, working formally has various disadvantages. The most important disadvantages of applying for a work permit are tax issues, the requirements of running a business premises out of the home, expenses, the administrative procedures of applying for a work permit, the required documentation, and the difficulties of running a business and producing goods under supervision, inspections, and regulations of related governmental organizations. For some of the participants in this study, importing goods, especially for home-based women entrepreneurs in the imported garment industry, caused further challenges. Other women who ran this type of business accessed their goods via connections, such as larger wholesale importers, or goods that were imported in passengers' luggage, or via other informal methods of importing goods, such as Kolbars, workers carrying goods on their back and transporting them illegally across the western borders of Iran to Iraq, Syria, and Turkey. Overall, a range of societal, structural, and organizational barriers were identified by interviewees in running their businesses, which resulted in the majority being run informally from home.

Motherhood Domain

The motherhood domain is the family and household context for women's entrepreneurship (Brush et al., 2009). This section focuses on the barriers that home-based women entrepreneurs experienced within this context. The motherhood domain is defined as the family and household context of women's entrepreneurship (Brush et al., 2009). This section focuses on the barriers that home-based women entrepreneurs experienced within this context, including the lack of family support, family responsibilities, and the husband's disapproval of women's employment (see Table 5.2).

Women managing home-based businesses face various challenges, including a lack of support from their families and gender roles related to motherhood. The disapproval of women's employment by husbands, based on male guardianship rules, is a significant barrier to women's entrepreneurship. Balancing work and home duties is also a challenge for some home-based women entrepreneurs:

> It is very rare for men and women to divide the work of the house between each other unless both work outside the house. But when the man is working outside the house, and women are working as entrepreneurs at home like me, the men do not say, for example, let's do the housework together today. My husband goes to work in the morning and comes back at one o'clock. When he leaves in the morning, he does not tell me let's do the home chores together and you start your work too. In most of our current works in our society, women are annoyed. Why? Because they have to take care of their children, they have to do the housework; they have to cook, and so on. Perhaps a small percentage of men are willing to help their spouse do the housework together. (Interviewee 18, Tehran 2018)

A few cases in this study also pointed out that the lack of family support and a husband's disapproval hindered the running of their business. Along with not having the support of the family, the women stated that their husband was worried about their financial independence. They stated that their husbands felt their independence jeopardized their power.

Individual Domain

The individual domain refers to the entrepreneurs' barriers in knowledge, personality traits, and skills. According to the theme found in this research, lack of skills, certificates, professional knowledge, and physical disabilities are barriers throughout their entrepreneurship trajectory, categorized in the individual domain. Although the interviewees insisted that their communication skills and social network, including the support of friends and family and social media in finding markets, enabled them to start their businesses, one of the most-identified barriers to women's home-based entrepreneurship related to a lack of marketing skills. The lack of professional certificates and professional knowledge in business industries also caused problems for some of the home-based women entrepreneurs in running their businesses, as this interviewee highlights:

> I don't really know about marketing, and I don't have much information about it. If I talk to a marketer or someone who has studied in this field, they will tell me the right ways to attract customers. This is a mistake of my own; I never sought to learn it and was always satisfied with the same customers I had. (Interviewee 16, Tehran 2018)

A heavy-duty workload was also highlighted, as well as taxing physical activities, ageing, fatigue, and decreased physical ability, which together made running their business difficult for a few home-based women entrepreneurs. This problem also affected accepting services and production offers.

In summary, in relation to the three domains considered in this study, the contextual domain explained the most critical challenges for home-based women entrepreneurs; capital, market access, and building customer trust were the most significant difficulties for businesses in the informal economy, and there were no significant differences regarding business type. However, the turbulent period of change in Iran set the context for the challenges, which home-based women entrepreneurs sought to navigate by running their businesses from home and mostly informally.

DISCUSSION

The barriers for home-based women entrepreneurs in Iran discussed in this chapter were categorised into three domains: contextual, motherhood, and individual, as summarized in Table 5.2. These domain barriers directly or indirectly influenced the opportunities for home-based women's entrepreneurship. One of the main obstacles faced by home-based women entrepreneurs in this study was running a business in the formal economy. Women who imported garments faced exclusion from work permits, resulting in limited income and high costs. Those who operate informally lack knowledge of the required documentation, while tax and guardianship laws further impeded their access. Similarly, women in the food industry struggled to enter the formal economy due to work permit procedures and male guardianship laws. Consequently, many entrepreneurs chose to operate informally. Therefore, running home-based businesses in the informal economy was one of the key strategies women deployed to navigate labour market barriers and to run a business in the formal context of the Islamic Republic. Despite the similarity in some of the barriers women entrepreneurs face worldwide, research indicates that it is essential to show how women entrepreneurs engage with entrepreneurship in specific contexts, which are more complicated and gendered (Henry & Lewis, 2023). Understanding the barriers to women entrepreneurs requires considering their context and the power structures they engage in, such as knowledge, experience and cultural values (Long & Buzzanell, 2022). Furthermore, understanding the context is essential to deploying the appropriate strategy and offer tailored solutions (Welsh et al., 2023).

This study found that the challenges faced by women entrepreneurs in home-based businesses in Iran were mainly related to the contextual domain. The research found the key challenges were at the macro level including bureaucracy, financing, gender discrimination, market access, costs, suppliers, role conflicts, business partners, managing the business, gender stereotypes, rent-seeking, the role of government in the economy, sanctions, business policies, and protectionism (Arasti, 2006; Javadian & Singh, 2012; Sarfaraz, 2017). Gender-related norms and stereotypes associated with familial social roles (Kliuchko, 2011), such as whether a woman should be a housewife and mother in the private sphere bound by family responsibilities, were identified as a barrier in this study. Gender stereotypes provide cognitive representations of category-based traits and attributes and normative beliefs about what is appropriate and inappropriate for them (Gupta et al., 2005). In this study, gender stereotypes related to family responsibilities affected women's home-based businesses, such as negative representations of self-employed women, as entrepreneurship was perceived to be a predominantly masculine activity, while a man's skill was more respected than a woman's skill, a finding supported by the wider literature (Modarresi & Arasti, 2021).

In this chapter, the contextual domain included societal-structural and organizational barriers to home-based women entrepreneurs' participation in the workforce. The societal-structural barriers included legal, cultural, economic, and political systems (Modarresi et al., 2017). Organizational barriers were identified based on the prevailing organizational practices, processes, policies, and designs of the business that mediate employment opportunities (Jamali, 2009; Ludewig & Sadowski, 2009; Modarresi et al., 2016). Nepotism, a sub-theme in social norms, is a cultural characteristic in the government sector of Iran, which also impacted on the opportunities for entrepreneurship amongst interviewees in this study (Farsi et al., 2014; Mujtaba et al., 2011). The governmental socio-cultural, political, and economic policies in Iran, following the Islamic revolution, coupled with the state's efforts to strengthen its ideologies, and the consequences of global sanctions, have collectively influenced different aspects of the entrepreneurial ecosystem. The Islamic revolution has also had an indirect impact on the entrepreneurial environment and resulted hindrances, such as restricted supply chains, elevated prices of imported goods, inflation, and censorship on social media. Women entrepreneurs faced challenges, such as unstable markets due to inflation, fluctuating currency value, economic sanctions, government import policies, taxes, intellectual property issues, while social media advertisements also threatened IP infringements (Collopy, 2017). Other issues identified included the following: social norms, financial capital issues, receiving payments, marketing, censorship of social media, disadvantages of running a home-based business and the challenges of importing goods.

Overall, it was found that home-based businesses in the informal economy have limited scope for market expansion and access to financial resources. Moreover, a lack of social security is one of the challenges for women in developing countries more broadly (Taib, 2014). However, the resilience of home-based women entrepreneurs in this study demonstrates that they found alternative sources, such as relying on their own investment capital and informal sources of finance, such as family and friends. Only a few received formal financial support through government. Despite these challenges, the women entrepreneurs in this study were mostly content and found strategies to overcome the barriers identified. However, the turbulent context, including the ongoing women–life–freedom revolution in Iran, will require home-based business entrepreneurs to continuously find alternative ways to navigate the changing business landscape.

This study contributes to the knowledge of women's home-based businesses in Iran by considering the barriers they face; however, it has some limitations. The scope of this research was limited to Iran; therefore, the findings and recommendations may not be generalizable to other countries. The research is grounded in a small-scale, qualitative dominant study of women home-based entrepreneurs. Testing these findings in future studies with diverse perspectives, involving other researchers and considering different business industries in a broader quantitative national study, and by conducting interviews with experts, scientists, and policymakers for small and home-based businesses, can expand and confirm the research results.

CONCLUSIONS

This research recommends the following initiatives that policymakers in Iran can implement to improve the entrepreneurial ecosystem. Firstly, the business registration process for home-based businesses needs to be streamlined to encourage women home-based entrepreneurs to register their businesses and move from the informal to the formal economy. This is because, according to this study's findings, the recent policies and support rules for these sorts of businesses were not sufficiently successful to encourage women to register their home-based businesses. This, in turn, will support efforts to socialize this practice and, over time, develop an understanding and acceptance of women entrepreneurs in Iran. However, alongside this effort, addressing, reassessing, and fundamentally changing economic, social, and legal systems, particularly regarding women's rights, are crucial steps towards ensuring equal rights and opportunities for women's economic participation and entrepreneurship. This will support efforts to develop an understanding and acceptance of women entrepreneurs in Iran. Secondly, formal data on women's businesses should be measured to clearly demonstrate their substantial value to the broader economy, society, and community. This will establish a compelling "business case" for supporting women entrepreneurs within the broader entrepreneurial ecosystem. Thirdly, further research should be conducted to study and unpack the self-identity and confidence of women home-based entrepreneurs. Fourthly, future studies are recommended to identify role models in successful home-based businesses and explore ways to share their knowledge and success with other women in Iran and similar contexts. Lastly, this chapter suggests funding workshops and skills development programmes for women entrepreneurs in Iran to close the knowledge gap and assist them in building successful business ventures.

REFERENCES

Adams-Prassl, A., Boneva, T., Golin, M., & Rauh, C. (2020). Inequality in the impact of the coronavirus shock: Evidence from real time surveys. *Journal of Public Economics*, *189*, 104245.

Ansell, C., & Boin, A. (2019). Taming deep uncertainty: The potential of pragmatist principles for understanding and improving strategic crisis management. *Administration & Society*, *51*(7), 1079–1112. https://doi.org/10.1177/0095399717747655.

Arasti, Z. (2006). Iranian women entrepreneurs: The effective socio-cultural structures of business start-up. *Women Research*, *4*(1–2), 93–119. [Persian language original.]

Arasti, Z., & Bahmani, N. (2017). Women's entrepreneurship in Iran. In S. Rezaei, L.-P. Dana, & V. Ramadani (Eds.), *Iranian Entrepreneurship: Deciphering the Entrepreneurial Ecosystem in Iran and in the Iranian Diaspora* (pp. 109–137). Cham: Springer International Publishing.

Arjomand, S. A. (1988). *The Turban for the Crown: The Islamic Revolution in Iran.* New York: Oxford University Press.

Bergman-Rosamond, A., Gammeltoft-Hansen, T., Hamza, M., Hearn, J., Ramasar, V., & Rydstrom, H. (2022). The case for interdisciplinary crisis studies. *Global Discourse, 12*(3–4), 465–486.

Bouguerra, N. (2015). An investigation of women entrepreneurship: Motives and barriers to business start-up in the Arab world. *Journal of Women's Entrepreneurship and Education,* 1–2, 86–104.

Brush, C. G., De Bruin, A., & Welter, F. (2009). A gender-aware framework for women's entrepreneurship. *International Journal of Gender and Entrepreneurship, 1*(1), 8–24.

Bryman, A. (2012). *Social Research Methods* (4th edn). New York: Oxford University Press.

Collopy, D. (2017). Social media's impact on intellectual property rights. In P. E. Chaudhry (Ed.), *Handbook of Research on Counterfeiting and Illicit Trade* (pp. 1–9). Cheltenham: Edward Elgar Publishing.

Costa, J., & Pita, M. (2020). Appraising entrepreneurship in Qatar under a gender perspective. *International Journal of Gender and Entrepreneurship, 12*(3), 233–251.

Crenshaw, K. (1990). Mapping the margins: Intersectionality, identity politics, and violence against women of color. *Stanford Law Review, 43,* 1241.

Creswell, J. W., & Clark, V. L. P. (2017). *Designing and Conducting Mixed Methods Research.* Thousand Oaks, CA: Sage Publications.

Esfandiari, H. (2022). The Iranian revolution of the women, by the women, for the people; How decades of women-led protest could bring a violent misogynist regime to its knees. Women without Borders, Policy Paper (No. 3). Retrieved from https://wwb.org/wp-content/uploads/2022/10/Esfandiari-Iranian-Revolution-of-the-Women-WwB-Policy-Paper.pdf.

Esfahani, H. S., & Shajari, P. (2012). Gender, education, family structure, and the allocation of labor in Iran. *Middle East Development Journal, 4*(2), 1–40.

Farsi, J., Modarresi, M., Motavaseli, M., & Salamzadeh, A. (2014). Institutional factors affecting academic entrepreneurship: The case of university of Tehran. *Economic Analysis, 47*(1–2), 139–159.

Fernandes, P., & Sanfilippo, M. (2022). Challenges faced by women entrepreneurs and some of the most successful women to follow. Retrieved from https://www.businessnewsdaily.com/5268-women-entrepreneur-challenges.html.

GEM [Global Entrepreneurship Monitor] (2020). *National Entrepreneurship Assessment for Iran 2019–2020.* Retrieved from https://www.gemconsortium.org/report/gem-iran-report-2019.

Grandy, G., Cukier, W., & Gagnon, S. (2020). (In)visibility in the margins: COVID-19, women entrepreneurs and the need for inclusive recovery. *Gender in Management: An International Journal,* 7–8, 667–675.

Gupta, V. K., Turban, D. B., Wasti, S. A., & Sikdar, A. (2005). Entrepreneurship and stereotypes: Are entrepreneurs from Mars or from Venus? In *Academy of Management Proceedings* (pp. C1–C6). Academy of Management Briarcliff Manor.

Hashemi, S. A., & Ebrahimpour, S. (2016). *Women in Informal Labour Market: Iran's Vice-President for Women and Family Affairs.* [Persian language original.]

Henry, C., & Lewis, K. V. (2023). The art of dramatic construction: Enhancing the context dimension in women's entrepreneurship research. *Journal of Business Research, 155*, 113440. https://doi.org/10.1016/j.jbusres.2022.113440.

Hoodfar, H., & Sadr, S. (2010). Islamic politics and women's quest for gender equality in Iran. *Third World Quarterly, 31*(6), 885–903.

Hoominfar, E., & Zanganeh, N. (2021). The brick wall to break: Women and the labor market under the hegemony of the Islamic Republic of Iran. *International Feminist Journal of Politics, 23*(2), 263–286. https://doi.org/10.1080/14616742.2021.1898286.

Jamali, D. (2009). Constraints and opportunities facing women entrepreneurs in developing countries: A relational perspective. *Gender in Management: An International Journal, 24*(4), 232–251.

Javadian, G., & Addae, I. Y. (2013). The impact of bureaucracies and occupational segregation on participation of Iranian women in the workforce. *Equality, Diversity and Inclusion: An International Journal, 32*(7), 654–670. http://www.emeraldinsight.com/doi/abs/10.1108/EDI-08-2012-0067.

Javadian, G., & Singh, R. P. (2012). Examining successful Iranian women entrepreneurs: An exploratory study. *Gender in Management: An International Journal, 27*(3), 148–164.

Joseph, S., & Slyomovics, S. (2011). *Women and Power in the Middle East.* Philadelphia: University of Pennsylvania Press.

Kargar, S., & McManamen, K. (2018). Censorship and collateral damage: Analyzing the Telegram ban in Iran. *Berkman Klein Center Research Publication* (2018–4). http://dx.doi.org/10.2139/ssrn.3244046.

Kelley, D., Brush, C., Greene, P., Herrington, M., Ali, A., & Kew, P. (2015). GEM 2014 Womens' Report. http://www.gemconsortium.org/report/49281.

Kliuchko, O. (2011). Gender stereotyping in studying pressing social problems. *Russian Social Science Review, 52*(2), 16–32.

Long, Z., & Buzzanell, P. M. (2022). Constituting intersectional politics of reinscription: women entrepreneurs' resistance practices in China, Denmark, and the United States. *Management Communication Quarterly, 36*(2), 207–234. https://doi.org/10.1177/08933189211030246.

Ludewig, O., & Sadowski, D. (2009). Measuring organizational capital. *Schmalenbach Business Review, 61*, 393–412. https://doi.org/10.1007/BF03396793.

Maloney, S. (2015). Sanctions and the Iranian nuclear deal: Silver bullet or blunt object? *Social Research, 82*(4), 887–911.

Martinez Dy, A., & Jayawarna, D. (2020). Bios, mythoi and women entrepreneurs: A Wynterian analysis of the intersectional impacts of the COVID-19 pandemic on self-employed women and women-owned businesses. *International Small Business Journal, 38*(5), 391–403.

Mason, M. (2010). Sample size and saturation in PhD studies using qualitative interviews. *Forum Qualitative Sozialforschung/Forum: Qualitative Social Research, 11*(3). https://doi.org/10.17169/fqs-11.3.1428.

Mensah, A. O., Fobih, N., & Adom, Y. (2019). Entrepreneurship development and new business start-ups: Challenges and prospects for Ghanaian entrepreneurs. *African Research Review, 13*(3), 27–41.

Modarresi, M., & Arasti, Z. (2021). Cultural challenges of women entrepreneurs in Iran. In S. Rezaei et al. (Eds.), *The Emerald Handbook of Women and Entrepreneurship in Developing Economies* (pp. 229–245). Leeds: Emerald Publishing.

Modarresi, M., Arasti, Z., Talebi, K., & Farasatkhah, M. (2016). Women's entrepreneurship in Iran: How are women owning and managing home-based businesses motivated to grow? *International Journal of Gender and Entrepreneurship*, *8*(4), 446–470.

Modarresi, M., Arasti, Z., Talebi, K., & Farasatkhah, M. (2017). Growth barriers of women-owned home-based businesses in Iran: An exploratory study. *Gender in Management: An International Journal*, *32*(4), 244–267.

Moghadam, V. M. (2004a). Patriarchy in transition: Women and the changing family in the Middle East. *Journal of Comparative Family Studies*, *35*(2), 137–162.

Moghadam, V. M. (2004b). Women in the Islamic Republic of Iran: Legal status, social positions, and collective action. Paper presented at the 'Iran after 25 years of revolution: A retrospective and a look ahead' conference for the Woodrow Wilson International Center for Scholars, November 16–17.

Moghadam, V. M. (2013). *Modernizing Women: Gender and Social Change in the Middle East* (3rd edn.). Boulder, CO: Lynne Rienner.

Mohajerani, A., Baptista, J., & Nandhakumar, J. (2015). Exploring the role of social media in importing logics across social contexts: The case of IT SMEs in Iran. *Technological Forecasting and Social Change*, *95*, 16–31.

Mujtaba, B. G., Tajaddini, R., & Chen, L. Y. (2011). Business ethics perceptions of public and private sector Iranians. *Journal of Business Ethics*, *104*(3), 433–447.

Ogundana, O., Akin-Akinyosoye, K., Ikhile, D., & Omodara, D. (2021). Women's entrepreneurship, health-related crisis, and a gender-sensitive crisis management model for sustainable development. In O. Adeola (Ed.), *Gendered Perspectives on Covid-19 Recovery in Africa: Towards Sustainable Development* (pp. 131–155). Cham: Springer International.

Organization of Petroleum Exporting Countries (2016). OPEC annual statistical bulletin. Retrieved from http://www.opec.org/opec_web/en/data_graphs/330.htm.

Paoloni, P. (2022). *Organizational Resilience and Female Entrepreneurship during Crises: Emerging Evidence and Future Agenda*. Cham: Springer Nature.

Poggesi, S., Mari, M., & De Vita, L. (2016). What's new in female entrepreneurship research? Answers from the literature. *International Entrepreneurship and Management Journal*, *12*(3), 735–764.

Saleh, A. (2022). One year on: Iran since President Raisi. Retrieved from https://studies .aljazeera.net/en/analyses/one-year-iran-president-raisi.

Sarfaraz, L. (2017). *Women's Entrepreneurship in Iran: Role Models of Growth-Oriented Iranian Women Entrepreneurs*. Cham: Springer International.

Shahrokni, N. (2020). Women in place. In *Women in Place: The Politics of Gender Segregation in Iran*. Oakland: University of California Press.

Sharafizad, J., & Coetzer, A. (2016). The networking interactions of Australian women small business owners. *Small Enterprise Research*, *23*(2), 135–150.

Sohrab, S. G., & Karambayya, R. (2016). Women in management in Iran. In A. M. Richardsen & R. J. Burke (Eds.), *Women in Management Worldwide: Signs of Progress* (3rd edn.) (pp. 285–309). London & New York: Routledge, Taylor & Francis Group.

Statistical Center of Iran (2022). Labor force survey results. Retrieved from https:// www.amar.org.ir/english/.

Taib, M. N. A. (2014). Psycho-social problems of female entrepreneurs in Pakistan: An analysis. *Journal of Progressive Research in Social Sciences*, *1*, 47–55.

The Guardian (2016). Telegram: The instant messaging app freeing up Iranians' conversations. Retrieved from https://www.theguardian.com/world/2016/feb/08/telegram-the-instant-messaging-app-freeing-up-iranians-conversations.

The World Bank (2013). *Opening Doors*. Washington, DC: The World Bank.

The World Bank (2022). Labor force participation rate. Retrieved from https://data.worldbank.org/indicator/SL.TLF.CACT.FE.ZS?locations=IR,2022.

The World Bank Group (2018). *Women, Business, and the Law 2018*. Washington, DC: The World Bank.

Vossenberg, S. (2013). Women entrepreneurship promotion in developing countries: What explains the gender gap in entrepreneurship and how to close it. Maastricht School of Management, Working Paper Series 8, 1–27.

Welsh, D. H. B., Kaciak, E., Fadairo, M., Doshi, V., & Lanchimba, C. (2023). How to erase gender differences in entrepreneurial success? Look at the ecosystem. *Journal of Business Research, 154*, 113320. https://doi.org/10.1016/j.jbusres.2022.113320.

PART II

Innovation and adaptation strategies

6. How women-led businesses fared in the Covid-19 pandemic

Rebecca Weicht, Rosemarie Kay, Markus Rieger-Fels and Friederike Welter

INTRODUCTION

While there has been an increasing number of research papers on how businesses, in general, fared in and handled the Covid-19 pandemic, few studies disaggregate the data by gender and consider how women-led businesses specifically weathered these turbulent times. Among the studies that do consider the issue, the findings are inconclusive. Given the somewhat contradictory nature of the findings, the question if women-led businesses were more affected by the pandemic must be regarded as still not thoroughly answered. Providing answers to these questions is crucial for evaluating policy proposals and determining how governments can support women entrepreneurs in turbulent times.

This chapter makes two contributions. First, we investigate the question of whether female-led firms were hit harder by the crisis. Given the period that our study covers, we can provide more than just a snapshot in time allowing us to discern whether and how differences in affectedness evolved. Second, there is still an ongoing debate about the possible causes that underlie differences between female- and male-led firms. Roughly, these can be differentiated into indirect and direct effects. As an example of an indirect effect, female-led businesses may have been affected stronger by the crisis simply because they are more prevalent in economic sectors that were hit particularly hard by the crisis (Kritikos et al., 2021). Additionally, female-led businesses are smaller, on average, and smaller firms may have had a harder time during the pandemic (Bundesministerium für Wirtschaft und Energie, 2021). For example, smaller firms often have limited financial resources compared to larger firms, making it difficult for them to weather a prolonged period of reduced revenue. Besides these indirect effects, there might be more direct effects. Female-led businesses may have responded differently to the crisis, thereby either ameliorating or exacerbating the crisis' impact on business outcomes (Buratti et al.,

2018; Manolova et al., 2020). Alternatively, female leaders might have been burdened more heavily by private obligations because of school and day-care closures, leaving them less time to attend to their struggling businesses (Hübgen et al., 2021).

Shedding light on these underlying causes is vital for informing a tailored policy response and designing appropriate support measures. If differences between female- and male-led firms are primarily driven by indirect effects, this calls for policies that address sector- or size-specific vulnerabilities directly. Female-led businesses will then benefit from such policies disproportionately. Alternatively, if differences between female- and male-led firms do not primarily result from such indirect effects, this calls for policies supporting female entrepreneurs more directly.

This chapter is structured as follows: first, the context of the Covid-19 pandemic in Germany is presented alongside a literature review that summarises the key findings on women-led businesses in the Covid-19 pandemic to date. Then, the empirical basis for the study, the German Business Panel (GBP), is introduced. In the section that follows, we present and discuss our findings.

CONTEXT AND REVIEW OF LITERATURE

Germany, like many countries, was caught off-guard when the Covid-19 pandemic hit in early 2020. The first case was reported on 27 January and by March the country had implemented strict lockdown measures. The federal government's response was guided by the advice of experts, including the Robert Koch Institute (RKI), Germany's federal disease control agency (Desson et al., 2020). The federal government also worked closely with the country's 16 states, which have significant autonomy in health policy (Desson et al., 2020).[1]

The federal government's initial response to the pandemic was swift and decisive (Forster and Heinzel, 2021). Chancellor Angela Merkel urged Germans to stay home and follow social distancing guidelines. The federal government implemented a series of measures to slow the spread of the virus, including closing schools, restaurants, and non-essential businesses.

Several business-support packages were implemented at both the federal and state levels in response to the Covid-19 pandemic. These support measures were aimed at helping businesses deal with the economic fallout from the pandemic and were designed to prevent layoffs and bankruptcy. One of the most significant federal-level packages was the Corona Aid Package, which included various measures to support businesses (Bundesministerium für Wirtschaft und Klimaschutz, 2022). It provided grants and loans to businesses that had to shut down due to lockdown measures or experienced significant revenue losses during the pandemic. The package also included tax relief measures, such as a temporary reduction in value-added tax and other taxes (Bundesministerium für Wirtschaft und Klimaschutz, 2022). In addition to these new support measures, short-time work benefits allowed businesses to reduce their employees' working hours instead of laying them off (Bundesministerium für Wirtschaft und Klimaschutz, 2022). The government covered a portion of the employees' lost wages, reducing the financial burden on businesses. Self-employed individuals were also eligible for financial support, including grants and loans.

At the state level, Germany's 16 states tended to implement additional business support measures. For example, the state of North Rhine-Westphalia provided support to businesses affected by the pandemic, including a package of grants, low-interest loans, and consultancy services (Ministerium für Wirtschaft, Industrie, Klimaschutz und Energie des Landes Nordrhein-Westfalen, 2020). The state of Bavaria provided aid to businesses affected by the pandemic, including emergency aid for small and medium-sized businesses, start-ups, and freelancers, as well as low-interest loans and grants for affected businesses (Bayerisches Staatsministerium für Wirtschaft, Landesentwicklung und Energie, n.d.). Against this background of how the Covid-19 pandemic played out in Germany and its policy support measures, we now turn to review the literature on how (women-led) businesses fared in the pandemic.

While many peer-reviewed papers (Torres et al., 2021), reports (Abel-Koch and Schwarz, 2021; Stephan et al., 2021), and ad hoc analyses (Verband deutscher Unternehmerinnen, 2020; Kritikos et al., 2020) have been published that considered the impact of the Covid-19 pandemic on small and medium-sized businesses, most publications were only able to consider a short time window. Among others, Graeber et al. (2021), Santos et al. (2021), and Yue and Cowling (2021) considered the time between April and July 2020. While the early months of the pandemic were times of particular turbulence and uncertainty, the pandemic affected firms for a much longer period of time and some of its adverse consequences may have manifested themselves only in later months.

Findings concerning how women-led businesses fared in the pandemic differ, as presented in Table 6.1. In Germany, drawing on data from the Socio-Economic Panel-CoV, researchers found that among the self-employed, who generally faced a higher likelihood of income losses due to Covid-19 than employees, women were about one-third more likely to experience income losses (Graeber et al., 2021). They explained this with women tending to work in industries that were more severely affected by the pandemic (Graeber et al., 2021). Self-employed women also reported a greater loss of income (63 per cent) than men (47 per cent; Seebauer et al., 2021). In contrast, Abel-Koch and Schwartz (2021) did not find a bigger impact of the pandemic on women-led businesses in Germany based on survey data from between April 2020 and

January 2021. Similarly, Kay and Welter (2021) traced the economic development in various sectors between January and December 2020 on official statistics and contrasted these data with the specifics of women's businesses. They did not find evidence suggesting women-led businesses were systematically more affected by the pandemic (specifically considering sales development). Kay and Welter (2021) reflected that it might rather be the case that women entrepreneurs suffer income losses because they tend to work in sectors that were affected more severely by social distancing regulations.

At the global level, women-led businesses surveyed across 23 countries tended to be impacted more adversely by Covid-19 (72 per cent vs. 56 per cent saw lower trading volume; Stephan et al., 2021). In low- and middle-income countries, the pandemic affected micro businesses, women-led businesses in the hospitality industry, and women-led businesses in 49 countries more severely (Torres et al., 2021). The authors also found that women-led businesses were less likely to have received some form of public support, although they have been hit harder in some domains (Torres et al., 2021). Similarly, Liu et al. (2021) found that the pandemic disproportionally affected women-led businesses in poorer countries. They found that women-led businesses were more likely to close (2.6 per cent more likely) and for a longer duration than men-led businesses (Liu et al., 2021). They also found no difference between women- and men-led businesses in terms of obtaining government support (Liu et al., 2021). However, their results revealed that women-led businesses were less likely to receive bank loans and were more likely to reduce the number of employees, especially female employees (Liu et al., 2021).

Given the somewhat contradictory nature of the findings, we believe that the question of whether women-led businesses were more severely affected by the pandemic and its accompanying policy measures must be regarded as still not being thoroughly answered.

METHOD

The empirical basis for our study is the German Business Panel (GBP), a representative ongoing online survey of 10,000 German businesses (Bischof et al., 2021, 2022). While there are other attractive data sources for the German context, for example the SOEP-CoV survey, we opted for the GBP data as it uses firms as sampling unit instead of households.[2]

Notably, the GBP is designed as a rolling panel. Businesses that no longer want to participate in the second and subsequent survey waves are replaced by structurally suitable, similar businesses. Also, businesses are contacted at different times during the survey period of each wave. In dynamic times, such as the Covid-19 pandemic, this meant that different responses within a wave could be examined.

Table 6.1   Overview of diversity of findings if and how women led-businesses were (not) affected by the Covid-19 pandemic

	Female businesses were more severely affected than male-led businesses	Female businesses were not more severely affected
Germany	Self-employed women were about one-third more likely to experience income losses than male self-employed; explanation: women tend to work in industries that were more severely affected by the Covid-19 pandemic (Graeber et al., 2021)	No impact on women-led businesses in Germany based on survey data from between April 2020 and January 2021 (Abel-Koch and Schwartz, 2021)
	Self-employed women reported a greater loss of income (63 per cent) than self-employed men (47 per cent; Seebauer et al., 2021)	No evidence suggesting women-led businesses were systematically more affected (specifically considering sales development); possible explanation: women entrepreneurs suffer income loss because they tend to work in sectors that were affected more severely by social distancing regulations (Kay and Welter, 2021)
Global level	Women-led businesses across 23 countries were affected more adversely (72 per cent vs. 56 per cent saw lower trading volume; Stephan et al., 2021)	
	Women-led micro businesses, women-led businesses in the hospitality industry, and women-led businesses in 49 countries are more severely affected (Torres et al., 2021)	
	Pandemic disproportionally affected women-led businesses in poorer countries: women-led businesses were more likely to close (2.6 per cent more likely) and for a longer duration (Liu et al., 2021)	

Source: Authors.

We use information from three waves of the survey. The first lasted from 6 July to 3 October 2020. The second lasted from 16 November 2020 to 24 June 2021. The third wave started on 30 June 2021 and was still ongoing when we retrieved the data. We have data up until March 2022. In all three waves, the pandemic played a major role. In addition to structural and performance data, rich information is available on which public-support measures were used and which measures were taken within the business in response to the crisis.

To ensure that the data is representative of the German corporate landscape, the panel offers weights that reflect the structure of the industry, firm size, and location (Bischof et al., 2022). We make use of these weights when calculating descriptive statistics.

The GBP data allow us to clearly categorize firms into micro, small, medium-sized, and large businesses according to the EU definition.[3] The GBP data do not contain direct information on whether a business is under female leadership. To identify differences between female- and male-led firms, we take the following steps. First, we restrict the sample to observations in which the respondent identified him or herself as the owner, managing director, board member, or general manager of the business. Within this restricted sample, we identify businesses as female-led if the respondent chose a female salutation. While our procedure does not perfectly identify female-led businesses, we use the presence of at least one female in a leading position as a proxy variable. Through our procedure, we identify a share of 20.2 per cent of businesses as female-led. This share is close to a recent estimate of 18.4 per cent of female-led businesses in the German economy (Fels and Wolter, 2022).

Our restrictions on the sample to only include observations where the respondent was the business owner/manager likely favours smaller businesses where survey response is less likely delegated to a subordinate. In addition, larger firms are considerably less likely to be under female leadership.[4] Hence, we control for firm size in all regression analyses. In addition, whenever possible, we derive estimates of the difference between female- and male-led firms for different firm sizes. We deem this differentiation important as some direct effects, such as the heavier burden on female entrepreneurs of private obligations through school and day-care closures, might be more pronounced for or even restricted to small businesses.[5]

We use either OLS or logit regressions in our multivariate analyses depending on whether the dependent variable of interest is continuous or binary. For OLS regressions, we report the estimated coefficients of the independent variables. For logit regressions, we report average marginal effects (in percentage points) of the independent variables.

FINDINGS

We present our findings under three over-arching headings: first, how women-led businesses were impacted by the Covid-19 pandemic; second, which business measures they took to manage the impact of the pandemic; and lastly, how they made use of state support offers.

Business Impact

During the first survey wave, female-led firms reported a decline in monthly revenue compared to January 2020 of, on average, 21.6 per cent compared to 20.0 per cent among male-led firms, as depicted in Figure 6.1. In the second survey wave, female-led firms reported an average decline of 27.0 per cent in monthly revenues compared to January 2020, while the average decline was 18.1 per cent among male-led firms. During the third survey wave, firms were asked to compare the annual revenues of 2021 to those of 2020. Female-led firms reported an average increase of 5.0 per cent, and male-led firms had an average increase of 7.5 per cent.

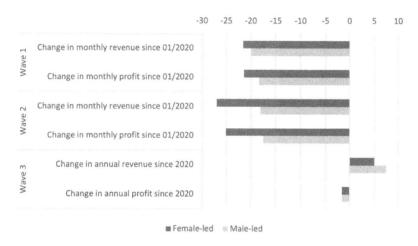

Source: German Business Panel, authors' calculations.

Figure 6.1   Change in monthly (annual) revenue/profit (in per cent)

Our regression analyses reveal that only the difference in the second wave is statistically significant once we control for firm size and sector (Table 6.2). This suggests that female- and male-led firms started out being affected roughly equally. Any observed difference in the early months of the crisis can be largely attributed to the different distributions of female- and male-led firms across sectors and firm sizes. The situation worsened considerably for female-led firms at the end of 2020/the beginning of 2021. In particular, the decline does not seem to be just an artefact of sector or size effects. Finally, the second pandemic year brought some relief. Still, given the prior difference in affectedness, the lacking difference in catch-up rates between female- and male-led firms suggests that female-led firms were still behind male-led firms in fully recovering from the crisis' impact.

We find a similar development when considering firm profits. Female-led businesses reported a decline in monthly profit during the first survey wave of, on average, 21.4 per cent compared to an average decline of 18.3 among their male-led counterparts. The gap widened in the second wave, with an average decline of 25.1 per cent among female-led firms and an average decline of 17.5 per cent among male-led firms. In the third wave, both female-led and male-led firms reported an average decline in annual profits of 1.6 per cent. Again, we find the differences not statistically significant in wave 1 and wave 3 (Table 6.2.). The statistical evidence for the second wave is more mixed. We find a significant negative effect for our female dummy variable and a significant positive interaction between female leadership and medium size. The interaction effect dominates the direct effect. This suggests that, apart from medium-sized enterprises, female-led firms suffered steeper losses. Among middle-sized enterprises, female-led firms suffered less severe losses.

Specifically, the costs associated with hygiene measures were the biggest financial burden during the Covid-19 pandemic for the businesses (Figure 6.2). It was cited most often and with a share of 42.9 per cent more frequently by female-led firms than male-led businesses (35.8 per cent). Firm closures and other sources were also cited more frequently by female-led firms (26.5 vs. 18.3 per cent and 29.5 vs. 23.4 per cent, respectively). We do not find strong differences between female- and male-led businesses in the share of firms citing home-office obligations (12.5 vs. 11.2 per cent), employee absence due to school or kindergarten closures (21.9 vs. 20.2 per cent) or due to sickness (18.8 vs. 19.2 per cent), supply chain disruptions (29.1 vs 33.2 per cent), or digitisation measures (23.4 vs. 20.3 per cent). Overall, and consistent with the data on revenue and profit development, the share of female firms that cited no financial burden due to the pandemic was considerably below the respective share among male-led firms (11.5 vs. 18.7 per cent). Once we control for sector and size effects, we find few differences between female- and male-led firms to be statistically significant (Table 6.3). Female-led micro enterprises were particularly burdened by investments due to hygiene measures. Female-led small firms reported home-office obligations more often, but employee absence less often as a source of burden. Overall, female-led firms were less likely to report no financial burden.[6]

Overall, our results on business impact indicate that, once size- and sector-related differences are controlled for, there were little discernible differences between male- and female-led firms during the first months of the pandemic. In later months, however, a gap between female- and male-led firms appeared that does not seem to be solely the result of size or sector differences. Given that the following recovery seemed equally strong at female- and

Table 6.2 Regression results: change in monthly (annual) revenue

	Wave 1		Wave 2		Wave 3	
	Change in monthly revenue since 01/2020	Change in monthly profit since 01/2020	Change in monthly revenue since 01/2020	Change in monthly profit since 01/2020	Change in annual revenue since 2020	Change in annual profit since 2020
	(in %)	(in %)	(in %)	(in %)	(in %)	(in %)
Small	6.86 ***	2.21	7.42 ***	3.65 **	2.49	0.27
Medium	12.10 ***	7.19 ***	7.41 ***	6.20 **	2.54	10.93 ***
Large	14.65 ***	4.56	12.39 **	5.43	2.54	11.50
Female	1.34	−1.33	−7.24 ***	−6.48 ***	−1.90	−3.75
Female x small	1.09	3.95	1.07	4.24	2.20	5.82
Female x medium	−6.49	−6.90	7.89	19.57 **	9.24	−3.02
Female x large	−13.11	−3.59	−15.02	−15.35	−5.81	−24.06
n	6,293	6,081	3,778	3,697	2,678	2,603
Adj. R2	0.0849	0.0861	0.1270	0.0952	0,0026	0.0161

Notes: OLS regressions including controls for economic sector, state, and month of response. * p-value< 0.1, ** p-value< 0.05, *** p-value< 0.01.

Source: Authors.

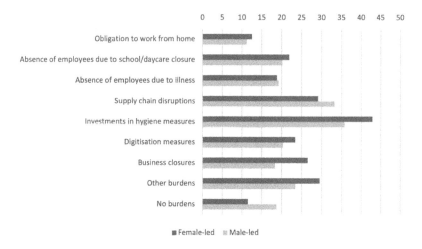

Source: German Business Panel, wave 3, authors' calculations.

Figure 6.2	*Share of businesses that cite the following source of financial burden during the pandemic (in per cent)*

male-led firms, this suggests that, at the beginning of 2022, female-led firms were still behind their male-led counterparts in making a full recovery.

Business Responses

Given the differences in affectedness, we expect that female-led firms had to react more strongly to the crisis. Alternatively, some of the later differences in business performance could have been the result of an earlier difference in behaviour. Therefore, we considered various operational measures that businesses might take in a situation of uncertainty or decline. Concretely, we investigated possible realignments of planned investments and a set of operational measures taken directly in response to the crisis.

During the first wave, we do not find strong differences in the share of female- and male-led firms which needed to postpone planned investment (44.8 vs 43.8 per cent, Figure 6.3) or cancel planned investment (33.2 vs. 33.16 per cent). During the second wave, this picture changed substantially: 60.0 per cent of female-led firms reported to have postponed and 45.3 per cent reported to have cancelled investment in wave 2 compared to 53.9 per cent and 43.2 per cent respectively among male-led firms. However, our regression results indicate that the difference between female- and male-led firms in their propensity

Table 6.3   Estimated difference between male- and female-led firms' propensity to identify sources of financial burden during the Covid-19 pandemic (in per cent)

	Home-office obligation	Employee absence due to school/daycare closures	Employee absence due to sickness	Supply-chain disruption	Investments in hygiene measures	Digitisation measures	Firm closures	No burden[+]
Female overall								−4.52 ***
Female at micro enterprise	1.88	2.28	0.39	−2.20	5.78 **	1.97	3.07	
Female at small enterprise	10.38 **	4.45 *	−7.83 *	−0.66	7.04	2.81	−3.03	
Female at medium-sized enterprise	0.74	−2.99	11.65	−5.12	10.46	3.10	13.25	
Female at large enterprise	39.59 *	−11.70	14.50	24.10	−9.31		47.57 *	
n	2,747	2,754	2,754	2,754	2,754	2,741	2,731	2,691
Pseudo R2	0.0884	0.1032	0.1254	0.1593	0.0789	0.0636	0.2194	0.0915

Notes: Results of a logistic regression. We show average marginal effects (in percentage points), i.e. the difference between female- and male-led firms (for firms of different sizes) in the predicted probability that a respondent answered affirmatively. Controls include economic sector, month of response, state, and a variable indicating a legal form that is strongly associated with family enterprises. [+] We report overall effects as estimation is not feasible for individual firm sizes. * p-value< 0.1, ** p-value< 0.05, *** p-value< 0.01.
Source: Authors.

Table 6.4   *Estimated difference between female- and male-led firms'*
                    propensity to postpone/cancel investments due to the
                    Covid-19 pandemic (in per cent)

	Postponed investment	Cancelled investment	Postponed investment	Cancelled investment
	Wave 1	Wave 2	Wave 2	Wave 2
Female at micro enterprise	0.91	−0.94	5.86 **	2.61
Female at small enterprise	−0.75	−0.66	0.02	0.18
Female at medium-sized enterprise	2.92	−4.54	4.50	−3.53
Female at large enterprise	−22.90 *	−8.32	−3.72	−22.56
n	5,871	5,818	3,378	3,231
Pseudo R2	0.0218	0.0222	0.0301	0.0281

Notes: Results of a logistic regression. We show average marginal effects (in percentage points), i.e. the difference between female- and male-led firms (for firms of different sizes) in the predicted probability that a respondent answered affirmatively. Controls include economic sector, month of response, state, and a variable indicating a legal form that is strongly associated with family enterprises. * p-value< 0.1, ** p-value< 0.05, ***p-value< 0.01.
Source: Authors.

to postpone investment is only statistically significant for micro enterprises in the second wave (Table 6.4).[7]

We also observe some differences concerning the measures taken directly in response to the crisis (Figure 6.4). During the first wave, we found that, in fact, many female-led firms have taken no business measures to respond to the crisis (36.5 vs 32.7 per cent). In comparison to male-led firms, female-led firms have implemented a variety of business measures less often. They have less often decreased wages/bonuses (35.6 vs. 39.7 per cent), reduced employment (13.8 vs 14.5 per cent), reduced retained earnings (20.4 vs 21.3), increased prices (20.2 vs 22.9), and reduced research and development expenses (5.7 vs 6.9 per cent). Notably, however, the differences appear not to be very large. Our regression results (Table 6.5) indicate that the differences are only significant for reducing wages/bonuses (though only for micro-enterprises) and for price increases (but confined to micro and small enterprises). During the second wave, female-led medium-sized businesses were less likely to use their retained earnings to deal with the crisis. In addition, female-led firms were significantly less likely to cut their R&D spending.

Overall, female-led and male-led businesses' responses to the crisis differed only slightly. If there were differences, they were largely concentrated in the first months of the crisis. Female entrepreneurs showed a more muted

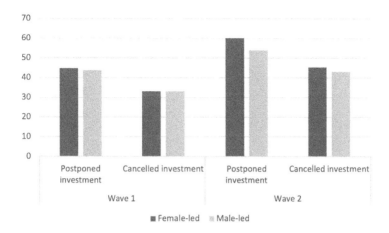

Source: German Business Panel, waves 1 and 2, authors' calculations.

Figure 6.3   *Share of businesses that reported to have postponed/
cancelled investment (in per cent)*

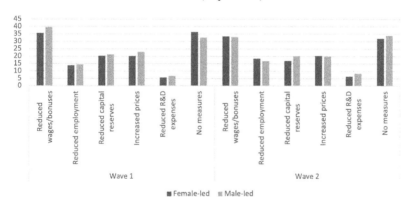

Source: German Business Panel, waves 1 and 2, authors' calculations.

Figure 6.4   *Business measures taken by male- and female-led businesses
(in per cent)*

response as they were overall less likely to take measures but particularly less likely to increase prices and reduce wages and bonuses. In the second wave, we find even fewer differences, except for a lower share of female-led firms that needed to reduce retained earnings. However, a larger share of female-led firms needed to postpone investment.

Table 6.5   Regression table showing estimated differences between female- and male-led firms' propensity to take a variety of business measures in response to the crisis (in per cent)

	Reduced wages/bonuses		Reduced employment		Reduced retained earnings	
	Wave 1	Wave 2	Wave 1	Wave 2	Wave 1	Wave 2
Female at micro enterprise	−3.68 *	1.95	0.29	1.11	−1.61	−2.48
Female at small enterprise	−1.28	−0.07	−3.03	−1.62	0.38	−4.39
Female at medium-sized enterprise	−2.09	−1.04	5.41	8.70	3.52	−13.98 ***
Female at large enterprise	−1.45	−32.92 **	−3.73	−14.41	3.09	−5.08
n	6,461	3,878	6,461	3,873	6,461	3,878
Pseudo R2	0.0484	0.0367	0.06	0.0503	0.0152	0.0170

	Increased prices		Reduced R&D expenses		Taken no measure	
	Wave 1	Wave 2	Wave 1	Wave 2	Wave 1	Wave 2
Female, overall				−2.39 **		
Female at micro enterprise	−2.83 *	−0.26	−0.81		1.89	−2.78
Female at small enterprise	−6.33 **	0.91	−1.03		6.11 *	0.21
Female at medium-sized enterprise	−5.99	−3.36	−0.12		1.67	1.12
Female at large enterprise	1.55	5.53	−3.12		2.60	20.12

	Reduced wages/bonuses		Reduced employment		Reduced retained earnings	
n	6,461	3,878	6,403	3,661	6,461	3,878
Pseudo R2	0.0470	0.0465	0.0361	0.0635	0.0407	0.0313

Notes: Results of a logistic regression. We show average marginal effects (in percentage points), i.e. the difference between female- and male-led firms (for firms of different sizes) in the predicted probability that a respondent answered affirmatively. Controls include economic sector, month of response, state, and a variable indicating a legal form that is strongly associated with family enterprises. [+] We report overall effects as estimation is not feasible for individual firm sizes. * p-value< 0.1, ** p-value< 0.05, ***p-value< 0.01.

Source: Authors.

Application for Government Aid

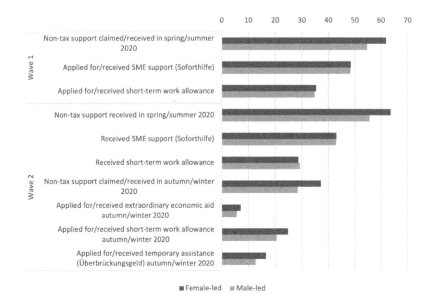

Source: German Business Panel, waves 1 and 2, authors' calculations.

Figure 6.5   *Non-tax support measures used by female- and male-led businesses (in per cent)*

The federal government and the state governments in Germany offered businesses several support measures to get them through the crisis and cushion the most severe restriction measures, such as mandated business closures. The measures included non-tax-related aid such as the Covid-19 emergency relief (*Soforthilfe*), interim aid (*Überbrückungshilfe*), extraordinary economic aid (e.g. *Novemberhilfe, Dezemberhilfe*), short-time work allowance (*Kurzarbeitergeld*), or generous credit lines through the German promotional bank KfW. Further assistance was provided through the tax system by granting a refund of the 2020 tax prepayment or the deferral of tax payments, among others. Our results indicate that most businesses needed to rely on such assistance.

Overall, 61.9 per cent of female-led businesses and 54.7 per cent of male-led businesses indicated in survey wave 1 that they applied for or received some non-tax-related government aid (Figure 6.5). The Covid-19 emergency relief programme and the short-time work allowance were particularly attractive. When asked whether they had received government support, 63.6 per cent of female-led businesses in survey wave 2 affirmed compared to 55.6 per cent among male-led businesses. The differences between female-led and male-led firms with respect to the reception of *Soforthilfe* (48.3 vs 42.9 per cent) and the reception of *Kurzarbeitergeld* (34.7 vs. 29.2 per cent) are quite close to the differences observed in the previous wave. Finally, fewer firms reported that they had applied for/received non-tax government support in the second half of 2020. Still, female-led firms remained more likely to have done so than male-led firms (37.1 vs. 28.5 per cent). Our regression results (Table 6.6) indicate that female-led micro enterprises had to rely more heavily on government assistance than their male counterparts throughout the year 2020. However, the evidence of a stronger need is not restricted to micro enterprises. Consistent with our evidence on a stronger affectedness, we also find evidence that female-led small and medium-sized businesses were more likely to have received aid.

Table 6.6   *Regression table showing estimated differences between female- and male-led firms' propensity to apply for and receive non-tax support*

	Applied for or received non-tax support		Received non-tax support[+]		Applied for/ received non-tax support in autumn/winter 2020	
	(wave 1)		(wave 2)		(wave 2)	
Female at micro enterprise	4.65	**	4.41	*	6.11	***
Female at small enterprise	2.97		8.90	**	0.14	
Female at medium-sized enterprise	−1.01		21.56	**	7.17	
Female at large enterprise	21.93	*	−20.43		−3.55	
n	6,459		3,877		3,858	
Pseudo R2	0.0772		0.0852		0.1244	

Notes: Results of a logistic regression. We show average marginal effects (in percentage points), i.e. the difference between female- and male-led firms (for firms of different sizes) in the predicted probability that a respondent answered affirmatively. Controls include economic sector, month of response, state, and a variable indicating a legal form that is strongly associated with family enterprises. [+] As in wave 1, restricted to support measures available in the first half of 2020. * p-value< 0.1, ** p-value< 0.05, ***p-value< 0.01. *Source:* Authors.

We find much lower differences when we consider the applications for tax-related government support (Figure 6.6): 34.5 per cent of female-led firms reported having applied for or received such aid in survey wave 1 compared to 26.2 per cent among male-led firms. In survey wave 2, the shares were equally similar with 28.6 and 26.2 per cent, respectively. Analysing the two most commonly claimed measures in more depth, we do not find strong differences, neither for the refund of the tax prepayment (15.5 vs. 14.5 per cent in wave 1; 8.4 vs. 10.5 per cent in wave 2) nor the deferral of tax payments (23.1 vs. 21.3 in wave 1; 20.7 vs 17.1 per cent in wave 2). We do not find any of these differences to be statistically significant (Table 6.7).

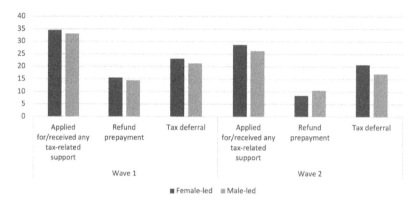

Source: German Business Panel, waves 1 and 2, authors' calculations.

Figure 6.6   Tax-related state support measures used by female- and male-led businesses (in per cent)

DISCUSSION

Our study contributes to the important discussion about women-led businesses during the Covid-19 pandemic. Our research focuses on possible differences compared to male-led businesses and whether these differences are attributable to mere sector or size effects.

Our results suggest that women- and men-led businesses in Germany experienced the shock of the Covid-19 pandemic differently. Women-led businesses tended to experience a higher loss of turnover and a slower recovery. To a large part, particularly early in the pandemic, this is because women tend to run businesses in sectors that were hit harder and tend to run smaller businesses. As such, our findings are consistent with early evidence (Graeber et al., 2021; Kay and Welter, 2021). Such evidence suggests that business support policies may, in fact, not need a specific focus on female entrepreneurship (e.g. Haverkamp and Dilekoglu, 2021) but policies that consider the sector as well

Table 6.7   *Regression table showing estimated differences between female- and male-led firms' propensity to apply for and receive tax-related government support*

	Applied for or received tax-related support (wave 1)	Applied for or received tax-related support (wave 2)
Female at micro enterprise	0.23	2.15
Female at small enterprise	−1.78	−0.00
Female at medium-sized enterprise	5.62	3.75
Female at large enterprise	−1.56	−21.87
n	6,413	3,845
Pseudo R2	0.0566	0.0445

Notes: Results of a logistic regression. We show average marginal effects (in percentage points), i.e. the difference in predicted probability of having applied for/received support between female- and male-led firms (for firms of different sizes). Controls include economic sector, month of response, state, and a variable indicating a legal form that is strongly associated with family enterprises. * p-value< 0.1, ** p-value< 0.05, *** p-value< 0.01.
Source: Authors.

as the size of the business. Given that the actual policy measures did exactly that, they can be considered tailored.

However, later developments indicate that the stronger affectedness of female-led businesses was not entirely driven by sector or size effects. This suggests that other factors drove a wedge between the situations of female- and male-led businesses. One possible explanation may be a different response to the crisis. We find some, but not overwhelmingly strong evidence for that explanation. Women entrepreneurs took fewer measures. Apart from that, we find few discernible differences in the measures taken between female- and male-led businesses. These were also largely concentrated in the first months of the crisis. At the same time, female-led businesses needed to rely more heavily on government support.

A final explanation might be that female entrepreneurs were inhibited stronger by the closure of schools and care facilities as they had to shoulder a larger part of the increased care work. This would be consistent with prior literature (Hübgen et al., 2021; Haverkamp and Dilekoglu, 2021). In addition, it would be broadly in line with some of our results. First, it would explain the more muted response of female-led businesses that we find as a heavier burden of private care work would leave less time to institute changes in a struggling business. Second, given that a more muted response would often take some time before affecting business outcomes, it would explain that the sector- and size-independent gap between female- and male-led firms is only observed later in the year. This suggests that policymakers may need to consider that a lack of social support (e.g. the closure of care infrastructure) leads to a re-traditionalisation. As a result, women entrepreneurs' labour is bound up more in comparison to male entrepreneurs (Bundesministerium für Familie, Senioren, Frauen und Jugend, 2020). If that reason is indeed underlying the different paths of female- and male-led firms, our findings may not support calls for a specific women entrepreneur-focused policy response (e.g. Haverkamp and Dilekoglu, 2021). Instead, it suggests that to heed the wider call for an inclusive recovery from the Covid-19 pandemic (Tang et al., 2021), we need to strengthen the social infrastructure that female entrepreneurs rely on. Among others, this means access to affordable childcare. Childcare is a major concern for many female entrepreneurs, particularly those with young children. Providing access to affordable, high-quality childcare can help female entrepreneurs balance the demands of running a business with the responsibilities of raising a family. Failing to provide this environment may ultimately backfire, as the stronger need of female-led businesses for government support indicates.

CONCLUSION

We investigated whether the fact that a business is led by women influenced business performance and business activity amid Covid-19. We address an ongoing debate on the causes underlying a different performance, specifically how much of any observed difference is attributable to a different sector and size distribution of female-led firms. Compared to previous studies seeking to address these and similar questions, we consider a longer time horizon.

We find that female- and male-led firms started out being affected roughly equally but that the situation worsened considerably for female-led firms in Germany at the end of 2020/the beginning of 2021. Overall, the results indicate that, once size- and sector-related differences are controlled for, there were no discernible differences between male- and female-led firms during the first months of the Covid-19 pandemic. In later months, however, a gap between female- and male-led firms appeared which does not seem to be solely the result of size or sector differences. Considering business measures, we find some evidence that women showed a more muted response early in the crisis. In contrast, we find rather strong evidence that women-led businesses needed to rely on public-support measures more heavily.

It is worthwhile to discuss policy measures in light of these findings. Overall, our results indicate that business support policies may not need a women's entrepreneurship-specific focus. Instead, policies that consider the sector, as well as the size of the business (as have often been in place), will help female-led businesses that are disproportionally represented in more heavily affected sectors and firm sizes. In addition, our results from the later months of the pandemic indicate that policymakers should seek to prevent a re-traditionalisation of society where, due to a lack of care options, women carry the burden of care work (i.e. unpaid labour) at the expense of their businesses. Again, this is not done by instituting policies directed solely at female entrepreneurs. Instead, it requires the provision of the social infrastructure on which female entrepreneurship, particularly in small businesses, but also female labour-force participation relies.

NOTES

1. In Germany, infection protection is a competence shared between the federal and state governments. The German Infection Protection Act (*Infektionsschutzgesetz*) regulates the tasks and cooperation of the federal, state, and local authorities, the health care system and other parties involved in combating infectious diseases in humans. While the federal government determines the framework conditions, the states are largely entrusted with determining and implementing an infection protection strategy.
2. While it is possible to identify the self-employed among the households in the SOEP-CoV survey, this naturally restricts the sample to owner-managed businesses. In addition, the GBP survey contains a large number of structural information on the firms such as size, sector affiliation, and location, and more detailed information on the support measures that were used.
3. A business is considered a micro enterprise if its revenue is below €2 million, and it has less than 10 employees. It is a small firm if its revenue is between €2 million and €10 million, and it has at least 10 and at most 49 employees. It is a medium-sized firm if its revenue is between €10 million and €50 million, and it has at least 50 but no more than 249 employees. A business is considered large if it has more than €50 million in revenue or at least 250 employees.
4. Fels and Wolter (2022) find a share of 18.8 per cent among firms with revenue below €2 million and a share of 8.5 per cent among firms with revenue above €50 million. We find a similar pattern in our data with a share of 20.5 per cent among micro enterprises and a share of 14.8 per cent among large enterprises.
5. This procedure also means that we derive estimates of differences between female- and male-led large enterprises. While we report those for sake of completeness, we refrain from interpreting any of them as we deem them insufficiently reliable due to the very small number of observations for large female-led firms.
6. As discussed in the methodology section, we disregard the results on differences at large businesses as we deem them less reliable due to the low number of observations of female-led large businesses.

7.   We also find a large, but marginally significant negative effect for large enterprises in the first wave. However, given the small number of observations we have for large enterprises (28 female-led large enterprises across all three waves) we caution not to over-interpret the results for large enterprises.

REFERENCES

Abel-Koch, J., & Schwartz., M. (2021). *Frauenquote im Mittelstand entwickelt sich in der Corona-Krise nur schleppend* (Volkswirtschaft Kompakt 209). KfW Research. https://www.kfw.de/PDF/Download-Center/Konzernthemen/Research/PDF-Dokumente-Volkswirtschaft-Kompakt/One-Pager-2021/VK-Nr.-209-Maerz-2021-Chefinnen.pdf.

Bayerisches Staatsministerium für Wirtschaft, Landesentwicklung und Energie (n.d.). *BayernFonds*. https://www.stmwi.bayern.de/foerderungen/bayernfonds/.

Bischof, J., Dörrenberg, P., Eble. F., Karlsson, C., Rostam-Afschar, D., Simons, D., & Voget, J. (2021). *German Business Panel: Empirische Evidenz zu den Auswirkungen der Corona-Krise auf deutsche Unternehmen* (18). Der Betrieb.

Bischof, J., Dörrenberg, P., Rostam-Afshar, D., Simons, D., & Voget, J. (2022). The German Business Panel: Evidence on accounting and business taxation (February 1, 2021). Available at https://papers.ssrn.com/sol3/papers.cfm?abstract_id=3777306.

Bundesministerium für Familie, Senioren, Frauen und Jugend (2020). Who takes care of children, household and the elderly? A dossier on the societal dimension of a private question. https://www.bmfsfj.de/bmfsfj/meta/en/publications-en/who-takes-care-of-children-household-and-the-elderly--160284.

Bundesministerium für Wirtschaft und Energie (2021). Deutsche Unternehmen von der Corona-Krise stark betroffen. Staatliche Hilfen und Unterstützungsmaßnahmen kommen an – Ergebnisse einer Unternehmensbefragung im Auftrag des BMWi. https://www.bmwk.de/Redaktion/DE/Pressemitteilungen/2020/20200507-deutsche-unternehmen-von-der-corona-krise-stark-betroffen-staatliche-hilfen-und-unterstuetzungsmassnahmen-kommen-an.html.

Bundesministerium für Wirtschaft und Klimaschutz (2022). Überblickspapier Corona-Hilfen; Rückblick – Bilanz – Lessons learned. https://www.bmwk.de/Redaktion/DE/Downloads/C-D/Corona/ueberblickspapier-corona-hilfen.pdf?__blob=publicationFile&v=8.

Buratti, A., Cesaroni, F. M., & Sentuti, A. (2018) Does gender matter in strategies adopted to face the economic crisis? A comparison between men and women entrepreneurs. In L. Mura (Ed.), *Entrepreneurship: Development Tendencies and Empirical Approach* (pp. 393–411). Rijeka: IntechOpen.

Desson, Z., Lambertz, L., Peters, J. W., Falkenbach, M., & Kauer, L. (2020). Europe's Covid-19 outliers: German, Austrian and Swiss policy responses during the early stages of the 2020 pandemic. *Health Policy and Technology* 9(4), 405–418.

Fels, M., & Wolter, H.-J. (2022). *Die volkswirtschaftliche Bedeutung von Familien- und Frauenunternehmen* (28). IfM Bonn. https://www.ifm-bonn.org/fileadmin/data/redaktion/publikationen/daten_und_fakten/dokumente/Daten-und-Fakten_28_2022.pdf.

Forster, T., & Heinzel, M. (2021). Reacting, fast and slow: How world leaders shaped government responses to the COVID-19 pandemic. *Journal of European Public Policy* 28(8), 1299–1320.

Graeber, D., Kritikos, A. S., & Seebauer, J. (2021). COVID-19: A crisis of the female self-employed. *Journal of Population Economics* 34, 1141–1187.

Haverkamp, K., & Dilekoglu, K. (2021). *Situation von frauengeführten Betrieben in der Corona-Krise* (49). Volkswirtschaftliches Institut für Mittelstand und Handwerk an der Universität Göttingen. https://doi.org/10.3249/2364-3897-gbh-49.

Hübgen, S., Eberlein, L., Munnes, S., Schlüter, C., & Unkel, N. S. (2021). Die Auswirkungen von COVID-19 auf die wirtschaftliche und soziale Situation von Frauen in Berlin (WZB Discussion Paper No. SP I 2021–504). Wissenschaftszentrum Berlin für Sozialforschung Berlin. https://www.econstor.eu/handle/10419/246270.

Kay, R., & Welter, F. (2021). Die Situation von Unternehmerinnen und Unternehmern in der Corona-Pandemie. *Sozialer Fortschritt* 70(5/6), 317–337.

Kritikos, A. S., Graeber, D., & Seebauer, J. (2020). *Corona-Pandemie wird zur Krise für Selbständige* (47). Deutsches Institut für Wirtschaftsforschung.

Kritikos, A. S., Graeber, D., & Seebauer, J. (2021). *Corona-Pandemie drängt Selbstständige vermehrt zur Geschäftsaufgabe – Frauen stärker betroffen* (69). Deutsches Institut für Wirtschaftsforschung.

Liu, Y., Wei, S., & Xu, J. (2021). COVID-19 and women-led businesses around the world. *Finance Research Letters* 43. https://doi:10.1016/j.frl.2021.102012.

Manolova, T. S. et al. (2020). Pivoting to stay the course: How women entrepreneurs take advantage of opportunities created by the COVID-19 pandemic. *International Small Business Journal* 38(6), 481–491. https://doi.org/10.1177/0266242620949136.

Ministerium für Wirtschaft, Industrie, Klimaschutz und Energie des Landes Nordrhein-Westfalen (2020). *Land startet "NRW Überbrückungshilfe Plus"*. https://www.wirtschaft.nrw/pressemitteilung/land-startet-nrw-ueberbrueckungshilfe-plus-und-sichert-existenz-von-solo#:~:text=Das%20Land%20erg%C3%A4nzt%20die%20Hilfen%20des%20Bundes%20um,1.000%20Euro%20pro%20Monat%20f%C3%BCr%20maximal%20drei%20Monate.

Santos, E., Ratten, V., Diogo, A., & Tavares, F. (2021). Positive and negative affect during the COVID-19 pandemic quarantine in Portugal. *Journal of Science and Technology Policy Management* 13(2), 195–212.

Seebauer, J., Kritikos, A. S., & Graeber, D. (2021). *Warum vor allem weibliche Selbstständige Verliererinnen der Covid-19-Krise sind* (DIW Wochenbericht 88). Deutsches Institut für Wirtschaftsforschung. https://doi.org/10.18723/DIW_WB:2021-15-3.

Stephan, U., Zbierowski, P., Pérez-Luño, A., Klausen, A., Alba Cabañas, M., Barki, E., Benzari, A., Bernhard-Oettel, C., Boekhorst, J., Dash, A., Efendic, A., Eib, C., Hanard, P.-J., Holienka, M., Iakovleva, T., Kawakatsu, S., Khalid, S., Kovacicová, Z., Leatherbee, M., Li, J., Parker, S., Qu, J., Rosati, F., Sahasranamam, S., Salusse, M., Sekiguchi, T., Thomas, N., Torres, O., Tran, M., Wach, D., Ward, M., Wiklund, J., Williamson, A., & Zahid, M. (2021). Entrepreneurship during the Covid-19 pandemic: A global study of entrepreneurs' challenges, resilience, and well-being (KBS Covid-19 Research Impact Papers 4). King's Business School. https://kclpure.kcl.ac.uk/portal/en/publications/entrepreneurship-during-the-covid19-pandemic-a-global-study-of-entrepreneurs-challenges-resilience-and-wellbeing(bc6bb6e3-053b-411d-8a54-137cf1605abc)/export.html.

Tang, V., Santiago, A., Khan, Z., Amaglobeli, D., Dugarova, E., Gifford, K., Gores, L., Honda, J., Klemm, A., Renteria, C., Soler, A., Staab, S., Osorio-Buitron, C., & Zhang, Q. (2021). Gender equality and COVID-19: Policies and institutions for mitigating the crisis. IMF Fiscal Affairs. https://www.imf.org/-/media/Files/

Publications/covid19-special-notes/en-special-series-on-covid-19-gender-equality -and-covid-19.ashx.

Torres, J., Maduko, F., Gaddis, I., Iacovone, L., & Beegle, K. (2021). The impact of the COVID-19 pandemic on women-led businesses (Policy Research Working Paper 9817). World Bank. https://openknowledge.worldbank.org/handle/10986/36435.

Verband deutscher Unternehmerinnen (2020). *Unternehmerinnenumfrage zur Corona-Pandemie*. Verband deutscher Unternehmerinnen.

Yue, W., & Cowling, M. (2021). The Covid-19 lockdown in the United Kingdom and subjective well-being: Have the self-employed suffered more due to hours and income reductions? *International Small Business Journal: Researching Entrepreneurship* 39(2), 93–108.

7. The influence of Covid-19-related entrepreneurial opportunities and difficulties on women entrepreneurs' business models

Anna Sörensson and Navid Ghannad

INTRODUCTION

The Covid-19 pandemic, which started in 2020 in China, had significant and varying effects globally on entrepreneurship and small business (Castro and Zermeño, 2020; Boter et al., 2021; Kuckertz, 2021). Sales in industries such as tourism and travel were negatively affected, while those in digital meetings and food stores significantly increased (Boter et al., 2021). However, even before the Covid-19 pandemic, women entrepreneurs faced tougher challenges than their male counterparts. Vossenberg defines the gender gap in entrepreneurship as "the difference between men and women in terms of numbers engaged in entrepreneurial activity, motives to start or run a business, industry choice and business performance and growth" (2013, p. 2).

Women entrepreneurs contribute to innovation, job creation, and income growth in developed countries (de Bruin et al., 2006, 2007; Brush et al., 2006; Brush et al., 2009; Lindvert et al., 2017). However, previous research has shown that women entrepreneurs are disadvantaged in different aspects (Brush et al., 2006; Brush et al., 2009). For example, definitions and stereotypes of entrepreneurs have historically been related to men and often to technology, with the best-known entrepreneurs including Bill Gates, Mark Zuckerberg, and Steve Jobs (Grandy et al., 2020). Furthermore, research has shown that women entrepreneurs are often disregarded, and experience completely different entrepreneurship conditions compared to the norm, namely male entrepreneurs (Grandy et al., 2020). This chapter aims to investigate how the pandemic has affected these conditions.

Ratten (2020) argues that there is a lack of studies examining the combination of crisis management, entrepreneurship, and Covid-19. Furthermore, few studies have examined how the Covid-19 pandemic has affected women entrepreneurs. Bartik et al. (2020) claim that small firms owned by women entrepreneurs have been major victims of the pandemic because women lack access to sufficient resources, particularly managerial and financial resources. Lack of financial resources is particularly problematic for women entrepreneurs because it is critical to starting and expanding their businesses (Villaseca et al., 2021). Women entrepreneurs also face significantly different issues depending on where in the world they operate their businesses, especially during turbulent times (Boter et al., 2021; Mustafa et al., 2021).

The few studies conducted on the effect of the pandemic on women in business have produced mixed results. Some studies show that women entrepreneurs identified opportunities and started new businesses because of the Covid-19 pandemic. Other studies have shown that the pandemic increased women's unemployment levels in some sectors, such as cleaning, due to decreased demand during lockdowns (Popović-Pantić et al., 2020). Many companies changed their business models during the pandemic, for example, by manufacturing face masks and hand sanitizers. There are many different definitions of a business model but a common view among researchers is that a business model explains how a company creates and captures value (Lahti et al., 2018).

> Every company has a business model, whether they articulate it or not. At its heart, a business model performs two important functions: value creation and value capture. First, it defines a series of activities, from procuring raw materials to satisfying the final consumer, which will yield a new product or service in such a way that there is net value created throughout the various activities. This is crucial, because if there is no net creation of value, the other companies involved in the set of activities won't participate. Second, a business model captures value from a portion of those activities for the firm developing and operating it. This is equally critical, for a company that cannot earn a profit from some portion of its activities cannot sustain those activities over time. (Chesbrough, 2007, p. 12)

Accordingly, a business model is often a balancing act between value creation and value capture.

The World Bank (Carranza et al., 2018) suggests that women entrepreneurs tend to operate more in the service, retail, and hospitality industries than their male counterparts. These sectors are more crowded with lower profits and growth potential than male-dominated sectors. Furthermore, there is a difference in how male and female entrepreneurs define success: male entrepreneurs try to achieve higher profits, while female entrepreneurs define success as having control over their own destinies, building relationships with clients, and achieving a better work–life balance (Caranza et al., 2018). These differences between male and female entrepreneurs create vulnerabilities during periods of crisis or rapidly changing circumstances. The Covid-19 pandemic was such a period, and it significantly impacted women entrepreneurs (Kumar and Singh, 2021). Yet, there are few studies on how women entrepreneurs adapted their businesses based on the new conditions created by the Covid-19 pandemic. Accordingly, this chapter aims to investigate how women entrepreneurs changed their business models during the Covid-19 pandemic by addressing the following research questions:

RQ1: What entrepreneurial opportunities did women entrepreneurs experience during Covid-19, and how did these influence their business models?

RQ2: What entrepreneurial difficulties did women entrepreneurs experience during Covid-19, and how did these influence their business models?

THEORETICAL BACKGROUND

Women Entrepreneurs and their Financial Conditions

This study defines women entrepreneurs as women who start, organize, and manage a business venture with the purpose of making a profit (Koontz, 2019). Using this definition, women entrepreneurs can be described as individuals who have played a role in establishing the business and are managers or owners of that business, or are both managers and owners.

Research has shown that women's entrepreneurship plays a key role in the expansion of businesses globally (Popović-Pantić et al., 2020). These women-owned businesses contribute to socio-economic development. However, women are less involved in entrepreneurship than men (Semenčenko et al., 2016). While there has been an increase in the percentage of women entrepreneurs, they still experience considerably less favourable positions compared to men (Popović-Pantić et al., 2020). They also face more difficulties when running their businesses than men. Thus, it is likely that they will be more vulnerable to challenges and crises (Popović-Pantić et al., 2020).

Research on women entrepreneurs often centres on issues such as how they seek growth financing (Grandy et al., 2020). Studies have found that they often seek credit from family and friends rather than banks. Furthermore, women often receive government loans, grants, or subsidies (Rosa and Sylla, 2016) rather than supplier credit or capital leases (Grandy et al., 2020).

Businesses owned by men are four times more likely to obtain venture capital than businesses owned by women (Brush et al., 2014; Grandy et al., 2020). Furthermore, male entrepreneurs are more likely to obtain trade credit, capital leasing, venture capital, or angel funding. Instead, women are more likely to obtain different types of government funding (Grandy et al., 2020). Women entrepreneurs are also more likely to get loans with higher interest rates and poorer term sheets than men, making the financial burden of borrowing higher for them (D'Espallier et al., 2011).

Women entrepreneurs do not rely on credit to finance their businesses to the same extent as male entrepreneurs. Research from the USA has shown that lending to women is less risky than lending to men. For example, women are more likely to repay their mortgages compared to men. However, financial institutions offer women higher interest rates (Grandy et al., 2020), and women entrepreneurs are less likely to be given a mortgage compared to male entrepreneurs (Goodman et al., 2016). All these differences impact women's entrepreneurship, especially during a crisis such as the Covid-19 pandemic.

Entrepreneurship during the Covid-19 Pandemic

The Covid-19 pandemic created difficulties for both female and male entrepreneurs (Boter et al., 2021). From an economic perspective, the pandemic caused sharp drops in demand and supply. Widespread lockdowns to control the pandemic resulted in shutdowns of businesses, leading to a decline in supply, while the reduction in consumption and investment led to a decline in demand (Seetharaman, 2020). This rapid change hit women entrepreneurs the hardest (OECD, 2020). Nonetheless, women entrepreneurs have shown remarkable resilience and adaptability in the face of the pandemic (OECD, 2020).

According to a report published by the American National Women's Business Council (2020), the pandemic has been more likely to impact women-owned businesses than male-owned businesses, as demonstrated by revenue loss and closures. This is partly because many women-owned businesses are concentrated in industries that have been hit the hardest by the pandemic, such as hospitality, retail, and personal services.

While the Covid-19 pandemic left many businesses struggling for survival, it also forced businesses to search for alternative strategic ideas. Thus, while creating significant challenges for businesses, the pandemic also forced them to innovate, presenting them with opportunities to identify new business models that would ensure they survived throughout the pandemic (Seetharaman, 2020). One way in which companies had to adapt their businesses is by following changes in demand during the pandemic. The pandemic produced permanent behavioural changes in consumers, such as increasing the use of digitalization (Zwanka and Buff, 2021). These changes significantly expanded the e-commerce sector globally, changing the nature of businesses at their core (Bhatti et al., 2020). E-commerce sales significantly increased during the pandemic because customers avoided leaving their houses, maintained social distance, and shopped and worked from home (Bhatti et al., 2020). Thus, the pandemic changed customer behaviours, spurring them to shop online (Ahmed, 2021).

The pandemic had a major impact on the hospitality and service sectors because customers had to stay at home during lockdowns; they could no longer go to restaurants and cafés (Seetharaman, 2020). Non-essential services, such as hotels, homestays, and leisure activities, had to shut down. In contrast, the food industry provided an essential service. Many restaurants changed their business models and offered off-premises dining, drive-through food pickups and ready-to-eat meals. Customers could get boxes of food delivered to their homes. Restaurants had to change their business models not only to ensure they could survive economically but also to keep up with changing customer demand. They had to quickly scale up and innovate to offer products that could remain fresh and interesting to their customers (Seetharaman, 2020). The widespread shift to delivery and take-out models for cafés and restaurants may mean that customers will maintain this practice even after the pandemic (Zwanka and Buff, 2021). These new ways of conducting business prompted by the Covid-19 pandemic meant that entrepreneurs had to be agile and possess dynamic capabilities (Tronvoll et al., 2020).

METHODOLOGY

The data on which this chapter draws were collected between September and October 2021. They consist of interviews with 131 entrepreneurs. Of these, 30 were women, and their interviews were separated from the rest of the data for the purpose of this chapter. Respondents were selected using a mix of systematic random sampling and convenient sampling. The sampling method used varied based on multiple factors, including country, culture, sample size, and number of respondents. The interviews were informal and were conducted either in person or digitally (via Zoom, Teams, or Skype), with each interview lasting 30–120 minutes. They were semi-structured and followed a common structure while allowing for follow-up questions. Question areas included financing, existing opportunities and difficulties, opportunity recognition and exploitation, and adaptation of business plans. The researcher took notes during the interviews; the interviews were recorded (unless the participant did not consent) and transcribed immediately afterwards.

Data were also obtained from secondary sources such as websites, annual reports, and other printed sources. The secondary data were important to gain more in-depth information and increase validity by triangulating the data (Eisenhardt and Graebner, 2007; Yin, 2003). The transcripts and the secondary data were pooled and thematically analysed using a model proposed by Gioia, Corley, and Hamilton (2013). The first step of the analysis was to carefully identify the terms used by the respondents and group the concepts. In the second step, the concepts and groups that were identified were connected to the theoretical framework guiding this research, keeping our purpose in mind.

Finally, in the third step of the analysis, the similarities and differences with the frame of reference and any new empirical findings not explained by the theoretical framework were identified and further explained.

Interviewee Profiles

Table 7.1 details the interview respondents. The women entrepreneurs were from various countries inside and outside Europe. Sweden was the most represented country; this was because foreign women entrepreneurs were more difficult to find and were also more reluctant to talk to us compared to their Swedish counterparts. While the definition of entrepreneurship we used did not require ownership of the company, 90 per cent of the respondents partly or fully owned their companies.

Our dataset consisted of 23 women entrepreneurs who owned their companies, and seven women entrepreneurs who either partially owned or were leading the business. Our analysis showed hardly any difference between these two types of women entrepreneurs. All the women acted entrepreneurially during Covid-19, regardless of whether they were company owners or company leaders. Therefore, we included both groups in our analysis.

FINDINGS

Problems Encountered during the Pandemic

The biggest challenge women entrepreneurs face when running a business, regardless of context, is ensuring they can survive financially. Table 7.2 illustrates the main issues our women interviewees mentioned when discussing Covid-19's economic impact on their businesses. Most of the women highlighted the importance of having a financial buffer when their company was exposed to a crisis of this magnitude, as most of their sales decreased dramatically during the pandemic (by up to 90 per cent). The decrease in sales was also evident in their companies' annual reports.

The respondents also addressed the issue of future uncertainties, as R6 stated: "we need to save for future uncertainties." It is not just about surviving financially during the pandemic itself, but respondents highlight the importance of thinking long-term and that economic security plays a role in the future. R1 states: "Make sure to have some liquidity to be able to meet a crisis."

For a few of the women entrepreneurs in our sample, their businesses grew during the Covid-19 pandemic since they already had an online sales channel. For example, R23 stated: "My business in an online store, we actually experienced much better sales with an increase of 80%."

Table 7.1   *Details of interviewee respondents*

Respondent	Founded	Role	Ownership (%)	Industry	Country
R1	2010	Owner	100	Consultant	Sweden
R2	2009	Owner	100	Home decoration	Sweden
R3	2017	Owner	100	Clothes sales	India
R4	2015	Owner	100	Clothes sales	India
R5	1986	Owner	100	Bookshop	Nepal
R6	2015	Owner	100	Clothes sales	India
R7	1989	Owner	50	Property development	Sweden
R8	2020	Owner	100	Beauty treatments	Sweden
R9	2013	Owner	100	Home decoration	Sweden
R10	2019	Manager	0	Restaurant	Germany
R11	2021	Owner	100	Consultant	Sweden
R12	2016	Manager	0	Clothes sales	Sweden
R13	2016	Owner	100	Service and maintenance	Sweden
R14	2016	Manager	0	Restaurant	Sweden
R15	2015	Owner	100	Restaurant	Finland
R16	2013	Manager	49	Consultant	Sweden
R17	2020	Owner	100	Accessories	Sweden
R18	2006	Manager	50	Service and maintenance	Sweden
R19	2015	Owner	82	Store	Sweden
R20	2008	Owner	50	Consultant	Sweden
R21	2001	Owner	100	Clothes sales	Pakistan
R22	2013	Owner	100	Consultant	Dubai
R23	2017	Manager	25	Home decoration	Pakistan
R24	2012	Manager	50	Consultant	Germany
R25	2014	Owner	100	Workout studio	Sweden
R26	2017	Owner	100	Clothes sales & consultant	Sweden
R27	2020	Owner	95	Farming	Pakistan
R28	2020	Owner	100	Farming	Pakistan

Respondent	Founded	Role	Ownership (%)	Industry	Country
R29	2019	Owner	100	Farming	Pakistan
R30	2019	Owner	100	Restaurant	Sweden

Source: Authors.

Table 7.2   *Women entrepreneurs and their financial resources during the Covid-19 pandemic*

Sales and liquidity in the short run (R1)

Make sure to have some liquidity to be able to meet a crisis (R1)

Never forget the economic part: you need money (R2)

Drop in sales (R3)

Decrease in total profit by 90% (R5)

I used my personal savings (R6)

I realized that economic support is really important, so we need to save for future uncertainties (R6)

Governmental support to receive grant 50% back (R7)

I have noticed that the liquidity in my company is worse than before (R9)

In the beginning, liquidity and financial backups were still good to pay salaries. After a while, it became more and more difficult to pay salaries on time due to accrued invoices from suppliers (R10)

Be careful how you spend your money; you do not know how this pandemic would affect you (R16)

Turnover was slightly lowered, [we had] fewer customers (R20)

Decline in demand (R21)

My earnings declined by almost 60% (R22)

My business is an online store, we actually experienced much better sales: an 80% increase (R23)

Profitability has increased (R26)

Source: Authors.

Support Received during the Covid-19 Pandemic

The women entrepreneurs have had mainly two different perspectives on their financial challenges during the pandemic. The first group of respondents received help from their family and friends to solve the liquidity that arose due to the pandemic. R5 explained her situation as "friends and family members who used the solidarity strategy". The other group has received various types of support from the state. R7 stated that she got "governmental support to

Table 7.3   Economic support for women entrepreneurs in Asia and Europe

No, not at all, nothing received from any sector nor any organizations (R3)
We did not receive any economic support from the government (R4)
Tax rates decreased by some margin (R4)
Family is my main support (R4)
Friends and family members who used the solidarity strategy (R5)
Got a loan from a friend of the family (R5)
The government provided loans to women [...] but I did not get any loan or help (R6)
I used my personal savings, and I got help from a friend to get some money (R6)
I took a bank loan at first, and after two years my family helped me pay off the bank loan (R21)
I did not receive any financial support (R22)
Economic support for women entrepreneurs in European countries
Did not need economic support (R2)
Have some liquidity to be able to meet a crisis (R1)
Governmental support to receive grant 50% back (R7)
Pay taxes later (R9)
Delayed payments to health insurance, as well as rent and energy costs (R10)
The support was rather small and very delayed (R10)
Government subsidies (R15)
I got helped with a certain percentage of the lost income (R20)

Source: Authors.

receive grant 50% back". There are also entrepreneurs who got better financial conditions when sales increased, although this group is a smaller number in this study. R2 explained that she "did not need economic support". We noted significant differences in the financial support that the women entrepreneurs received during the pandemic. The women who run businesses in Asia did not receive any support from the state. Rather, their businesses survived financially because they borrowed money from friends and family and, in a few cases, from banks. These findings align with previous studies that discuss how women entrepreneurs obtain capital when starting a business: they mostly rely on connections (Lindvert, 2018; Lindvert et al., 2019), as illustrated in Table 7.3.

Adapting Business Models

The women entrepreneurs highlighted other aspects of how the pandemic affected their businesses. For example, they had to ensure their companies adapted during the Covid-19 pandemic. Many women entrepreneurs changed their communication channels during the pandemic and showed this on their homepages and social media channels. The women entrepreneurs, regardless of their personal context or the country in which they operated, chose to use social media when communicating with their customers: "Having a Facebook page helped us by [allowing us to give] our contact info to the customer and also show when we were available to deliver" (R5). The advantage of social media is that it is cheap, which is especially useful when women entrepreneurs are struggling with scarce financial resources.

The women entrepreneurs' marketing also changed during the pandemic from traditional marketing channels to social media channels. R19 stated that her business chose to "increase […] social media advertising instead of [advertising in] local magazines. We have tried to increase our marketing of our online store." Women entrepreneurs with access to digital channels found it easier to adapt during the pandemic than those without this access. The lack of capital forced the entrepreneurs to use different communication channels.

Our finding also revealed small differences in how women entrepreneurs ran their businesses depending on which country they were based in, although most turned to social media as their main communication channel during the Covid-19 pandemic. The women also emphasized that investing in digital channels was a profitable long-term investment for their company. As R24 stated, "We have used the time to make our company safe for the digital future and to respond to the changing digital behaviour of our customers."

The women also highlighted that they had difficulties with deliveries, and that their customers made fewer physical visits to their stores but purchased larger quantities during those visits. The interviewees were mainly concerned with two areas of distribution. The first was how the company distributed its goods to its customers (e.g. how customers could buy the products and how businesses could arrange distribution and delivery). The second was how distribution, in the form of supply, changed during the pandemic. Businesses had to determine how they could access the raw materials or products they needed to sell their products. A common theme in the interviews was that the women identified new ways of distributing their products to customers. A common solution was home delivery in various forms. One respondent stated: "Our customers are more into takeaways and deliveries" (R14). Another respondent stated: "I started [delivering] food [from] my restaurant" (R30), and another said that "We deliver the orders to the doorstep of our customers and leave the food in front of their house and call them to inform them that their order has arrived" (R14).

The home deliveries solution is not gender-specific or location-specific. Home delivery became a standard solution during the Covid-19 pandemic; since customers could not go to stores or restaurants, businesses had to deliver products to the customers in their home.

Another difficulty that these women entrepreneurs faced during Covid-19 was how to access raw materials. Since there were lockdowns in many parts of the world, factories closed, and customers did not receive products. Study respondents who had to send goods to customers faced issues with deliveries because lockdowns led to delays. One respondent said: "We were unable to send our deliveries to other countries as there was no transportation" (R21), while another stated that "There was no transportation system to import or export raw material" (R4). Lockdowns globally affected supply chains, and women entrepreneurs could not rely on having products delivered on time. This situation affected entrepreneurs globally, regardless of whether they were operating in Asia or Europe.

However, all these issues created opportunities and benefits for some of the women entrepreneurs. For example, the reduction in transport and deliveries positively impacted environmental sustainability as well as costs; as one respondent stated: "We lowered our transport cost by 80 per cent [when] delivering products" (R5).

DISCUSSION

This study focuses on highlighting the opportunities and challenges that women entrepreneurs were exposed to during the Covid-19 pandemic. The women were forced to change their business models in order to survive financially.

The major challenge for all respondents was the economy. Previous research has often dealt with how women entrepreneurs obtain capital to start businesses (Grandy et al., 2020). However, this study focuses on economic survival at a time when the whole world was in lockdown. One difference between women entrepreneurs in Asia compared women entrepreneurs in Europe is government support. In Asia there was a significant lack of government support, while in Europe various government supports and loans were available.

Previous studies have shown that women entrepreneurs are more exposed to crises (Popović-Pantić et al., 2020) and find it more difficult to get loans (Goodman et al., 2016). This study has shown similar results. For example, the women entrepreneurs in Asia had no opportunity to access loans from banks but managed to secure crisis loans through family and friends.

This study has also shown that women entrepreneurs faced several challenges during the Covid-19 pandemic. Examples included customers not being able to come to their stores or restaurants. Similar results were shown in other studies as more women than men run companies within the service, retail, and hospitality industries (Carranza et al., 2018). It was precisely these industries that had the toughest time during the Covid-19 pandemic. Some of the changes made to the women's business models will probably remain in place after the pandemic, such as the widespread shift to delivery and take-out models for cafés and restaurants (Zwanka and Buff, 2021).

The women in our sample were able to identify opportunities despite the challenges created by the Covid-19 pandemic. They secured alternative communication channels that were more accessible to their customer base at a lower cost. Other opportunities identified included other ways of distributing products and services. Our findings also show that the changes the women made to their business models were similar regardless of whether they were based in Asia or Europe. Finally, the study shows that the women have exhibited similar entrepreneurial behaviours regardless of whether they were the owner or leader of the company.

Limitations

While our study provides valuable insights into the impact of the Covid-19 pandemic on women entrepreneurs, we acknowledge its limitations. First, our data are confined to interviews conducted between September and October 2021. As the pandemic continued to evolve beyond this timeframe, there may have been ongoing developments and long-term impacts that were not captured in our study. To fully comprehend the lasting effects of the crisis on women entrepreneurs, it would be beneficial to conduct follow-up interviews and observations over an extended period.

Second, our study examined women entrepreneurs from various countries, encompassing diverse economic conditions, cultural norms, legal frameworks, and government support systems. These regional variations and contextual factors could have influenced the experiences and outcomes of women entrepreneurs during the pandemic. Considering the heterogeneity in support measures and economic contexts across different regions is crucial when interpreting the findings and understanding the nuances of their responses to the crisis.

Third, our sample of 30 women entrepreneurs might be considered relatively small, limiting the generalizability of the findings to a broader population. Additionally, while the respondents represented various countries, the distribution of participants might not be proportionally representative of all regions, potentially skewing the research outcomes. Expanding the sample size and ensuring a more balanced representation of diverse regions would strengthen the study's validity.

Finally, as the pandemic unfolded, its consequences evolved continuously. While our study provided insights into the immediate impact of the crisis on women entrepreneurs, understanding the long-term effects and the sustained change in their businesses is essential. Future research should investigate how women entrepreneurs' strategies and adaptations during the pandemic influenced their business performance and trajectory beyond the immediate crisis period.

CONCLUSIONS

This chapter presents insights into the impact of the Covid-19 pandemic on women entrepreneurs and their businesses. The findings shed light on the challenges and opportunities that women entrepreneurs faced during the crisis, and highlights the importance of financial resources, adaptability, and digital integration. The key messages to emerge from our study include the following:

Financial Challenges: Women entrepreneurs faced significant financial challenges during the pandemic, with some industries experiencing a sharp decline in sales.

Importance of Financial Resources: Access to financial resources emerged as a crucial factor in determining the survival and resilience of women-owned businesses during the crisis.

Digital Integration and Communication: Leveraging digital solutions and social media platforms played a vital role in facilitating communication with customers and providing a competitive edge for women entrepreneurs.

Innovation and Business Model Adaptation: The pandemic forced women entrepreneurs to innovate and adapt their business models, leading to the emergence of new strategies for reaching customers and delivering products.

Valuable Research Questions for the Future

To enhance our understanding of the impact of the Covid-19 pandemic on women entrepreneurs it is essential to expand the scope of research and explore specific aspects in depth. Several future research questions can be formulated to shed light on various dimensions of this phenomenon.

One interesting area to study further is to investigate the long-term effects of the Covid-19 pandemic on women entrepreneurs' business performance, growth, and sustainability. Understanding the enduring implications of the pandemic on women entrepreneurs is crucial. By examining how their businesses have evolved beyond the initial disruption, we can identify factors that contributed to their post-pandemic growth and resilience. Additionally, investigating the challenges they encountered in sustaining their businesses alongside any potential changes in their business models for increased resilience would provide valuable insights.

Another interesting future question would be how the women entrepreneurs' access to financial resources during the pandemic influenced their ability to adapt and innovate in response to challenges. This study has identified the importance of financial resources for women entrepreneur's survival but we believe that the role of financial resources in women entrepreneurs' ability to navigate the crisis deserves further exploration. Investigating whether those with sufficient financial buffers or access to diverse funding sources were better equipped to innovate and adapt to changing market conditions would provide valuable knowledge for fostering their future preparedness.

Another interesting area would be to investigate the extent to which the utilization of digital channels and technology played a role in women entrepreneurs' pandemic response and post-pandemic growth. The findings of this study show that the pandemic accelerated the adoption of digital tools, and its impact on women entrepreneurs' strategies merits detailed examination. Studying how they leveraged digital channels, e-commerce platforms, and technology to connect with customers, explore new markets, and optimize operations would offer critical insights into their business transformations.

While not the focus of this study, our data identified that the industry in which women entrepreneurs operate plays a role in their ability to secure financial resources and their overall survival during a crisis. The pandemic's impact varied across industries, and this discrepancy influenced women entrepreneurs differently. Delving into the experiences of entrepreneurs in sectors such as hospitality, retail, technology, and others would enable us to understand how they adapted their business models to navigate challenges and capitalize on emerging opportunities. Therefore, as a future research question it would be interesting to further study what distinct challenges and opportunities women entrepreneurs face in different industries during the pandemic, and how they adapted their business models accordingly.

Finally, we suggest that in the future scholars investigate the role of networking for women entrepreneurs. During times of crisis, support systems can be of vital importance in helping entrepreneurs persevere. Examining the significance of networking, mentorship, and peer communities in sharing knowledge, accessing resources, and providing emotional support would offer insights into its importance for women entrepreneurs. Such knowledge could help us develop targeted and effective support measures that strengthen women entrepreneurs' resilience, growth, and contribution to the global economy in the face of future challenges.

Implications

The findings of this study have several practical implications for policymakers and stakeholders in supporting women entrepreneurs during times of crisis. Policymakers should recognize the vital role women entrepreneurs play in the economy and design targeted support measures, including financial assistance and access to resources. Furthermore, policymakers should work with digital empowerment for women entrepreneurs because encouraging women entrepreneurs to embrace digital solutions and integrate social media into their business models can enhance their resilience and adaptability in the face of uncertainty. Finally, policymakers should also have a long term-focus and encourage women's entrepreneurship. Implementing capacity-building programmes and training initiatives can equip women entrepreneurs with dynamic capabilities to innovate and seize opportunities during crises.

By including these key messages, acknowledging limitations, posing valuable research questions, and offering practical implications, this study contributes to a comprehensive understanding of how women entrepreneurs navigate crises. Moreover, it provides actionable guidance for policymakers and stakeholders to provide targeted support to the essential segment of women's entrepreneurship.

REFERENCES

Ahmed, M. (2021). COVID-19 impact on consumer behaviour, demand and consumption. *International Journal for Innovative Research in Multidisciplinary Fields*, 7(1), 63–67.

Bartik, A. W., Bertrand, M., Cullen, Z., Glaeser, E. L., Luca, M., & Stanton, C. (2020). The impact of COVID-19 on small business outcomes and expectations. *Proceedings of the National Academy of Sciences*, 117(30), 17656–17666.

Bhatti, A., Akram, H., Basit, H. M., Khan, A. U., Raza, S. M., & Naqvi, M. B. (2020). E-commerce trends during COVID-19 pandemic. *International Journal of Future Generation Communication and Networking*, 13(2), 1449–1452.

Boter, H., Lundström, A., & Sörensson, A. (2021). Experiences of small businesses due to the COVID-19 pandemic. In A. Sörensson et al. (Eds.), *Corporate Responsibility and Sustainability during the Coronavirus Crisis* (pp. 135–160). Palgrave Macmillan, Cham.

Brush, C. G., Carter, N. M., Gatewood, E. J., Greene, P. G., & Hart, M. M. (2006). The use of bootstrapping by women entrepreneurs in positioning for growth. *Venture Capital*, 8(1), 15–31.

Brush, C. G., De Bruin, A., & Welter, F. (2009). A gender-aware framework for women's entrepreneurship. *International Journal of Gender and Entrepreneurship*, 1(1), 8–24.

Brush, C., Greene, P., Balachandra, L., Davis, A., & Blank, A. M. (2014). Women entrepreneurs 2014: Bridging the gender gap in venture capital. Arthur M. Blank Center for Entrepreneurship Babson College, 28.

Carranza, E., Dhakal, C., & Love, I. (2018). *Female Entrepreneurs: How and Why Are they Different?* World Bank Group. Issue 20. https://documents1.worldbank.org/curated/en/400121542883319809/pdf/Female-Entrepreneurs-How-and-Why-are-They-Different.pdf.

Castro, M. P., & Zermeño, M. G. G. (2020). Being an entrepreneur post-COVID-19– resilience in times of crisis: A systematic literature review. *Journal of Entrepreneurship in Emerging Economies*. https://doi.org/10.1108/JEEE-07–2020–0246.

Chesbrough, H. (2007). Business model innovation: It's not just about technology anymore. *Strategy & Leadership*, 35(6), 12–17.

De Bruin, A., Brush, C. G., & Welter, F. (2006). Introduction to the special issue: Towards building cumulative knowledge on women's entrepreneurship. *Entrepreneurship Theory and Practice*, 30(5), 585–593.

De Bruin, A., Brush, C. G., & Welter, F. (2007). Advancing a framework for coherent research on women's entrepreneurship. *Entrepreneurship Theory and Practice*, 31(3), 323–339.

D'Espallier, B., Guerin, I., & Mersland, R. (2011). Women and repayment in microfinance: A global analysis. *World Development*, 39(5), 758–772. https://doi.org/10.1016/j.worlddev.2010.10.008.

Eisenhardt, K. M. & Graebner, M. E. (2007). Theory building from cases: Opportunities and challenges. *Academy of Management Review*, 50(1), 25–32.

Gioia, D. A., Corley, K. G., & Hamilton, A. L. (2013). Seeking qualitative rigor in inductive research: Notes on the Gioia methodology. *Organizational Research Methods*, 16(1), 15–31.

Goodman, L., Zhu, J., & Bai, B. (2016). Women are better than men at paying their mortgages. Urban Institute, September. https://www.urban.org/sites/default/files/publication/84206/2000930-Women-Are-Better-Than-Men-At-Paying-Their-Mortgages.pdf.

Grandy, G., Cukier, W., & Gagnon, S. (2020). (In)visibility in the margins: COVID-19, women entrepreneurs and the need for inclusive recovery. *Gender in Management: An International Journal*, 7–8, 667–675.

Koontz, S. (2019). Women entrepreneurs: Defining success, overcoming barriers, and thriving in the business world. *Journal of Business and Entrepreneurship: Research, Practice, and Teaching*, 11(2), 67–83.

Kuckertz, A. (2021). Standing up against crisis-induced entrepreneurial uncertainty: Fewer teams, more habitual entrepreneurs. *International Small Business Journal*, 39(3), 191–201. https://doi.org/10.1177/0266242621997782.

Kumar, S., & Singh, N. (2021). Entrepreneurial prospects and challenges for women amidst COVID-19: A case study of Delhi, India. *Fulbright Review of Economic Policy*, 1, 205–226. https://doi.org/10.1108/FREP-09–2021–0057.

Lahti, T., Wincent, J., & Parida, V. (2018). A definition and theoretical review of the circular economy, value creation, and sustainable business models: Where are we now and where should research move in the future? *Sustainability*, 10(8), 2799.

Lindvert, M. (2018). Resource acquisition and the complexity of social capital: Perspectives from women entrepreneurs in Tanzania and Pakistan (doctoral dissertation, Mid Sweden University).

Lindvert, M., Patel, P. C., Smith, C., & Wincent, J. (2019). Microfinance traps and relational exchange norms: A field study of women entrepreneurs in Tanzania. *Journal of Small Business Management*, 57(1), 230–254.

Lindvert, M., Patel, P. C., & Wincent, J. (2017). Struggling with social capital: Pakistani women micro entrepreneurs' challenges in acquiring resources. *Entrepreneurship & Regional Development*, 29(7–8), 759–790.

Mustafa, F., Khursheed, A., Fatima, M., & Rao, M. (2021). Exploring the impact of COVID-19 pandemic on women entrepreneurs in Pakistan. *International Journal of Gender and Entrepreneurship*, 13(2), 187–203. https:// doi .org/ 10 .1108/ IJGE -09–2020–0149.

National Women's Business Council (2020). COVID-19 and women-owned businesses: Before and during the pandemic. https://www.nwbc.gov/research/covid-19 -and-women-owned-businesses-pandemic.

OECD [Organisation for Economic Co-operation and Development] (2020). COVID-19 and women entrepreneurs: Impact and policy responses. https:// www .oecd.org/coronavirus/policy-responses/covid-19-and-women-entrepreneurs-impact -and-policy-responses-0518de6a/.

Popović-Pantić, S., Semenčenko, D., & Vasilić, N. (2020). Women entrepreneurship in the time of COVID-19 pandemic: The case of Serbia. *Journal of Women's Entrepreneurship & Education*. https://doi.org/10.28934/jwee20.34.pp23-40.

Ratten, V. (2020). Coronavirus (Covid-19) and entrepreneurship: Cultural, lifestyle and societal changes. *Journal of Entrepreneurship in Emerging Economies*, 13(4), 747–761. https://doi-org.proxybib.miun.se/10.1108/JEEE-06–2020–0163.

Rosa, J. M., & Sylla, D. (2016). A comparison of the performance of majority female-owned and majority male-owned small and medium-sized enterprises. Innovation, Science and Economic Development Canada.

Seetharaman, P. (2020). Business models shifts: Impact of Covid-19. *International Journal of Information Management*, 54, 102173.

Semenčenko, D., Popović-Pantić, S., & Živković, L. (2016). Training as the indicator of female entrepreneurship development, and training needs analysis. *Journal of Women's Entrepreneurship and Education*, 1–2, 18–36.

Tronvoll, B., Sklyar, A., Sörhammar, D., & Kowalkowski, C. (2020). Transformational shifts through digital servitization. *Industrial Marketing Management*, 89, 293–305.

Villaseca, D., Navío-Marco, J., & Gimeno, R. (2021). Money for female entrepreneurs does not grow on trees: Start-ups' financing implications in times of COVID-19. *Journal of Entrepreneurship in Emerging Economies*, 13(4), 698–720. https:// doi .org/10.1108/JEEE-06–2020–0172.

Vossenberg, S. (2013). Women entrepreneurship promotion in developing countries: What explains the gender gap in entrepreneurship and how to close it. Maastricht School of Management Working Paper Series, 8(1), 1–27.

Yin, R. K. (2003). *Case Study Research: Design and Methods*. SAGE, Thousand Oaks, CA.

Zwanka, R. J., & Buff, C. (2021). COVID-19 generation: A conceptual framework of the consumer behavioral shifts to be caused by the COVID-19 pandemic. *Journal of International Consumer Marketing*, 33(1), 58–67. https://doi.org/10.1080/08961530 .2020.1771646.

PART III

Societal impact and global contexts

8. Legitimacy of women entrepreneurs: forced to behave according to rules?

Susanne Schlepphorst, Siegrun Brink and Friederike Welter

INTRODUCTION

In the late 1990s, pharmaceutical companies were in the spotlight for neglecting the AIDS epidemic in Africa and for being too concerned with protecting their patent rights and profits (McNeil Jr., 2000). This behavior became a challenge to the world's pharmaceutical giants who feared for their legitimacy as a result of key stakeholders defining their behavior as problematic to society (Mahon & Waddock, 1992; Oliver, 1997; Trullen & Stevenson, 2006). This caused considerable damage to the industry and is a prime example of a loss of legitimacy resulting from undesirable, improper and inappropriate behavior. Subject to stakeholders' approval of entrepreneurs' behavior, entrepreneurs gain their consent of being competent, trustworthy, and needed (Fisher et al., 2016; Suchman, 1995; Zimmerman & Zeitz, 2002). With its intangible nature, legitimacy, therefore, is a prerequisite of stakeholders' willingness to provide a business with the resources necessary for its further existence (Shepherd & Zacharakis, 2003; Tornikoski & Newbert, 2007). Therefore, it should be in the best interest of entrepreneurs to gain and maintain legitimacy once it has been achieved.

Even in today's turbulent times, companies still face challenge in keeping discrepancies between stakeholder expectations and entrepreneurial actions low. With the climate crisis, for example, consumers are paying more attention to the production methods of companies. Companies that do not act in an environmentally friendly and sustainable manner increasingly lose support and legitimacy (Vătămănescu et al., 2021). A similar picture emerged with the start of Russia's war against Ukraine. Many companies ceased their business with Russia under stakeholder pressure (*The New York Times*, 2022). So, the value of legitimacy to businesses is undeniable, whether in turbulent or tranquil times. Accordingly, research into the relationship between legitimacy and entrepreneurial behavior is well developed, although knowledge stems mostly from research on the attainment of legitimacy by new ventures (e.g., Choi & Shepherd, 2005; Delmar & Shane, 2004; Nagy et al., 2012; O'Neil & Ucbasaran, 2016; Parhankangas & Ehrlich, 2014; Tracey et al., 2018; Truong & Nagy, 2021). Research addressing the behavior of established companies to maintain their legitimacy is, in contrast, sparse (Nagy et al., 2017). Likewise, little research has been done on how the gender of the entrepreneur influences entrepreneurial legitimacy (Swail & Marlow, 2018). Knowledge about whether there are differences between women and men in terms of acquiring and maintaining their entrepreneurial legitimacy helps advance debates about gender models and further opens the perspective of entrepreneurship research to overcome what is still often a traditional understanding of entrepreneurship.

Indications that women and men differ in terms of their entrepreneurial behavior, lead us to the question of whether differences between women and men entrepreneurs are also evident in their behavior in gaining and maintaining entrepreneurial legitimacy. Díaz-García & Jiménez-Moreno (2010), for example, provide empirical evidence that men have stronger entrepreneurial intentions than women. In addition, men tend to show higher risk-taking and self-efficacy, but have a lower need for entrepreneurial education (Wilson et al., 2007). Such differences are thought to be related to socially and culturally constructed gender (Henry et al., 2016; Yukongdi & Lopa, 2017). That is, the context in which entrepreneurs do business plays a role in how they operate (Brush et al., 2009; Welter, 2011, 2020). Gender roles prescribe what is considered typically male and typically female behavior in a society. If societies have a traditional understanding of roles and women are ascribed domestic and family-related roles, they are socialized to be passive and rule-abiding, rather than play leading roles. In this respect, Germany is particularly suitable to study gender differences within entrepreneurial legitimation processes. Although family policies have become more supportive of women's employment and employment rates have risen, Germany still represents a male breadwinner regime with persistent inequalities in paid and unpaid work (Zoch, 2021). In such contexts, entrepreneurship is described as a less desirable career choice for women (Welter, 2020). This understanding ultimately plays a major role in womens' strategic decisions on their choice of career, division of labor, and employment biography (Edmeades et al., 2012; Marlow & McAdam, 2013; Thapa Karki et al., 2021). Gender may also play a key role in stakeholders' judgment on the appropriate behavior of men and women (entrepreneurs). In settings where a traditional understanding of roles persists, women entrepreneurs may face more difficulties in gaining and maintaining legitimacy (Swail & Marlow, 2018). We therefore argue that under such conditions, women entrepreneurs engage in behaviors that are more in line with the expectations of appropriate behavior in order to gain and maintain their legitimacy.

To reveal whether women entrepreneurs behave strategically different from their male counterparts to gain and maintain legitimacy, we analyze the ways they handle formal rules (i.e., bureaucratic requirements) in Germany. Dealing with bureaucracy is particularly well suited for this purpose, because it is a discipline that supposedly addresses women and men entrepreneurs equally, regardless of their sex and whether times are turbulent or tranquil. The gendered interaction between behavior and legitimacy that we observe in this perceived neutral environment of fulfilling bureaucratic requirements illustrates how institutionally embedded gender perceptions influence entrepreneurial identity and processes. Thus, this chapter aims to extend our knowledge of the influence of gender on women entrepreneurs' entrepreneurial behavior and legitimation strategies.

To this end, we first explain the concept of legitimacy as well as legitimation strategies in general and with respect to women entrepreneurs. This explanation is followed by a description of the methodology we employ. We then analyze our findings. Finally, we conclude with a discussion of our results and point out the contributions of this study. We then summarize the limitations of our work and offer suggestions for future research.

ENTREPRENEURIAL LEGITIMACY, LEGITIMATION STRATEGIES, AND TURBULENT TIMES

A considerable number of studies have identified the relationship between legitimacy and business success (Baum & Oliver, 1992; Díez-Martín et al., 2016; Díez-Martín et al., 2013; Ruef & Scott, 1998), and organizational survival and growth (Beelitz & Merkl-Davies, 2012; Cruz-Suarez et al., 2014; Meyer & Rowan, 1977; Tornikoski & Newbert, 2007; Zimmerman & Zeitz, 2002).

As mentioned, entrepreneurial legitimacy is of general importance in ensuring the continued existence of companies, whether in turbulent or tranquil times. In turbulent times, when, for example, pandemics, disruptions, and social issues can seriously jeopardize the profitability of companies and possibly tarnish their images (Dawkins, 2005), entrepreneurial legitimacy is likely to be all the more important. This was impressively evident during the Covid-19 pandemic, when employment opportunities, interorganizational relationships, supply chains, and innovation ecosystems were disrupted. Many workflows and routines no longer worked. At the same time, the duration and dynamics of the pandemic led to great planning uncertainty (Agarwal & Audretsch, 2020; Alvarez & Barney, 2020; Breier et al., 2021). Many entrepreneurs had to overcome additional challenges and barriers during the pandemic, including financial difficulties and obtaining access to resources to ensure survival. To address these and other challenges, and the associated uncertainty of turbulent environments, legitimacy has been noted as a key factor (Carli, 2020; Díez-Martín et al., 2016). For example, citizens initiated online campaigns to support local businesses, freelancers, and self-employed individuals to help them generate income and show appreciation for them. However, crisis situations have also been noted to cause internal and external stakeholders to scrutinize the legitimacy of companies more closely. For example, with the climate crisis worsening, stakeholders are paying increasing attention to how sustainably companies conduct their businesses and, if necessary, sanctioning behavior that is harmful to the environment. When faced with a crisis, entrepreneurs are therefore more than ever forced to behave strategically towards their stakeholders to manage their legitimacy (Massey, 2001).

There are two approaches to researching entrepreneurial legitimacy: the institutional approach and the strategic approach. The institutional approach interprets legitimacy as congruence with a set of constitutive beliefs in a company's institutional environment (e.g., DiMaggio & Powell, 1983; Jeong & Kim, 2019; Meyer & Rowan, 1977; Oliver, 1991; Scott, 1987, 2005). According to this view, institutional norms, values, and expectations act as the unwritten rules in a society to which companies must adhere (Robin & Reidenbach, 1987). Societies ascribe convictions to entrepreneurship with normative notions of who and what an entrepreneur is and associate certain characteristics, ideals, expectations, and role models with entrepreneurs (Swail & Marlow, 2018). The entrepreneurs who meet these institutional norms demonstrate cultural allegiance, attain legitimacy, and avoid illegitimacy penalties. In contrast to this institutional tradition, the strategic approach posits legitimacy as an operational resource that entrepreneurs draw from their environment and use in an instrumental, calculated, and frequently oppositional manner in pursuit of their goals (Ashforth & Gibbs, 1990; Dowling & Pfeffer, 1975; Zimmerman & Zeitz, 2002). Taking a middle stance similar to, for example, Suchman (1995) and Du & Vieira (2012), while we assume that entrepreneurs (can) formulate strategies to promote the legitimizing perceptions of desirability, propriety, and appropriateness among stakeholders, we consider the institutional environment constitutive for companies. Once gained, legitimacy is far from being permanently secured. In fact, the opposite is true: gaining and maintaining legitimacy is a dynamic and ongoing process. Just as stakeholders confer legitimacy to entrepreneurs and reward them with support and access to resources (e.g., financial capital, technology, competent employees, customers, or networks) (Tornikoski & Newbert, 2007), the same stakeholders can withdraw legitimacy if they no longer judge entrepreneurs' behavior appropriate (Demil & Bensédrine, 2005).

Based on this assumption, entrepreneurs can strategically influence the extent of legitimacy by influencing the perception of their stakeholders through their choices and own behavior (Zimmerman & Zeitz, 2002). They may respond to stakeholders' expectations via acquiescence, compromise, or avoidance (Oliver, 1991; Suchman, 1995). Suchman (1995) refers to these three behaviors as legitimation strategies, which fall along a continuum that ranges from passive behavior to highly active resistance. To gain and maintain legitimacy through acquiescence, entrepreneurs conform to existing institutional requirements and expectations by, for example, following invisible, self-evident values and norms and submitting to institutional rules or existing models. Such behavior signals affiliation with the social structures in which a company operates. However, as entrepreneurs are often confronted with multiple, sometimes conflicting institutional requirements, they have to find ways to deal with these situations through compromise. Compromise-behavior involves a certain degree of conformity to the environment but allows entrepreneurs to be more active in promoting their own interests. They can resist full adequacy but show partial conformity. Entrepreneurs select environments whose requirements are easily met or are particularly important, which makes entrepreneurial behavior appear desirable and appropriate (Zimmerman & Zeitz, 2002). Entrepreneurs can also gain and maintain legitimacy through avoidance-behavior. That is, entrepreneurs can take measures aimed at circumventing the conditions that require conforming behavior (Oliver, 1991). By doing so, they evade institutional requirements and mitigate institutional pressures.

Entrepreneurs' decisions of which legitimation strategy to pursue, especially in turbulent times, depend on their willingness and ability to (fully) meet or resist prevailing rules and expectations. This is influenced by a variety of factors, including entrepreneurs' resource endowments, their power to choose between strategies and/or their need to (sufficiently) differentiate themselves from others to secure comparative advantages (De Clercq & Voronov, 2009; Zimmerman & Zeitz, 2002). An under-explored element in this context is how the gender of the entrepreneur influences the choice of the legitimation strategy (Swail & Marlow, 2018). To fill this research gap, we explain how societies' understanding of role models influences women entrepreneurs and their legitimacy.

WOMEN ENTREPRENEURS AND THEIR LEGITIMATION: HYPOTHESES

In settings where women are exposed to traditional understanding of roles, instilled beliefs of what constitutes a "good girl" raises expectations about their behavior. On the one hand, women are expected to be passive and compliant (Coffé & Bolzendahl, 2010) as well as caring, kind, and supportive (Gupta et al., 2009; Hancock et al., 2014; Liñán et al., 2022). On the other hand, entrepreneurship is a masculine domain, so simply being a man better fits the contemporary entrepreneurial prototype (Bird & Brush, 2002; Hamilton, 2013; Swail & Marlow, 2018). In this regard, research has confirmed that women take into account what society considers desirable and "correct" for their gender when choosing careers (Holst, 2001). Just as pivotal stakeholders like investors, cooperation partners, or customers judge women's behavior from their gendered perspective, women themselves enact these expectations (Elam & Terjesen, 2010) with long-term implications for their actions (Edmeades et al., 2012; Marlow & McAdam, 2013; Thapa Karki et al., 2021). If we assume that gender is embedded both in how society is structured and in individual choices, it is important to study its impact on entrepreneurial behavior (Martínez-Rodríguez et al., 2022). What this entails in terms of entrepreneurial activities can be illustrated in the context of Germany, a country that can be considered conservative "with a strong societal pressure to conform to traditional gender roles" (Eib & Siegert, 2019, p. 3). In Germany, there is still widespread understanding of a traditional labor distribution where men contribute income and women are mainly responsible for childcare (Welter, 2004). For example, in a recent survey, 87 percent of mothers report they do more than half of the care tasks and only 17 percent report that childcare is shared equally (Institut für Demoskopie Allensbach, 2021). This traditional understanding of roles is reflected in the labor force participation of German women. In 2018, 76 percent of working-age women were in employment; this amounted to 84 percent of men of the same age (Destatis, 2020), and the share of women entrepreneurs also remains below that of men entrepreneurs: 6.6 percent of the total labor force in 2019, compared to 9.3 percent for men (IfM Bonn, 2021). Regardless of whether they are employed or self-employed, women tend to prefer part-time employment in Germany (Institut für Demoskopie Allensbach, 2021; Jurczyk et al., 2019). Furthermore, the share of women-led companies among all small and medium-sized enterprises was 16.8 percent in 2019 (Abel-Koch & Schwartz, 2021).

As in other countries, despite efforts to achieve gender equality, women are still underrepresented as entrepreneurs, on the executive boards of private sector companies and in family businesses (Hytti et al., 2017; Martinez Jimenez, 2009; Ughetto et al., 2020). In short, women entrepreneurship is still not the norm and entrepreneurship is still attributed with male characteristics (Rubio-Bañón & Esteban-Lloret, 2016; Welter, 2004). Since achieving gender equality is a long-term process, women need to learn to put themselves more to the fore, just as society needs to adjust its understanding of role models.

Women who have already taken the step to pursue entrepreneurship run counter to traditional roles that define women mainly through roles connected to family and household responsibilities. Thus, society implicitly views women entrepreneurship as less desirable (Rubio-Bañón & Esteban-Lloret, 2016; Welter, 2004). As a consequence, the public scrutinizes their actions more critically, which gives rise to a particular challenge for women entrepreneurs to gain and maintain legitimacy (Swail & Marlow, 2018). Therefore, they still need to devote much effort, more than men, to convince both pivotal stakeholders and society in general that they are competent, trustworthy, appropriate, and needed (Fisher et al., 2016; Suchman, 1995; Zimmerman & Zeitz, 2002). Accordingly, we expect that women entrepreneurs are more concerned with conforming to rules to gain or maintain legitimacy. We thus formulate the following hypothesis:

H1: Women entrepreneurs are more likely than men entrepreneurs to fully acquiesce to the formal rules imposed on them.

Because it is more difficult for women entrepreneurs to attain entrepreneurial legitimacy, they have more to lose once they gain it. Against this backdrop, we assume that women entrepreneurs are more concerned with and more engaged in preserving the legitimacy they have gained. However, due to the traditional understanding of roles in Germany, women entrepreneurs tend to be passive in their doings. Therefore, they resort to passive behavior to gain and maintain entrepreneurial legitimacy (Coffé & Bolzendahl, 2010; Suchman, 1995; Zimmerman & Zeitz, 2002). Compared to their male counterparts, they are more likely to simply conform to stakeholders' expectations and avoid being more active in promoting their own interests through compromise. Following this argumentation, we formulate our second hypothesis as follows:

H2: Women entrepreneurs are less likely than men entrepreneurs to compromise the formal rules imposed on them.

Following on from this, women entrepreneurs are even less likely to influence their environment and circumvent the conditions that require conforming behavior. Thus, we hypothesize the following:

H3: Women entrepreneurs are less likely than men entrepreneurs to avoid the formal rules imposed on them by deliberately not complying with them.

METHODOLOGY AND RESEARCH APPROACH

To explore our assumptions of how women entrepreneurs behave strategically, we analyze the ways they handle formal rules prescribed by authorities. To this end, we make use of a questionnaire-based survey that examined how entrepreneurs perceive bureaucracy. The survey was conducted in November/ December 2018, and thus at a time when there was no severe crisis in Germany. The survey targeted owners and managers of companies of all sizes and sectors registered in Germany. The addresses for the business survey were supplied by Markus database of the credit reporting agency Creditreform and Bureau van Dijk which contains 2.2 million addresses of companies of all sizes, ownership, and management structures located in Germany. A stratified random sample of 29,173 companies was drawn, whose executives were then invited to participate in the survey by email. To further increase the number of participants, the survey was also supported by intermediaries and media representatives. These supporters drew attention to the survey via various channels, such as newsletters or homepages. Ultimately, a total of 1,483 executives completed the survey.

To test our hypotheses, how women and men entrepreneurs strategically behave to gain and maintain legitimacy, questions on how they deal with bureaucratic requirements serve as proxy variables of legitimacy. We refer to bureaucratic requirements as formal rules "created, applied and enforced by state and state-supported organisations" (Kitching, 2018, p. 393). They are closely intertwined with informal rules because they codify the informal, widely accepted beliefs and expectations in a society. Conversely, informal rules emerge in response to these formal rules (Helmke & Levitsky, 2004). For both kinds of rules (i.e., formal and informal), entrepreneurs are free to decide whether to comply with them (Kitching, 2018). Using self-reported data on the ways entrepreneurs deal with bureaucratic requirements, we can thus approximate the ways they deal with the informal rules informed by society's expectations, and provide specific indications on their strategic behavior to gain and maintain legitimacy. The use of self-reported data is common and widely accepted in entrepreneurship research (Peng & Luo, 2000).

To capture what strategic behavior entrepreneurs apply to respond to expectations, we asked them whether they fully implement bureaucratic requirements (acquiescence), whether they weigh up bureaucratic requirements and fulfill the most important ones (compromise) and whether they do not meet single bureaucratic requirements deliberately (avoidance). The strategic behavior was captured using separate statements, with each dependent variable taking the value 1 in case of affirmation and 0 otherwise (Table 8.1 provides an overview of the variables used). They represent an increase from rule-abiding handling to active as well as conscious non-compliance with bureaucratic requirements.

We applied strict rules to unambiguously identify women entrepreneurs and only used data from companies owned and run by women. To be categorized as women entrepreneurs, the respondents were required to meet certain criteria: they had to be women and to either be the sole owner of a company and belong to its management or be co-owners of their company with a management function (Bell, 2005). Our dataset includes 889 completed responses meeting these criteria. Of them, 153 companies are owned and led by women

Table 8.1   Variable descriptions

Variable	Coding
Woman owner-manager	0 = no; 1 = yes
Acquiesce-behavior	0 = no; 1 = yes
Compromise-behavior	0 = no; 1 = yes
Avoidance-behavior	0 = no; 1 = yes
Company size	1 = 0 to 9 employees
	2 = 10 to 49 employees
	3 = 50 to 249 employees
	4 = 250 to 499 employees
	5 = 500 and more employees
Annual sales	1 = Up to 250,000 euros
	2 = 250,000 to 1 million euros
	3 = 1 million to 2 million euros
	4 = 2 million to 10 million euros
	5 = 10 million euros and more
Age of company	in years (metric)
Industry affiliation	1 = manufacturing
	2 = trade/transport/catering
	3 = business-related services
	4 = person-related services
	5 = others
Current company situation	1 = (very) good
	2 = satisfactory
	3 = (very) bad
Availability resources	metric from 1 to 100
Experiences with bureaucracy	0 = (very) good experiences
	1 = (very) bad experiences

Source: Authors.

entrepreneurs and 736 are owned and led by men entrepreneurs. These data are our independent variable, coded 1 for women entrepreneurs and 0 for men entrepreneurs.

Finally, we added a set of control variables in our model that may affect the choice of legitimation strategy. We accounted for company size, age, industry affiliation, and current company situation. We further controlled for the resources available to meet the bureaucratic requirements and the experiences that entrepreneurs had made with bureaucracy up to the time of the survey. To test the simultaneous influence of the variables, we applied a logistic regression model.

FINDINGS

The descriptive results, presented in Table 8.2, show that 17.2 percent of the participating entrepreneurs are women, and that 82.8 percent are men. For comparison, the companies run and led by women entrepreneurs are, on average, smaller and generate fewer annual sales than those run and led by men entrepreneurs. Additionally, they are more likely to offer person-related services and much less likely to be involved in manufacturing. Both the ratio of women and men entrepreneurs in our sample and the demographic characteristics roughly correspond to the distribution in the entrepreneurial landscape (Haunschild & Wolter, 2010) and are consistent with other studies on women entrepreneurship in Germany. This indicates that the specific characteristics of our data are not biasing our results (e.g., Abel-Koch & Schwartz, 2021; Kay et al., 2018).

In terms of the three legitimation strategies, the results show only marginal differences between the behavior of women and men entrepreneurs. Entrepreneurs of both sexes mostly behave in acquiescence with formal rules. A total of 51 percent of women entrepreneurs and 46 percent of men entrepreneurs fully implement bureaucratic requirements. The large majority of both groups of entrepreneurs weigh up bureaucratic requirements and comply with those they consider most important (women entrepreneurs 83.9 percent and men entrepreneurs 80.9 percent). Differences only become obvious if entrepreneurs need to take proactive measures aimed at influencing their environment and circumventing the conditions that require conforming behavior. A total of 28 percent of women entrepreneurs deliberately do not comply with single bureaucratic requirements, compared to 35 percent of men entrepreneurs.

The results of the logistic regression model concur with these descriptive results. There are no statistically significant differences between women and men entrepreneurs for acquiesce- and compromise-behavior (Table 8.3). These results lead us to reject Hypotheses H1 and H2. That is, as regards both legitimation strategies that require less proactive behavior when compared to men entrepreneurs, women entrepreneurs are neither more acquiescent nor more compromising when dealing with formal rules.

With respect to the third strategy, namely avoidance-behavior, a significant gender difference is reported. This result suggests that women entrepreneurs are less likely to manipulate their environment via avoidance-behavior than their male counterparts, thus supporting Hypothesis H3.

Table 8.2   *Characteristics of women and men entrepreneurs*

Variable	Women entrepreneurs (%)	Men entrepreneurs (%)
Share of companies	17.2	82.8
Acquiesce-behavior	50.8	45.5
Compromise-behavior	83.9	80.9
Avoidance-behavior	27.7	34.5
0 to 9 employees	43.1	43.3
10 to 49 employees	36.6	33.0
50 to 499 employees	19.0	21.5
500 and more employees	1.3	2.2
Up to 250,000 euros annual sales	22.8	15.9
250,000 to 1 million euros annual sales	28.9	24.8
1 million to 2 million euros annual sales	16.1	17.7
2 million to 10 million euros annual sales	22.8	27.0
10 million euros and more annual sales	9.4	14.7
Manufacturing	24.1	41.6
Trade/transport/catering	25.5	24.2
Business-related services	22.7	21.6
Person-related services	27.7	12.7
(Very) good company situation	54.3	59.5
Satisfactory company situation	33.8	28.4
(Very) bad company situation	11.9	12.2
Average age of company	34.4 years	35.9 years
Negative experience	73.2	73.6
Resources held available	35.2	42.8
n	153	736

Source: Authors.

The findings demonstrate that the three strategies are not mutually exclusive but overlap. Institutional rules, such as bureaucratic requirements, are found in different areas of entrepreneurial activity. Consequently, companies pursue different strategies in different areas to gain legitimacy. Regardless of gender, the share of entrepreneurs who reported weighting up bureaucratic requirements and meeting the most important ones exceeds the share of those who meet all bureaucratic requirements. This indicates that compliant behavior is not always feasible. Unlike entrepreneurs, however, women entrepreneurs are

Table 8.3   Results of logistic regression (average marginal effects)

Variables	(H1) Acquiesce-behavior	(H2) Compromise-behavior	(H3) Avoidance-behavior
Woman owner-manager	0.061	0.035	−0.100**
	(0.052)	(0.036)	(0.043)
Negative experience	−0.214***	0.046	0.188***
	(0.044)	(0.034)	(0.035)
Resources held available	0.002*	−0.001*	−0.002***
	(0.001)	(0.000)	(0.001)
Numbers of employees (Ref.: 0 to 9 employees)			
10 to 49 employees	0.008	−0.017	−0.029
	(0.046)	(0.033)	(0.040)
50 to 499 employees	0.202***	−0.018	−0.093**
	(0.052)	(0.037)	(0.045)
500 and more employees	0.092	−0.105	−0.020
	(0.135)	(0.110)	(0.122)
Age of company	−0.001	−0.000	0.001
	(0.001)	(0.000)	(0.000)
Industry affiliation (Ref.: manufacturing)			
Trade/transport/catering	0.107**	−0.055	−0.030
	(0.051)	(0.037)	(0.046)
Business-related services	0.055	−0.083**	−0.064
	(0.056)	(0.041)	(0.048)
Person-related services	0.019	−0.030	−0.072
	(0.064)	(0.043)	(0.055)
Others	0.097	−0.032	−0.046
	(0.090)	(0.060)	(0.073)
Current company situation (Ref.: (very) good)			
Satisfactory	0.057	−0.002	−0.105**
	(0.044)	(0.032)	(0.037)
(Very) bad	0.002**	0.033	0.016
	(0.063)	(0.044)	(0.057)

Variables	(H1) Acquiesce-behavior	(H2) Compromise-behavior	(H3) Avoidance-behavior
LR-Chi2Test	53.0***	18.4*	55.3***
PseudoR2	0.060	0.025	0.060

Note: Robust standard errors in parentheses. Results are statistically significant at the *** 1% level, ** 5% level, and * 10% level.
Source: Authors' calculations.

less likely to go that far and evade bureaucratic requirements. This reflects the passive roles that the society in a traditional context like Germany ascribes to women entrepreneurs.

Gender does not exert the sole influence on the respective behavior of entrepreneurs. It is, among other things, influenced by available resources and experiences. The probability of acquiesce-behavior decreases if entrepreneurs have had negative experiences when dealing with bureaucracy. In contrast, acquiesce-behavior increases if companies are larger and have more resources at their disposal. If, on the other hand, companies have had a better experience when dealing with formal rules, the probability of avoidance-behavior increases. If a company has fewer resources at its disposal and is rather small, this decreases the probability of avoidance-behavior.

DISCUSSION

Our concern in this chapter is whether women entrepreneurs behave strategically differently from men entrepreneurs to gain and maintain legitimacy. Using data collected on how entrepreneurs of both sexes handle bureaucracy in Germany, we attempted to understand, whether they respond to expectations via acquiescence, compromise, or avoidance. Our empirical findings reveal that to a certain extent and in tranquil times, women entrepreneurs apply similar legitimation strategies as men entrepreneurs. This is, first of all, in line with previous research that women do not behave fundamentally differently from their male counterparts (Díaz-García & Jiménez-Moreno, 2010). Both women and men entrepreneurs show similar rule-abiding behavior. Both tend to adhere to rules. Yet, women entrepreneurs are less rebellious when a more active legitimation strategy is needed. When it comes to circumventing conditions, men entrepreneurs show more activity. This leads us to conclude that women entrepreneurs have a higher threshold of inhibition before they are willing to circumvent rules and expectations. Compliant behavior through acquiescence or compromise is a low-effort strategy and avoids clashes about whether behavior is appropriate. In sum, the findings indicate that women entrepreneurs enact according to the collective patterns of thought and behavior based on culturally shaped gender roles. The achievements in terms of gender equality made so far, however, remain fragile, as the Covid-19 pandemic revealed. The pandemic triggered a regression in equality and a revival of traditional roles, with men the main bread-winners and women as main caregivers (Carli, 2020; Reichelt et al., 2021).

In a sense, then, legitimacy serves as a guideline for women entrepreneurs in their decision-making. As long as women entrepreneurs abide by the rules, stakeholders recognize women entrepreneurs as competent, trustworthy, and needed and do not question their legitimacy, finally serving the future viability of the company. Although the study results are based on data collected during a non-crisis period, it must be noted that bureaucratic requirements are equally valid regardless of whether times are turbulent or tranquil. It can therefore be assumed that the overall findings in how women and men entrepreneurs deal with bureaucracy remain just as valid and applicable regardless of when the survey was conducted. However, the implications arising from the choice of legitimation strategies may differ in turbulent times from those in tranquil times.

Previous studies have already shown that the maintenance of legitimacy in times of crises depends on the reliability of entrepreneurs' behavior (Massey, 2001). Turbulent times are uncertain times and legitimacy can reduce uncertainties and ultimately increase women entrepreneurs' routine in making fast decisions. This was particularly relevant in the Covid-19 pandemic, when women entrepreneurs fulfilled multiple roles relating to work and family. Their less rebellious behavior may simply have been for pragmatic reasons, considering that scarce time resources leave little room for active resistance. But it does offer reliability and orientation, which is in line with stakeholders' desire for consistency in times of crisis.

Depending on the reason for turbulent times, stakeholders' views on what is reliable, appropriate, trustworthy, and competent entrepreneurial behavior may change. In this way, turbulent times can put pressure on entrepreneurs to change certain behavior and activities, such as ceasing business relations with Russia. Otherwise, entrepreneurs lose legitimacy. Besides, in turbulent times it can also be advantageous to skirt rules in order to leave opportunities for creativity, which may lead to innovation and renewal.

CONCLUSIONS

The aim of this study is to determine whether women entrepreneurs behave in a strategically different fashion from men entrepreneurs to gain and maintain legitimacy. Our deliberations follow prior research, which has established that entrepreneurs modulate their legitimacy through their behavior (Tornikoski & Newbert, 2007). Stakeholders' judgment of appropriate behavior determines their willingness to provide necessary resources to entrepreneurs. In settings where a traditional understanding of roles persists, women entrepreneurs need to devote more effort to gain and maintain legitimacy (Fisher et al., 2016; Swail & Marlow, 2018). Once they achieve it, they are more careful to maintain it. We therefore surmise that women entrepreneurs are more engaged in simply conforming to the rules and expectations of stakeholders than in trying to circumvent or actively resist them. As legitimacy is essentially intangible, we approximate the strategies for gaining and maintaining legitimacy through the ways women and men entrepreneurs handle the formal rules issued by authorities. Results indicate that women entrepreneurs behave less rebelliously than men entrepreneurs. They are less active when it comes to circumventing rules and expectations. By using a perceived neutral environment, in which rules apply equally to both sexes, this study illustrates how institutionally embedded gender perceptions influence entrepreneurial identity and processes. The gender of the entrepreneur plays a critical role in the entrepreneurial legitimation process and influences the legitimation strategy employed. This should be given even more attention in entrepreneurship research than it has been in the past.

We are aware that this study is not without limitations, leaving avenues for future research. The focus of this study was on the German context. As culture encourages individuals to carry out certain behavior that may not be obvious or desirable in other societies (Mueller & Conway Dato-on, 2013), we invite researchers to conduct follow-up research on the relationship between the influence of gender on entrepreneurial behavior and the legitimacy of women entrepreneurs in other cultural contexts. Moreover, measuring legitimacy is neither simple nor has it been a subject of much quantitative research. While legitimacy strategies are important to understand behavior, it challenges researchers to develop an analytical framework to operationalize it. This is certainly an important endeavor for the future. Following on from this, future research could also shed light on the relationship between strategic behavior and the actual extent of legitimacy (Nagy et al., 2017). In particular, with regard to the legitimacy of women entrepreneurs, a self-reinforcing behavior among them can be surmised. That is, in professional terms, women entrepreneurs are more likely to be involved in an environment characterized by women entrepreneurship. This can lead women entrepreneurs to discipline each other in terms of their behavior, as they have developed with a similar understanding of their roles. The question of how to counteract this entrenched behavior is subject of future research.

Finally, this study is one of few that fails to focus on the legitimacy strategies of young companies. In their early beginnings, new ventures are particularly confronted with uncertainties and turbulences, and challenged to gain legitimacy in markets (Delmar & Shane, 2004). The legitimacy of young companies seeking to establish themselves is an important issue, particularly in turbulent times such as pandemics or geopolitical conflicts (Massey, 2001). Given the importance of legitimacy in maintaining competitiveness even in turbulent times, it is of particular importance to learn more about how entrepreneurs of young and establishing companies maintain their legitimacy under these very special circumstances.

REFERENCES

Abel-Koch, J., & Schwartz, M. (2021). Frauenquote im Mittelstand entwickelt sich in der Corona-Krise nur schleppend. *KfW Research, Volkswirtschaft Kompakt*, No. 209.

Agarwal, R., & Audretsch, D. (2020). Looking forward: Creative construction as a road to recovery from the COVID-19 crisis. *Strategic Entrepreneurship Journal*, *14*(4), 549–551.

Alvarez, S. A., & Barney, J. B. (2020). Insights from creation theory: The uncertain context rendered by the COVID-19 pandemic. *Strategic Entrepreneurship Journal*, *14*(4), 552–555.

Ashforth, B. E., & Gibbs, B. W. (1990). The double-edge of organizational legitimation. *Organization Science*, *1*(2), 177–194.

Baum, J. A., & Oliver, C. (1992). Institutional embeddedness and the dynamics of organizational populations. *American Sociological Review*, *57*(4), 540–559.

Beelitz, A., & Merkl-Davies, D. M. (2012). Using discourse to restore organisational legitimacy: 'CEO-speak' after an incident in a German nuclear power plant. *Journal of Business Ethics*, *108*, 101–120.

Bell, L. A. (2005). Women-led firms and the gender gap in top executive jobs. Institute for Study of Labor (IZA), IZA Discussion Papers, No. 1689.

Bird, B., & Brush, C. (2002). A gendered perspective on organizational creation. *Entrepreneurship Theory and Practice*, *26*(3), 41–65.

Breier, M., Kallmuenzer, A., Clauss, T., Gast, J., Kraus, S., & Tiberius, V. (2021). The role of business model innovation in the hospitality industry during the COVID-19 crisis. *International Journal of Hospitality Management*, *92*, 102723.

Brush, C. G., Bruin, A. d., & Welter, F. (2009). A gender-aware framework for women's entrepreneurship. *International Journal of Gender and Entrepreneurship*, *1*(1), 8–24.

Carli, L. L. (2020). Women, gender equality and COVID-19. *Gender in Management: An International Journal*, *35*(7–8), 647–655.

Choi, Y. R., & Shepherd, D. A. (2005). Stakeholder perceptions of age and other dimensions of newness. *Journal of Management*, *31*(4), 573–596.

Coffé, H., & Bolzendahl, C. (2010). Same game, different rules? Gender differences in political participation. *Sex Roles*, *62*(5), 318–333.

Cruz-Suarez, A., Prado-Román, A., & Prado-Román, M. (2014). Cognitive legitimacy, resource access, and organizational outcomes. *Revista de Administração de Empresas*, *54*(5), 575–584.

Dawkins, C. E. (2005). First to market: Issue management pacesetters and the pharmaceutical industry response to AIDS in Africa. *Business & Society*, *44*(3), 244–282.

De Clercq, D., & Voronov, M. (2009). Toward a practice perspective of entrepreneurship: Entrepreneurial legitimacy as habitus. *International Small Business Journal, 27*(4), 395–419.

Delmar, F., & Shane, S. (2004). Legitimating first: Organizing activities and the survival of new ventures. *Journal of Business Venturing, 19*(3), 385–410.

Demil, B., & Bensédrine, J. (2005). Processes of legitimization and pressure toward regulation: Corporate conformity and strategic behavior. *International Studies of Management & Organization, 35*(2), 56–77.

Destatis (2020). Drei von vier Frauen in Deutschland sind erwerbstätig – dritthöchster Wert in der EU. Press Release No. 010, 6 March. Retrieved from https://www.destatis.de/DE/Presse/Pressemitteilungen/2020/03/PD20_N010_132.html.

Díaz-García, M. C., & Jiménez-Moreno, J. (2010). Entrepreneurial intention: The role of gender. *International Entrepreneurship and Management Journal, 6*, 261–283.

Díez-Martín, F., Blanco-González, A., & Prado-Román, C. (2016). Explaining nation-wide differences in entrepreneurial activity: A legitimacy perspective. *International Entrepreneurship and Management Journal, 12*, 1079–1102.

Díez-Martín, F., Prado-Román, C., & Blanco-González, A. (2013). Beyond legitimacy: Legitimacy types and organizational success. *Management Decision, 51*(10), 1954–1969.

DiMaggio, P. J., & Powell, W. W. (1983). The iron cage revisited: Institutional isomorphism and collective rationality in organizational fields. *American Sociological Review, 48*(2), 147–160.

Dowling, J., & Pfeffer, J. (1975). Organizational legitimacy: Social values and organizational behavior. *The Pacific Sociological Review, 18*(1), 122–136.

Du, S., & Vieira, E. T. (2012). Striving for legitimacy through corporate social responsibility: Insights from oil companies. *Journal of Business Ethics, 110*(4), 413–427.

Edmeades, J., Hayes, R., Hollingworth, G., & Warner, A. (2012). *The Girl Effect: What Do Boys Have to Do With It?* International Center for Research on Women (ICRW), Washington, DC.

Eib, C., & Siegert, S. (2019). Is female entrepreneurship only empowering for single women? Evidence from France and Germany. *Social Sciences, 8*(4), 1–19.

Elam, A., & Terjesen, S. (2010). Gendered institutions and cross-national patterns of business creation for men and women. *European Journal of Development Research, 22*(3), 331–348.

Fisher, G., Kotha, S., & Lahiri, A. (2016). Changing with the times: An integrated view of identity, legitimacy, and new venture life cycles. *Academy of Management Review, 41*(3), 383–409.

Gupta, V. K., Turban, D. B., Wasti, S. A., & Sikdar, A. (2009). The role of gender stereotypes in perceptions of entrepreneurs and intentions to become an entrepreneur. *Entrepreneurship Theory and Practice, 33*(2), 397–417.

Hamilton, E. (2013). The discourse of entrepreneurial masculinities (and femininities). *Entrepreneurship & Regional Development, 25*(1–2), 90–99.

Hancock, C., Pérez-Quintana, A., & Hormiga, E. (2014). Stereotypical notions of the entrepreneur: An analysis from a perspective of gender. *Journal of Promotion Management, 20*(1), 82–94.

Haunschild, L., & Wolter, H. J. (2010). Volkswirtschaftliche Bedeutung von Familien- und Frauenunternehmen. Institut für Mittelstandsforschung Bonn, IfM-Materialien, No. 199.

Helmke, G., & Levitsky, S. (2004). Informal institutions and comparative politics: A research agenda. *Perspectives on Politics, 2*(4), 725–740.

Henry, C., Foss, L., & Ahl, H. (2016). Gender and entrepreneurship research: A review of methodological approaches. *International Small Business Journal, 34*(3), 217–241.

Holst, E. (2001). Institutionelle Determinanten der Erwerbsarbeit zur Notwendigkeit einer Gender-Perspektive in den Wirtschaftswissenschaften. DIW Discussion Papers No. 237.

Hytti, U., Alsos, G. A., Heinonen, J., & Ljunggren, E. (2017). Navigating the family business: A gendered analysis of identity construction of daughters. *International Small Business Journal, 35*(6), 665–686.

IfM Bonn (2021). *Selbstständige/Freie Berufe*. Retrieved from https://www.ifm-bonn .org/statistiken/selbststaendigefreie-berufe/selbststaendige#accordion=0&tab=0.

Institut für Demoskopie Allensbach (2021). *Elternzeit, Elterngeld und Partnerschaftlichkeit. Eine repräsentative Onlinebefragung von Eltern mit ältestem Kind unter 10 Jahren.* Retrieved from https://www.ifd-allensbach.de/fileadmin/IfD/ sonstige_pdfs/8251_Bericht_Elternzeit_final.pdf.

Jeong, Y.-C., & Kim, T.-Y. (2019). Between legitimacy and efficiency: An institutional theory of corporate giving. *Academy of Management Journal, 62*(5), 1583–1608.

Jurczyk, K., Jentsch, B., Sailer, J., & Schier, M. (2019). Female-breadwinner families in Germany: New gender roles? *Journal of Family Issues, 40*(13), 1731–1754.

Kay, R., Pahnke, A., & Schlepphorst, S. (2018). Business transferability chances: Does the gender of the owner-manager matter? In S. Birkner, K. Ettl, F. Welter, & I. Ebbers (Eds.), *Women's Entrepreneurship in Europe: Multidimensional Research and Case Study Insights* (pp. 39–64). Cham: Springer International.

Kitching, J. (2018). Exploring firm-level effects of regulation: Going beyond survey approaches. In R. Blackburn, D. De Clercq, & J. Heinonen (Eds.), *The SAGE Handbook of Small Business and Entrepreneurship* (pp. 391–406). London: Sage.

Liñán, F., Jaén, I., & Martín, D. (2022). Does entrepreneurship fit her? Women entrepreneurs, gender-role orientation, and entrepreneurial culture. *Small Business Economics, 58*(2), 1051–1071.

Mahon, J. F., & Waddock, S. A. (1992). Strategic issues management: An integration of issue life cycle perspectives. *Business & Society, 31*(1), 19–32.

Marlow, S., & McAdam, M. (2013). Gender and entrepreneurship. *International Journal of Entrepreneurial Behavior & Research, 19*(1), 114–124.

Martinez Jimenez, R. (2009). Research on women in family firms: Current status and future directions. *Family Business Review, 22*(1), 53–64.

Martínez-Rodríguez, I., Quintana-Rojo, C., Gento, P., & Callejas-Albinana, F.-E. (2022). Public policy recommendations for promoting female entrepreneurship in Europe. *International Entrepreneurship and Management Journal, 18*(3), 1235–1262.

Massey, J. E. (2001). Managing organizational legitimacy: Communication strategies for organizations in crisis. *The Journal of Business Communication, 38*(2), 153–182.

McNeil Jr., D. (2000, 9 July). Medicine merchants: Patents and patients. *The New York Times*. Retrieved from https://www.nytimes.com/2000/07/09/world/medicine -merchants-patents-patients-devastating-epidemics-increase-nations-take.html.

Meyer, J. W., & Rowan, B. (1977). Institutionalized organizations: Formal structure as myth and ceremony. *American Journal of Sociology, 83*(2), 340–363.

Mueller, S., & Conway Dato-on, M. (2013). A cross cultural study of gender-role orientation and entrepreneurial self-efficacy. *International Entrepreneurship and Management Journal, 9*, 1–20.

Nagy, B., Rutherford, M., Truong, Y., & Pollack, J. (2017). Development of the legitimacy threshold scale. *Journal of Small Business Strategy, 27*(3), 50–58.

Nagy, B. G., Pollack, J. M., Rutherford, M. W., & Lohrke, F. T. (2012). The influence of entrepreneurs' credentials and impression management behaviors on perceptions of new venture legitimacy. *Entrepreneurship Theory and Practice, 36*(5), 941–965.

Oliver, C. (1991). Strategic responses to institutional processes. *Academy of Management Review, 16*(1), 145–179.

Oliver, C. (1997). The influence of institutional and task environment relationships on organizational performance: The Canadian construction industry. *Journal of Management Studies, 34*(1), 99–124.

O'Neil, I., & Ucbasaran, D. (2016). Balancing "what matters to me" with "what matters to them": Exploring the legitimation process of environmental entrepreneurs. *Journal of Business Venturing, 31*(2), 133–152.

Parhankangas, A., & Ehrlich, M. (2014). How entrepreneurs seduce business angels: An impression management approach. *Journal of Business Venturing, 29*(4), 543–564.

Peng, M. W., & Luo, Y. (2000). Managerial ties and firm performance in a transition economy: The nature of a micro-macro link. *Academy of Management Journal, 43*(3), 486–501.

Reichelt, M., Makovi, K., & Sargsyan, A. (2021). The impact of COVID-19 on gender inequality in the labor market and gender-role attitudes. *European Societies, 23*(1), 228–245.

Robin, D. P., & Reidenbach, R. E. (1987). Social responsibility, ethics, and marketing strategy: Closing the gap between concept and application. *Journal of Marketing, 51*(1), 44–58.

Rubio-Bañón, A., & Esteban-Lloret, N. (2016). Cultural factors and gender role in female entrepreneurship. *Suma de Negocios, 7*, 9–17.

Ruef, M., & Scott, W. R. (1998). A multidimensional model of organizational legitimacy: Hospital survival in changing institutional environments. *Administrative Science Quarterly, 43*(4), 877–904.

Scott, W. R. (1987). The adolescence of institutional theory. *Administrative Science Quarterly, 32*(4), 493–511.

Scott, W. R. (2005). Institutional theory: Contributing to a theoretical research program. In K. G. Smith & M. A. Hitt (Eds.), *Great Minds in Management: The Process of Theory Development* (pp. 460–484). London: Oxford University Press.

Shepherd, D. A., & Zacharakis, A. (2003). A new venture's cognitive legitimacy: An assessment by customers. *Journal of Small Business Management, 41*(2), 148–167.

Suchman, M. C. (1995). Managing legitimacy: Strategic and institutional approaches. *Academy of Management Review, 20*(3), 571–610.

Swail, J., & Marlow, S. (2018). 'Embrace the masculine; attenuate the feminine' – gender, identity work and entrepreneurial legitimation in the nascent context. *Entrepreneurship & Regional Development, 30*(1–2), 256–282.

Thapa Karki, S., Xheneti, M., & Madden, A. (2021). To formalize or not to formalize: Women entrepreneurs' sensemaking of business registration in the context of Nepal. *Journal of Business Ethics, 173*(4), 687–708.

The New York Times (2022, 14 October). Companies are getting out of Russia, sometimes at a cost. Retrieved from https://www.nytimes.com/article/russia-invasion-companies.html.

Tornikoski, E. T., & Newbert, S. L. (2007). Exploring the determinants of organizational emergence: A legitimacy perspective. *Journal of Business Venturing, 22*(2), 311–335.

Tracey, P., Dalpiaz, E., & Phillips, N. (2018). Fish out of water: Translation, legitimation, and new venture creation. *Academy of Management Journal, 61*(5), 1627–1666.

Trullen, J., & Stevenson, W. B. (2006). Strategy and legitimacy: Pharmaceutical companies' reaction to the HIV crisis. *Business & Society, 45*(2), 178–210.

Truong, Y., & Nagy, B. G. (2021). Nascent ventures' green initiatives and angel investor judgments of legitimacy and funding. *Small Business Economics, 57*(4), 1801–1818.

Ughetto, E., Rossi, M., Audretsch, D., & Lehmann, E. E. (2020). Female entrepreneurship in the digital era. *Small Business Economics, 55*(2), 305–312.

Vătămănescu, E.-M., Dabija, D.-C., Gazzola, P., Cegarro-Navarro, J. G., & Buzzi, T. (2021). Before and after the outbreak of Covid-19: Linking fashion companies' corporate social responsibility approach to consumers' demand for sustainable products. *Journal of Cleaner Production, 321*, 128945.

Welter, F. (2004). The environment for female entrepreneurship in Germany. *Journal of Small Business and Enterprise Development, 11*(2), 212–221.

Welter, F. (2011). Contextualizing entrepreneurship – conceptual challenges and ways forward. *Entrepreneurship Theory and Practice, 35*(1), 165–184.

Welter, F. (2020). Contexts and gender – looking back and thinking forward. *International Journal of Gender and Entrepreneurship, 12*(1), 27–38.

Wilson, F., Kickul, J., & Marlino, D. (2007). Gender, entrepreneurial self-efficacy, and entrepreneurial career intentions: Implications for entrepreneurship education. *Entrepreneurship Theory and Practice, 31*(3), 387–406.

Yukongdi, V., & Lopa, N. Z. (2017). Entrepreneurial intention: A study of individual, situational and gender differences. *Journal of Small Business and Enterprise Development, 24*(2), 333–352.

Zimmerman, M. A., & Zeitz, G. J. (2002). Beyond survival: Achieving new venture growth by building legitimacy. *Academy of Management Review, 27*(3), 414–431.

Zoch, G. (2021). Thirty years after the fall of the Berlin Wall – do East and West Germans still differ in their attitudes to female employment and the division of housework? *European Sociological Review, 37*(5), 731–750.

9. Women as shock absorbers in turbulent times

Bettina Lynda Bastian, Melissa Langworthy and Bronwyn P. Wood

INTRODUCTION

Modern efforts to promote women's entry into the labor force have never been about women alone. From the first arguments justifying a focus on women's economic engagement, women have been consistently positioned to carry more than simply their own interests. In 1973, Maureen Woodhall offered the following rationale for investing in women's human capital:

> For society, the education of women offers benefits in the form of increased productivity of working women, increased labor force participation and indirect benefits, including the 'inter-generation' effect on children's education and subsequent occupational performance, higher standards of family health and childcare, a lower birth rate, and possibly the fostering of family attitudes conducive to economic growth. (Woodhall, 1973, p. 25)

Women's economic inclusion has been embedded in wider discourses of economic, social, and political turbulence, with women themselves becoming saviors of the neoliberal, capitalist system. Starting with the 1980s debt crisis, the extent to which women's unpaid labor has been repeatedly utilized as a 'shock absorber' during times of economic downturn has been well documented by feminist researchers (Elias, 2016). As such, the daily struggles of women and their households cannot be sidelined in a discussion of crisis (e.g., Hozic & True, 2016) and greater attention needs to be paid to "the gendered everyday forms of crisis and crisis management" that women and vulnerable populations experience in their daily lives (Elias, 2016). For example, Asia's economic dynamism is closely related to the dynamisms of Asian women as both 'shock absorbers' during economic downturns, and drivers of economic recovery, at the same time as cascading crises of precarity, impoverishment, and disenfranchisement simmer in the background (Hozic & True, 2016).

In this chapter, we examine this market positioning of women's roles and contributions.

Shock absorption by women can take different forms. In this chapter, we will refer to shock absorption in three circumstances: first, through women as a 'reserve army' of cheap and vulnerable labor for neoliberal markets, which includes women's "infinitely elastic" (Elson, 1988) provision of household labor, each of which effectively subsidize neoliberal policies. Second, women serve as shock absorbers during times of crisis, such as the crisis of the financial system or the recent Covid-19 pandemic. In that context, it also places women, as Silvia Federici (2012, p. 108 in Seri, 2016, p. 128) explains, in a position to serve as "shock absorbers for the bumps in the global economy," particularly given the inherent tension between production and social reproduction in a context of deteriorating economic and political conditions (Fraser, 2017; Steans & Tepe, 2010). Third, women are frequently employed as shock absorbers during economic restructuring, as frequently witnessed in developmental contexts which face this necessity with an aim of becoming less natural resource dependent. Economic diversification in such contexts becomes an antecedent for economic growth and the creation of private sector employment (Ennis, 2015, 2019). Entrepreneurship has been promoted, worldwide, as growth engine that creates hundreds of thousands of jobs and, via innovation, solves the world's and regions' biggest and most pressing problems (Acs & Szerb, 2007; Al-Dajani et al., 2015; Anderson & Ronteau, 2017; Bastian et al., 2020; Schumpeter, 1983; Wennekers & Thurik, 1999). In many countries worldwide entrepreneurship has become a way to involve citizens in private sector activities and to incite individuals to create their own employment (Bastian et al., 2019; Ennis, 2019).

The present chapter focuses on female entrepreneurs who are prime exemplars of women as shock absorbers, as they carry the responsibilities of social reproduction and the precarity of financialization, which tethers them to the fluctuations and downturns of the global markets, and external shocks as well as economic change and restructuration. We address how women's entrepreneurship has been instrumentalized for shock absorption as defined above, as well as discussing the consequences for female venturing. The text is structured as follows: first, we will introduce the different forms of shock absorption and place them in their historical and normative context. In each case, we will provide examples of shock absorption with regards to women's entrepreneurship. We then critically discuss our findings and offer potential directions for future analysis, as well as for future policymaking.

WOMEN AS INCOME GENERATORS AND THE 'RESERVE ARMY' IN A NEOLIBERAL WORLD

When the World Bank and the international community (e.g., USAID) needed to redesign their interventions and policy recommendations to focus away from the large industrial projects of the post-World War II period, women were targeted as an 'untapped resource' that could expediently produce results across many sectors. As Meyerowitz (2021, p. 99) explains, these policies "downplayed feminism and argued that women as 'income generators' were crucial to productivity, population control, the satisfaction of basic needs, and the alleviation of poverty." In this way, the value of large infrastructure projects would be more easily identified and impacts more easily claimed, than if issues of justice were scrutinized.

By the mid-1970s, governments had become important employers of women in nearly all regions of the world. Women were especially represented in public-welfare agencies (e.g., education and healthcare) which made them more susceptible to retrenchment, a neoliberal policy prescription for shrinking social safety nets. By the 1980s, women as 'income generators' were largely reflected in the microcredit revolution. A decade of structural adjustment policies by the World Bank had left many countries in need of economic salvation. At a time when countries were facing unprecedented austerity measures that gutted many social programs, women were being prioritized as essential agents of economic recovery (Hozic & True, 2016). Women's enterprise has emerged as a key driver of both shock absorption and recovery of neoliberal markets. As explained by Juanita Elias (2016, p. 115), "women were positioned as those best able to deliver sustainable pro-poor economic growth – essentially providing the 'human face' of globalization in ways that do not alter the underlying structures of capital accumulation in any meaningful sense." In that sense, women's self-employment has been largely motivated by the need to balance work and increasing family demands (Carr et al., 1996). Indeed, family has remained a central component of the gendered incentive structures for persons entering self-employment (McManus, 2001).[1]

In this economic context, the rise of microcredit especially targeting poor women in the global South further entrenched these strategies. Microcredit programs have strategically utilized women's roles as mothers in their outreach and aimed to cultivate gendered neoliberal and entrepreneurial subjectivities among these women that would, in turn, bring widespread progress for their families, communities, and countries (Altan-Olcay, 2014; Radhakrishnan, 2022; Rankin, 2001). By engaging women in the economic market through microenterprise and access to credit markets, such strategies both established poor women as surplus value generators for the global credit markets and exposed them to the vagaries of the financial markets (Mader, 2015; Radhakrishnan, 2022). In these places, men were not seen to bring the complex benefits to family and community well-being that women do; nor were they drawn to small business – given women's largely information economic enterprise, which did not threaten men's access to more stable and secure wage labor. And, where "Men could avoid the informal economy; women had fewer options. In the search for the smallest enterprise and the most indigent workers, women were hard to avoid" (Meyerowitz, 2021, p. 157).

From a Women in Development (WID) perspective, microfinance also represents an approach to reduce what is seen as main cause for gender inequality. It basically supports poor women's necessity-driven and often subsistence-based businesses and so should help in reducing overall poverty by providing women with more opportunities to participate in the production process and to gain access to essential production resources (Islam, 2007; Mazzone, 2022; Roy, 2010). The WID logic has been widely criticized for its disregard of gendered norms both prevalent in the economic system and which have profoundly handicapped and limited female agency and economic opportunities (De Jong, 2017; Radhakrishnan, 2022; Wilson, 2011). The aim that women starting their own little business, and participating in producing economic value for them, their families, and society, would change power relations in their households and increasingly participate in the public realm was not achieved (Langworthy, 2023; Mazzone, 2022). On the contrary, the women's responsibilities as business owners, in addition to their traditional roles as caretakers for their families, would result in substantially higher workloads for women (Ennis, 2019).

A second pivotal objective of microfinance and microcredit has been women's empowerment, which should not be considered at the individual female level only, as it also entails the objective of social change in terms of societal power structures, social mobilization, and power of communities (Calás et al., 2009; Kabeer, 2005). Propagated by gender and development (GAD) programs, these approaches went beyond female participation in the production process and female access to production resources toward strategic gender needs (Vaessen et al., 2014) by instrumentalizing women for social transformative purposes (Edgcomb & Barton, 1998). To achieve this empowerment, the capacity building and training of women is undertaken, along with investing in their organizational capacities and helping construct their social capital and networks. Groups of women entrepreneurs would then become collective social change agents (Holvoet, 2005). However, evidence regarding the effect of microcredit on women's advancements in economies and women's empowerment to date is mixed. Contrary to its 'promise,' access to microcredits have not substantially changed power relations within households, or led to substantial changes in female social status (Vaessen et al., 2014). There are also no generalizable conclusions possible regarding the relationship between microcredit and empowerment (Al Hakim et al., 2022; Fernando, 2006; Radhakrishnan, 2022). Several researchers have argued that microfinance has improved women's socio-economic status and conditions and helped women to leave extreme poverty (Akhter & Cheng 2020; Parwez & Patel, 2022). However, many studies find that despite the general poverty reduction women's decision-making power remained inferior to that of men (Al-Shami et al., 2021).

Microfinance and women's engagement in it have, in fact, been able to buffer the constraints of institutional voids and related market dysfunctionalities (Chakrabarty & Bass, 2015); they resulted in increased income generation for households, and served economic growth as well as promoting active participation of people at the bottom of the pyramid in liberal markets (Mair & Marti, 2009). Yet, microfinance seems to have had little to no impact on women's social situations, since it has not facilitated more female household decisions or female mobility and has kept concerned entrepreneurial women firmly locked into the constraints of a gender discriminating patriarchal system (Al-Shami et al., 2021; Quibria, 2012). Female empowerment in the context of microfinance seems to be closely related to entrepreneurial success trajectories (Quibria, 2012), which seem to have little to do with the entrepreneurial mindsets of the women concerned and more with persisting class inequalities among women that give access to different knowledge and different social capital and reinforce persisting gender inequalities (Altan-Olcay, 2016).

WOMEN ENTREPRENEURS AS SHOCK ABSORBERS DURING TIMES OF CRISIS

Women as Shock Absorbers during Financial Crisis

Fifty years of expanding microcredit operations focusing on women has coincided with the rise of a 'privatization bias' among states that have deepened financialization and privatization of many social programs (Sennett, 1977). This shift had immediate effects on women due to individualization of risk and women's integration into financial markets, primarily as debtors (Elson, 2014). The rise of women's self-employment and entrepreneurship during this period of increasing economic and financial turbulence was, and continues to be, actively encouraged to increase the economic productivity of women while concomitantly increasing gender equality (Nadin et al., 2020). Indeed, women entrepreneurs and their position as "rational economic women" (Rankin, 2001) have come to embody "the resilient economic subject – providing essential income and socially reproductive labor of their households" (p. 116) – labor which enables the kinds of risky financial behaviors that trigger crises in the first place (Elias, 2016). Critical feminist analysis of the 1997 Asian Financial Crisis shows how the "financial system had developed so that risk was off-loaded from those who took risks (mainly high income men) to women, especially low income women, who had to absorb the risks because they could not liquidate their responsibilities for their children" (Elson, 2014, p. 193).

By 2008, the history of women as economic and social shock absorbers was well entrenched in the global political economy. Analysis drew heavily on the gendered dynamics of finance (de Goede, 2005) to position a "rational economic woman" who was poised to rescue the global economy (Elias, 2013) once again as a counterweight to mean-hearted masculine capitalism economy (Elias, 2013). Financial actors and international policy organizations (e.g., the World Economic Forum) sought recovery through adding more women to the ranks of banks and commercial finance organizations. Backed by empirical studies, the presence of gender diverse boards was praised for stronger company performance during the crises because of better counter cyclical strategic decisions and more cautious investments (Fernandes et al., 2017; Sun et al., 2015). The World Bank sold the 'business case' for investing in women as 'smart economics,' once again drawing on women's 'innate' risk aversion and sense of responsibility (Calkin, 2015). This discourse was also bolstered by the fact that in 2008 and 2009, microfinance portfolios of the global top ten funds grew by 31 percent and 23 percent, respectively (Radhakrishnan, 2022). These assets looked like better investments precisely because they were lent to women in noncyclical trades (Radhakrishnan, 2022). Research about women entrepreneurship during adverse conditions, such as the global financial crisis, is scarce but empirical analysis agrees that women from crisis-affected households were more willing to engage in self-employment and start their own business compared with their male counterparts (GEM, 2023). However, their motivations were mainly necessity driven and focused both on compensating for deteriorating financial and living conditions and increasing livelihood choices for their families (Giotopoulos et al., 2017; Paul & Sarma, 2013). Men who started businesses during a financial crisis were much more growth- and export-oriented than their female peers (Giotopoulos et al., 2017). In particular, women's embeddedness with local communities made them prone to emphasize contributing to their communities' well-being and to deliberately increasing the wealth of local economies (del Mar Alonso-Almeida, 2012; Zapalska & Brozik 2014).

The situation for female entrepreneurs during crises has been quite challenging. Historical analysis has shown that in the global financial crisis, like all other economic recoveries since 1970, women fared better than men in the first two years (Kochhar, 2011). However, analysis of World Bank Enterprise Surveys found that female-managed ventures were more likely to exit the market because of the crisis as sales deteriorated disproportionately for women, reflecting a limited ability to adapt (Ahmed et al., 2018).[2] In fact, gendered structural inequalities faced by women entrepreneurs (Ahl & Marlow, 2012), such as limited access to necessary resources and incompatibilities of entrepreneurial and care-giver responsibilities/"motherhood" (Brush et al., 2009) were exacerbated during times of crisis, creating substantial challenges for female entrepreneurs in creating a sustainable business with a growth perspective (Ozkazanc-Pan & Clark Muntean, 2018).

Covid-19
With the onset of the Covid-19 pandemic, women's daily 'small "t" turbulence' was once again illuminated. The pandemic affected service sectors especially, such as hospitality, retail, personal care, and the like, which suffered under long lockdowns and shop closures. As women dominate work in such fields, this was a bigger problem for women than for men. According to a McKinsey study (McKinsey, 2022) women were 1.8 times more vulnerable during the Covid-19 crisis: Although worldwide women represent only 39 percent of global employment, they accounted for 54 percent of overall job losses. Moreover, the pandemic more negatively affected workers with lower educational achievements who were unable to work from their home office (Goldin et al., 2022). In the U.S.A., 25 percent of women without a college degree, compared with 14 percent of men (Goldin et al., 2022), were affected in this way. In fact, the gendered labor markets worldwide accounted for a substantial number of female job losses (McKinsey, 2022). In addition, persisting societal inequalities regarding the share of care work led to a disproportionally large burden for women who, during lockdowns of schools and childcare facilities, were charged with the brunt of unpaid childcare and care for relatives, as well as household labor. Again, mothers are expected to be shock absorbers, even when doing so comes at the cost of their economic life: mothers must "make decisions that are sensible for their families' in the near-term, but these can be emotionally devastating and have long-lasting consequences" (Grose, 2020).

In this context, Covid-19 also stressed the shrinking social policy spaces (e.g., social protection, healthcare, and education), transferring these responsibilities directly to women in the household. In the U.S.A., a "great resignation" by women proved how women's unpaid care responsibilities conflicted with the market and were driving labor market trends (McKinsey, 2022). The Covid-19 pandemic also affected women entrepreneurs, who were disproportionally affected for the same reasons as the rest of the female labor force. The Global Entrepreneurship Monitor (GEM) states that between 2019 and 2021 established business ownership by women in upper- and middle-income countries showed the starkest ever recorded decrease of 43 percent. Worldwide, the descending numbers of established firms by female entrepreneurs' risks completely undoing decades of progress in closing the gender gap in entrepreneurship (OECD, 2024). The most frequently provided reason by women for exiting their venture was the pandemic situation, followed by a lack of profitability (GEM, 2023). In addition, women were 27 percent more likely to report their exit as being for "family reasons" (GEM, 2023).

Research by the World Bank (2021, 2022) shows that female managers and owners in different regions of the world are less likely to benefit from policy measures that cushioned the pandemic impact; moreover, this research found that women had substantially less access to finance. Despite the limited focus within Covid policies on the needs of women entrepreneurs, and the steep social reproductive demands of the past few years, women's enterprises are once again positioned to drive economic recovery after Covid (Blumburg, 2022; Cofield, 2022; Gilbert et al., 2022). In this context, the GEM survey (2023) reveals that half of the women who are early-stage entrepreneurs considered the pandemic a period that created new business opportunities (compared to one-third of established female business owners). It is also very interesting to see how women entrepreneurs make increasing use of digital technologies to overcome barriers of entry (to international markets) or to address new customer groups. According to the GEM survey (2023) one-quarter of female early-stage entrepreneurs reported a strong reliance on digital technologies, and more than 50 percent of women entrepreneurs expect to digitalize substantial parts of their operations in the coming months. In many developmental contexts, digital technologies mitigate cultural barriers that assign the role of a homemaker to women and which expect them to stay in the house even until they are married (Welter & Smallbone, 2008). Digital technology enables them a chance to build, and grow, a business from the safe space that connects them to the outside world and to markets which they otherwise would not have been able to enter (Kelley & McAdam, 2022)

Women as Shock Absorbers in Times of Economic Restructuring

Economies cyclically undergo restructuring, which can sometimes result in dramatic changes to the economy's main pillars and constituents. Economic restructuring impacts a wide range of macro-environmental elements, such as institutional arrangements, social hierarchies, demographics, consumer behavior, geographic spacing (rural versus urban), and more. For example, with the fall of the Soviet empire, former Eastern Bloc countries went through an economic transition process toward liberal economies, which included the development of private business ownership. In this context, the formation of new businesses was encouraged, since small and medium-sized companies were considered crucial for development based on innovation and entrepreneurship (European Bank for Reconstruction and Development, 1997). Most transition states actively promoted entrepreneurship and made it an intrinsic part of their development agenda, supporting an increase in employment, private sector development, economic diversification, and innovation strategies. Research on female ventures in transition contexts assigned additional value creation to women businesses, such as solidarity and support with other women in challenging economic circumstances by both employing and engaging more women, and by reducing substantially female unemployment (Aidis et al., 2007). For example, this view has been empirically supported by research from Tanzania, an emerging development context, where women "are stronger together" and where female entrepreneurs and owners advocate actively for other women, providing employment for them (Madison et al., 2022). In exchange, a greater representation of women is involved in new product development, bringing female experiences and knowledge to the fore and bringing forward innovation (Madison et al., 2022).

In such a restructuring context, policymaking tries to establish formal institutions that encourage the creation of new firms. Besides that, formal institutions influence the type of entrepreneurial ventures women (and men) engage in, and to what extent (Peng, 2003; Welter & Smallbone, 2003). For example, founder rates of women were substantially higher than those of men in seven of the 11 countries in Middle East & North Africa (MENA) region, establishing the meaningful and high-value interpretation of enterprise for MENA women (GEM, 2023). In countries such as Saudi Arabia, the UAE, and Oman, there is near gender parity when it comes to entrepreneurial intentions and to starting a business (GEM, 2023). The Arab Gulf countries, especially, have provided favorable regulations for women entrepreneurs; their practical and financial support initiatives have created an enabling environment for women ventures and all countries include entrepreneurship and women's advancement as a vital part of their 2030 economic development agendas (Bastian et al., 2023; Wood et al., 2021). Nevertheless, informal pressures such as culture and gender expectations were shown to strongly impact women's entrepreneurial intentions as well as female perception of entrepreneurial legitimacy. Furthermore, research by Welter and Smallbone (2003) on transition countries in Eastern Europe showed how formal institutions' positive effect on female venturing might be overridden by the effects of informal institutions that reflect patriarchic values which typically restrict and limit women's entrepreneurial activities. Research about women's entrepreneurship in different restructuring contexts agrees that women must negotiate their entrepreneurial and gender assigned roles: in Pakistan women were shown to use religious justifications to support their entrepreneurial choices (Roomi et al., 2018). Additionally, Palestinian embroiderers in Jordan had to negotiate their entrepreneurial activities alongside their family responsibilities and homemaker work with their families and husbands over and over again (Al-Dajani & Marlow, 2013).

In the Middle East, the Gulf monarchies in particular are undergoing tremendous economic and social changes as these countries look to diversify their economies having relied heavily on hydrocarbons. The Gulf Cooperation Council (GCC) countries have used public sector employment for citizens to redistribute the oil wealth and to ensure employment for nationals. However, since oil and gas revenues have been unstable and have not been able to keep pace with both population growth and associated needs, governments have challenged themselves to privatize their economies. With this they seek to assign responsibility for economic growth and employment to the private sector, and in this way, to individuals (Forstenlechner & Rutledge, 2010), creating an externality of the issue. In the Gulf States the private sector relies on expat employees, which leaves very little space in the labor market for nationals and especially for women (Ennis, 2019). In this way, entrepreneurship has become a means to assign government responsibilities for job and wealth creation to the individual. In particular, women's entrepreneurship is promoted with a normative narrative of women's advancement and emancipation via the power female venturing (Bastian et al., 2023; Ng et al., 2022) and with a narrative of female entrepreneurs being patriotic role models (Ennis, 2018). Yet, female entrepreneurs are still expected to fulfill multiple tasks and responsibilities, such as their traditional family roles (e.g., caretaking), be successful as business women, and also show loyalty to their country (Ennis, 2019).

CONCLUSION

As our discussion reveals, women have been positioned as 'supporters' and 'saviors' of the economy and society in times of uncertainty, crisis and fundamental change. Women (entrepreneurs) are ascribed responsible and risk-averse characteristics that also keep them from fully engaging in the labor force while being valorized to rebalance the economy after 'masculine' excesses (Hozic & True, 2016). The discourse of women as shock absorbers/saviors of the family and the economy at large, due to neoliberal market adjustment, as well as adaptation to times of crisis or economic restructuring, is a result of women being "viewed as able to easily cope with and support policies of welfare retrenchment, liberalization, and privatization" (Elias, 2016, p. 123). Further, strains on social reproduction (caring labor) as was illuminated by the Covid-19 pandemic, are not accidental, but have deep systematic roots in the structure of things: care crises are a distinctive feature of neoliberal capitalism (Fraser, 2017). For example, in middle-class families in the Middle East, women's work participation and also men's domestic participation are often symptomatic of necessity and economic decline rather than economic growth, changing gender norms, and expansion of new opportunities for women (Bargawi et al., 2022).

Women entrepreneurs are the prime exemplars of women as shock absorber/ savior as they carry both the responsibility of social reproduction and the precarity of financialization, which tethers them to the fluctuations and downturns of the global markets. Deeply intertwined with this instrumentalist treatment of women is the expectation that women will bring value, not just within the economic system but will also continually prioritize, and attend to, the socially reproductive labor that maintains both family and community wellbeing. This expectation was – and continues to be – codified in macroeconomic policies that exhibit gender bias, such as the "male breadwinner bias" (Elson & Cagatay, 2000). This bias brings to the forefront the paradox of promoting women's economic engagement whilst also closely tethering this engagement to women's instrumental roles inside the household. Women can (and should) work because it is good for their families and also to provide an army of reserve labor to support society in general.

The subject of women entrepreneurs as shock absorber leaves space for several interesting research pathways: What are the costs of the correlation between women entrepreneurs as shock absorbers (e.g. 'mumpreneurship' (in which women are mothers, and enterprise is good for mothers) and social reproducers? Since crises are not a one-off 'traumatic event' (Brassett & Clarke, 2012), it is important to focus on women's working lives both within and outside the household to observe the way in which economic and social crises associated with state restructuring, and the increased strains on the socially reproductive sphere, are continually reproduced and sustained. Or, as pointed out by Diane Elson (Elson, 2000, p. 28): "If too much pressure is put upon the domestic sector to provide unpaid care work to make up for deficiencies elsewhere, the result may be a depletion of human capabilities." This raises calls to look at 'depletion' in the context of social reproduction (e.g., to account for the depletion in women and their capacities from subsidizing political and economic systems).

Basic policy changes which could support women in their 'small "t" turbulence' are those which are regularly called for: an easing of childcare demands through publicly funded quality childcare, or tax breaks for women entrepreneurs; redistribution of childcare responsibilities through ensuring men have access to care leave in addition to paternity leave. Overall, an easing of other social reproduction demands through the provisioning of adequate social protection and the inclusion of entrepreneurs in these protections (e.g., healthcare to families of women entrepreneurs, minimum wage floors for entrepreneurs and the like), and ensuring that state tax policies do not reinforce male breadwinner biases within families in ways that discourage or devalue women's enterprise, would significantly improve the work lives of, particularly, entrepreneurial women.

To this end, we encourage (and strive) to complete more research on women's entrepreneurship and the costs in time and income incurred to them from daily social reproduction responsibilities and care crises and services to help women entrepreneurs manage businesses during turbulence (e.g., with well-trained substitutes or collaborative groups who can cover for each other as needed).

NOTES

1. Both self-employed men and women are more likely to be married and living with a spouse than counterparts working wage employment (see Boden & Nucci, 1997).
2. Research in Bulgaria, Hungary, Latvia, Lithuania, Romania, and Turkey.

REFERENCES

Acs, Z. J., & Szerb, L. (2007). Entrepreneurship, economic growth and public policy. *Small Business Economics, 28*, 109–122.

Ahl, H., & Marlow, S. (2012). Exploring the dynamics of gender, feminism and entrepreneurship: Advancing the debate to escape a dead end? *Organization, 19*(5), 543–562.

Ahmed, G., Amponsah, C. T., & Deasi, S. S. (2018). Exploring the dynamics of women entrepreneurship: A case study of UAE. *International Journal of Business Science and Applied Management, 7*(3), 13–24.

Aidis, R., Welter, F., Smallbone, D., & Isakova, N. (2007). Female entrepreneurship in transition economies: The case of Lithuania and Ukraine. *Feminist Economics, 13*(2), 157–183.

Akhter, J., & Cheng, K. (2020). Sustainable empowerment initiatives among rural women through microcredit borrowings in Bangladesh. *Sustainability, 12*(6), 2275.

Al-Dajani, H., Carter, S., Shaw, E., & Marlow, S. (2015). Entrepreneurship among the displaced and dispossessed: Exploring the limits of emancipatory entrepreneuring. *British Journal of Management, 26*(4), 713–730.

Al-Dajani, H., & Marlow, S. (2013). Empowerment and entrepreneurship: A theoretical framework. *International Journal of Entrepreneurial Behaviour & Research, 19*(5), 503–524.

Al Hakim, G., Bastian, B. L., Ng, P. Y., & Wood, B. P. (2022). Women's empowerment as an outcome of NGO projects: Is the current approach sustainable? *Administrative Sciences, 12*(2), 62.

Al-Shami, S. A., Al Mamun, A., Rashid, N., & Al-shami, M. (2021). Microcredit impact on socio-economic development and women empowerment in low-income countries: Evidence from Yemen. *Sustainability, 13*(16), 9326.

Altan-Olcay, Ö. (2014). Entreneurial subjectivities and gendered complexities: Neoliberal citizenship in Turkey. *Feminist Economics, 20*(4), 235–259.

Altan-Olcay, Ö. (2016). The entrepreneurial woman in development programs: Thinking through class differences. *Social Politics: International Studies in Gender, State & Society, 23*(3), 389–414.

Anderson, A., & Ronteau, S. (2017). Towards an entrepreneurial theory of practice: Emerging ideas for emerging economies. *Journal of Entrepreneurship in Emerging Economies, 9*(2), 110–120.

Bargawi, H., Alami, R., & Ziada, H. (2022). Re-negotiating social reproduction, work and gender roles in occupied Palestine. *Review of International Political Economy, 29*(6), 1917–1944.

Bastian, B. L., Khoury, C. M., Issa, I. A., & Ghattas, P. (2020). Key success factors of social entrepreneurs in Lebanon. *World Review of Entrepreneurship, Management and Sustainable Development, 16*(3), 329–357.

Bastian, B. L., Metcalfe, B. D., & Zali, M. R. (2019). Gender inequality: Entrepreneurship development in the MENA region. *Sustainability, 11*(22), 6472.

Bastian, B. L., Wood, B. P., & Ng, P. Y. (2023). The role of strong ties in empowering women entrepreneurs in collectivist contexts. *International Journal of Gender and Entrepreneurship, 15*(1), 122–146.

Blumburg, D. L. (2022). Female entrepreneurs could drive a global economic recovery. All they need are the digital keys. Retrieved March 3, 2023 from https://www.mastercard.com/news/perspectives/2022/inez-murray-financial-alliance-for-women/.

Boden, R. J., & Nucci, A. R. (1997). Counting the self-employed using household and business sample data. *Small Business Economics, 9*, 427–436.

Brassett, J. & Clarke, C. (2012). Performing the sub-prime crisis: Trauma and the financial event. *International Political Sociology, 6*(1), 4–20.

Brush, C., de Bruin, A., & Welter, F. (2009). A gender-aware framework for women's entrepreneurship. *International Journal of Gender and Entrepreneurship, 1*(1), 8–24.

Calás, M. B., Smircich, L., & Bourne, K. A. (2009). Extending the boundaries: Reframing 'entrepreneurship as social change' through feminist perspectives. *Academy of Management Review, 34*(3), 552–569.

Calkin, S. (2015). 'Tapping' women for post-crisis capitalism: Evidence from the 2012 World Development Report. *International Feminist Journal of Politics, 17*(4), 611–629.

Carr, M., Chen, M. A., & Jhabvala, R. (1996). *Speaking Out: Women's Economic Empowerment in South Asia*. London: IT Publications on behalf of Aga Khan Foundation Canada and United Nations Development Fund for Women (UNIFEM).

Chakrabarty, S., & Erin Bass, A. (2015). Comparing virtue, consequentialist, and deontological ethics-based corporate social responsibility: Mitigating microfinance risk in institutional voids. *Journal of Business Ethics, 126*, 487–512.

Cofield, N. M. (2022). Women entrepreneurs are critical to America's economic recovery. Retrieved March 3, 2023 from https://www.inc.com/natalie-madeira-cofield/women-entrepreneurs-are-critical-to-americas-economic-recovery.html.

de Goede, M. (2005). *Virtue, Fortune, and Faith: A Genealogy of Finance*. University of Minnesota Press.

De Jong, S. (2017). *Complicit Sisters: Gender and Women's Issues across North–South Divides*. Oxford University Press.

del Mar Alonso-Almeida, M. (2012, September). Water and waste management in the Moroccan tourism industry: The case of three women entrepreneurs. *Women's Studies International Forum, 35*(5), 343–353.

Edgcomb, E., & Barton, L. (1998). Social intermediation and microfinance programs: A literature review. Bethesda: Microenterprise Best Practices. Retrieved May 9, 2024 from https://pdf.usaid.gov/pdf_docs/PNACD060.pdf.

Elias, J. (2013). Davos woman to the rescue of of global capitalism: Postfeminist politics and competitiveness promotion at the World Economic Forum. *International Political Sociology, 7*(2), 152–169.

Elias, J. (2016). Whose Crisis? Whose Recovery? Lessons learned (and not) from the Asian crisis. In A. Hozic & J. True (Eds.), *Scandelous Economics: Gender and the Politics of Financial Crises* (pp. 109–25). Oxford University Press.

Elson, D. (1988). The impact of structural adjustment on women: Concepts and issues. Manchester Discussion Papers in Development Studies (23236).

Elson, D. (2000). The progress of women: Empowerment and economics. In *The Progress of the World's Women* (pp. 15–36). New York: UNIFEM.

Elson, D. (2014). Economic crises from the 1980s to the 2010s. In S. Rai & G. Waylen (Eds.), *New Frontiers in Feminist Political Economy* (pp. 189–212). Abingdon: Routledge.

Elson, D., & Cagatay, N. (2000). The social content of macroeconomic politices. *World Development, 28*(7), 1347–1364.

Ennis, C. A. (2018). Reading entrepreneurial power in small Gulf states: Qatar and the UAE. *International Journal, 73*(4), 573–595.

Ennis, C. A. (2019). The gendered complexities of promoting female entrepreneurship in the Gulf. *New Political Economy, 24*(3), 365–354.

Ennis, C. D. (2015). Knowledge, transfer, and innovation in physical literacy curricula. *Journal of Sport and Health Science, 4*(2), 119–124.

European Bank for Reconstruction and Development (1997). *Transition report 1997: Enterprise Performance and Growth.* London: European Bank for Reconstruction and Development.

Fernandes, C., Farinha, J., Martins, F. V., & Mateus, C. (2017). Supervisory boards, financial crisis and bank performance: Do board characteristics matter? *Journal of Banking Regulation, 18,* 310–337.

Fernando, J. L. (2006). Microcredit and empowerment. In J. L. Fernando (Ed.), *Microfinance: Perils and prospects* (pp. 187–238). London: Routledge.

Forstenlechner, I., & Rutledge, E. (2010). Unemployment in the Gulf: Time to update the 'social contract'. *Middle East Policy, 17*(2), 38–51.

Fraser, N. (2017). Crisis of care? On the social-reproductive contradictions of contemporary capitalism. In T. Bhattacharya (Ed.), *Social Reproduction Theory: Remapping Class, Recentering Oppression* (pp. 21–36). London: Pluto.

Gilbert, J., Nyadjroh, A., & Kamara, G. (2022). Investing in women and diverse entrepreneurs to boost the post-pandemic recovery. Retrieved March 3, 2023 from https://www.weforum.org/agenda/2022/05/investing-in-women-and-diverse-entrepreneurs-to-boost-the-post-pandemic-recovery/.

GEM [Global Entrepreneurship Monitor] (2023). *GEM 2022/23: Women's Entrepreneurship Report: Challenging Bias and Stereotypes.* Retrieved May 9, 2024 from https:// www .gemconsortium .org/ report/ gem -20222023 -womens -entrepreneurship-challenging-bias-and-stereotypes-2.

Giotopoulos, I., Kontolaimou, A., & Tsakanikas, A. (2017). Antecedents of growth-oriented entrepreneurship before and during the Greek economic crisis. *Journal of Small Business and Enterprise Development, 24*(3), 528–544.

Goldin, C., Albanesi, S., & Olmstead-Rumsey, J. (2022). Understanding the economic impact of COVID-19 on women. Retrieved March 3, 2023 from https:// www .brookings.edu/ bpea -articles/ understanding -the -economic -impact -of -covid -19 -on -women/.

Grose, J. (2020). Mothers are the 'shock absorbers' of our society. *New York Times*, 14th October 2020. https://www.nytimes.com/2020/10/14/parenting/working-moms -job-loss-coronavirus.html.

Holvoet, N. (2005). Credit and women's group membership in south India: Testing models of intrahousehold allocative behavior. *Feminist Economics*, *11*(3), 27–62.

Hozic, A. A., & True, J. (Eds.) (2016). *Scandalous Economics: Gender and the Politics of Financial Crises*. Oxford: Oxford University Press.

Islam, T. (2007). *Microcredit and Poverty Alleviation*. Aldershot: Ashgate Publishing.

Kabeer, N. (2005). Is microfinance a 'magic bullet' for women's empowerment? Analysis of findings from South Asia. *Economic and Political Weekly*, *40*(44/45), 4709–4718. Retrieved May 9, 2024 from http://www.jstor.org/stable/4417357.

Kelly, G., & McAdam, M. (2022). Women entrepreneurs negotiating identities in liminal digital spaces. *Entrepreneurship Theory and Practice*. https:// doi .org/ 10 .1177/10422587221115363.

Kochhar, R. (2011). Two years of economic recovery: Women lose jobs, men find them. Retrieved March 3, 2023 from https:// www .pewresearch .org/ social -trends/ 2011/07/06/two-years-of-economic-recovery-women-lose-jobs-men-find-them/.

Langworthy, M. (2023). Women's (micro)enterprise and the SDGs: Reframing success in women's economic development in Sri Lanka. *Journal of International Women's Studies*, 26(1), article 7. https://vc.bridgew.edu/jiws/vol26/iss1/7.

Mader, P. (2015). *The Political Economy of Microfinance: Financializing Poverty*. Basingstoke: Palgrave Macmillan.

Madison, K., Moore, C. B., Daspit, J. J., & Nabisaalu, J. K. (2022). The influence of women on SME innovation in emerging markets. *Strategic Entrepreneurship Journal*, *16*(2), 281–313.

Mair, J., & Marti, I. (2009). Entrepreneurship in and around institutional voids: A case study from Bangladesh. *Journal of Business Venturing*, *24*(5), 419–435.

Mazzone, A. (2022). Gender and energy in international development: Is there a return of the 'feminization' of poverty discourse? *Development*, *65*(1), 17–28.

McKinsey (2022). Women in the workplace report. Retrieved March 3, 2023 from https://womenintheworkplace.com/.

McManus, P. A. (2001). Women's participation in self-employment in Western industrialized nations. *International Journal of Sociology*, *31*(2), 70–97.

Meyerowitz, J. (2021). *A War on Global Poverty: The Lost Promise of Redistribution and the Rise of Microcredit*. Princeton, NJ: Princeton University Press.

Nadin, S., Smith, R., & Jones, S. (2020). Heroines of enterprise: Post-recession media representations of women and entrepreneurship in a UK newspaper 2008–2016. *International Small Business Journal*, *38*(6), 557–577.

Ng, P. Y., Wood, B. P., & Bastian, B. L. (2022). Reformulating the empowerment process through women entrepreneurship in a collective context. *International Journal of Entrepreneurial Behavior & Research*, *28*(9), 154–176.

OECD (2024). Is the gender gap closing? Retrieved May 9, 2024 from https:// www .oecd.org/cfe/smes/inclusive-entrepreneurship/gender.htm.

Ozkazanc-Pan, B., & Clark Muntean, S. (2018). Networking towards (in)equality: Women entrepreneurs in technology. *Gender, Work & Organization*, *25*(4), 379–400.

Parwez, S. & Patel, R. (2022). Augmenting women empowerment: A systematic literature review on microfinance-led developmental interventions. *Journal of Global Responsibility*, *13*(3), 338–360.

Paul, S., & Sarma, V. (2013). Economic crisis and female entrepreneurship: Evidence from countries in Eastern Europe and Central Asia. CREDIT Research Paper No. 13/08. Retrieved May 9, 2024 from https://www.econstor.eu/bitstream/10419/96357/1/779706439.pdf.

Peng, M. W. (2003). Institutional transitions and strategic choices. *Academy of Management Review, 28*(2), 275–296.

Quibria, M. G. (2012). Microcredit and poverty alleviation: Can microcredit close the deal? WIDER Working Paper No. 2012/78. Retrieved May 9, 2024 from https://ideas.repec.org/p/unu/wpaper/wp-2012-078.html.

Radhakrishnan, S. (2022). *Making Women Pay: Microfinance in Urban India.* Durham, NC: Duke University Press.

Rankin, K. N. (2001). Governing development: Neoliberalism, microcredit, and rational economic woman. *Economy and Society, 30*(1), 18–37.

Roomi, M. A., Rehman, S., & Henry, C. (2018). Exploring the normative context for women's entrepreneurship in Pakistan: A critical analysis. *International Journal of Gender and Entrepreneurship, 10*(2), 158–180.

Roy, A. (2010). *Poverty Capital: Microfinance and the Making of Development.* New York: Routledge.

Schumpeter, J. A. (1983). *The Theory of Economic Development.* Hoboken, NJ: Routledge.

Sennett, R. (1977). *The Fall of Public Man.* WW Norton & Company.

Sennett, R. (2020). The public realm. In R. Sennett, *Being Urban* (pp. 35–58). New York: Routledge.

Seri, G. (2016). 'To double oppression, double rebellion': Women, capital and crisis in 'post-neoliberal' Latin America. In A. Hozic & J. True (Eds.), *Scandalous Economics: Gender and the Politics of Financial Crises* (pp. 126–142). New York: Oxford University Press.

Steans, J., & Tepe, D. (2010). Introduction – social reproduction in international political economy: Theoretical insights and international, transnational and local sitings. *Review of International Political Economy, 17*(5), 807–815.

Sun, S. L., Zhu, J., & Ye, K. (2015). Board openness during an economic crisis. *Journal of Business Ethics, 129*, 363–377.

Vaessen, J., Rivas, A., Duvendack, M., Palmer Jones, R., Leeuw, F., Van Gils, G., Lukach, R. et al. (2014). The effects of microcredit on women's control over household spending in developing countries: A systematic review and meta-analysis. *Campbell Systematic Reviews, 10*(1), 1–205.

Welter, F., & Smallbone, D. (2003). Entrepreneurship and enterprise strategies in transition economies: an institutional perspective. In David Kirby and Anna Watson (Eds.), *Small Firms and Economic Development in Developed and Transition Economies: A Reader* (pp. 95–114). Aldershot: Ashgate Publishing.

Welter, F., & Smallbone, D. (2008). Women's entrepreneurship from an institutional perspective: The case of Uzbekistan. *International Entrepreneurship and Management Journal, 4*, 505–520.

Wennekers, S., & Thurik, R. (1999). Linking entrepreneurship and economic growth. *Small Business Economics, 13*(4), 27–56.

Wilson, K. (2011). 'Race', gender and neoliberalism: Changing visual representations in development. *Third World Quarterly, 32*(2), 315–331.

Wood, B. P., Ng, P. Y., & Bastian, B. L. (2021). Hegemonic conceptualizations of empowerment in entrepreneurship and their sustainability for collective contexts. *Administrative Sciences, 11*(1), 28.

Woodhall, M. (1973). Investment in women: A reappraisal of the concept of human capital. *International Review of Education, 19*(1), 9–29.

World Bank (2021). *Women, Business and the Law 2021*. Retrieved May 9, 2024 from https://openknowledge.worldbank.org/bitstream/handle/10986/35094/9781464816529 .pdf.

World Bank (2022). *Women, Business and the Law 2022*. Retrieved May 9, 2024 from https://wbl.worldbank.org/en/wbl.

Zapalska, A. M., & Brozik, D. (2014). Female entrepreneurship businesses in tourism and hospitality industry in Poland. *Problems and Perspectives in Management, 12*(2), 7–13.

10. Pivoting and positionality: entrepreneurship, care, and the Covid-19 pandemic in Czechia and the U.S.A.

Alena Křížková, Nancy C. Jurik, Marie Pospíšilová, Gray Cavender and Dongling Zhang

INTRODUCTION

The Covid-19 pandemic produced crises in human care and economic survival. Efforts to stop its spread prompted business and government shutdowns in many countries. Shutdowns produced uncertainty and supply chain issues, and fuelled economic crises (World Bank, 2022). Closures also produced a care crisis. Parents experienced expanded care responsibilities as schools and child-care facilities closed. Online schooling helped continue education, but required access to technology and parental supervision (Schilder and Sandstrom, 2021).

Covid-19 effects and the opportunities to defend against them were uneven both within and across countries (Ferreira, 2021). Variations can only be understood by examining the intersecting dynamics that position people based on gender, class, race/ethnicity, family situation, occupation, and geographical context (Maestripieri, 2021). Individuals working in fields that required face-time with customers (mostly women) risked infection, government closure, and job loss. Covid-19 effects were gendered, and poor women were among the hardest hit. Women were disproportionately made unemployed by Covid-19, likely because they worked in industries that were newer, smaller, and required face-time with customers (Madgavkar et al., 2020). Women bore the brunt of routine unpaid care work of children and elders heightened by the closure of schools, playgrounds, and care facilities (Gromada et al., 2020).

As previous literature has focused primarily on employees (Mun et al., 2022), the study presented in this chapter attends to Covid-19 effects on self-employed and small business owners (SEBOs). The authors examined women SEBOs and care responsibilities during Covid-19's first two years. Because women SEBOs tend to be smaller, newer, and located in industries vulnerable to closure, and because demands for increased unpaid care work tend to fall disproportionately on women, it is important that research examines women SEBOs' survival strategies (Torres et al., 2021). It has been acknowledged that the impacts of the pandemic were intersectional and policy measures that were taken failed to account for resulting inequalities (Al-Dajani et al., 2020). Covid-19 effects varied across countries, and Czechia and the United States offer interesting sites to compare SEBOs' responses. Compared to Czechia, the USA has a long, consistent history of entrepreneurship, while Czechia has more developed welfare state support, and different levels of gender inequalities as well as gender norms.

This chapter's conceptual framework combines business pivoting research (Manolova et al., 2020) with theories of intersectionality (Romero, 2018), social positionality (Anthias, 2008; Martinez Dy, 2020; Zavella, 1991), and cultural embeddedness (Yousafzai et al., 2019). We extend Martinez Dy's (2020) social positionality perspective on the complex interplay between structure and agency in shaping enterprise opportunities and practices. These theories are empirically employed to examine SEBOs' pivot opportunities and strategies not simply as the provenance of atomistic entrepreneurial agents, but intertwined with, and embedded within, their lived experiences. Entrepreneurship and pivoting are thereby subject to social conditions and conditioning, as well as the advantages and disadvantages that ensue. We respond to Manolova et al.'s (2020) call for further investigation of how pivots vary and are shaped by the economic and social structures in which businesses operate. Thus, we address two core research questions: How did women SEBOs pivot their businesses and families during Covid-19? How were pivots shaped by their social positions, intersecting social identities, and contextual embeddedness?

Our research reveals how family and business pivot opportunities and decisions are intertwined and shaped by respondent social positionality in two country contexts—the USA and Czechia. Our findings underline the need for intersectional, contextual, and comparative analyses as they relate to positionality and entrepreneurship generally as well as to specific women SEBOs' Covid-19 survival strategies. We offer policy insights for supporting women as diverse SEBOs, with a specific focus on crises influencing both the economy and families, and on post-crisis recovery.

In the next section, we review the relevant literature and outline our analytical framework on contextual intersectionality and social positionality. This is followed by our methodology and findings sections. Finally, we present our conclusions and identify their policy implications.

LITERATURE AND ANALYTICAL FRAMEWORK

Extant research reports more negative Covid-19 impacts for women SEBOs including closures, reduced hours, and decreased revenues. Women's ventures are typically younger, smaller, and more concentrated in retail, personal service, and highly competitive sectors (Elam et al., 2019). Disproportionately, women perform more unpaid care work (OECD/GWEP, 2021). Covid-19 increased these burdens through school/day-care closures. Self-employed women were more likely to suffer income losses than women employees or self-employed men (Graeber et al., 2021). Even within-gender groups, there is considerable variation of Covid-19 effects. Low income, less-educated SEBOs who are people of colour or recent immigrants were most affected, facing a triple whammy of increased health risks, SEBO challenges, and care demands (Torres et al., 2021). There are also variations across and within countries (OECD/GWEP, 2021). Although relief policies aided SEBOs in many countries, including Czechia and the USA, governments did not design programmes in a gender-aware manner, attend to economic inequalities, or provide adequate social services (Manolova et al., 2020).

The literature documents the survival strategies of SEBOs in uncertainty during economic crises and natural disasters (Li et al., 2019). Research on SEBO strategies during Covid-19 is emerging, but few studies focus on the experiences of women SEBOs (Abbate et al., 2021). The term "pivot" applies to changes undertaken in business models to defend against challenges and seize crisis-generated opportunities (Manolova et al., 2020). Pivoting entails experimentation to modify products or services, incorporate alternative technologies, shift target markets, or modify labour utilization. Some pivots are temporary; others become permanent (Sadeghiani, et al., 2021).

Manolova et al. (2020) suggest that pivot patterns may be gendered, but it is unclear whether differences are gender-based or just due to women's business characteristics. They stress that survival entails *defensive pivoting* to reduce risk (e.g. reducing product lines, reducing employees), and *offensive pivoting* seizing new opportunities created by crisis (Manolova et al., 2020). This study asks how women SEBOs in Czechia and the USA pivoted their ventures and family care strategies during Covid-19. It examines the ways in which SEBO and family strategies are interconnected and impacted by differentiated positions of SEBOs in the two countries. The significant differences between the USA and Czechia make comparing entrepreneurial experiences of Covid-19 a worthy undertaking. Business ownership is newer to Czechia than to the USA because it was prohibited for decades and reinitiated when state socialism ended in 1989. The USA has a long and consistent history of entrepreneurship. Data also suggest significant US–CZ differences in gender inequality measures (e.g. gender pay gaps, occupational segregation), and that relative to US respondents, Czech survey respondents favour more traditional gendered divisions of labour (Jurik et al. 2019; Parker, 2012). The US government, however, offers significantly fewer social services such as health care and paid family leave than does Czechia.

The study also extends the pivoting concept to understand how SEBOs combined family with business responsibilities. For example, Kalenkoski and Pabilonia (2022) report that self-employed married mothers were less likely to be employed and worked fewer hours during Covid-19 than married fathers. Remote work, being in an essential industry, or being incorporated mitigated some negative effects. Other research concurs: SEBO women were more likely to reduce work hours and took on more care duties than men regardless of occupation (Daniel et al., 2021; Reuschke et al., 2021).

Gender alone is insufficient to explain Covid-19 business/family pivoting. Strategies are shaped by systems of inequality that dominate social relationships and contexts, thereby positioning SEBOs' pivot opportunities (Romero and Valdez, 2016). Understanding the multiplicity of factors that simultaneously shape business and family (dis)advantage in disasters such as Covid-19 requires avoiding single-source analyses of inequality. Covid-19 effects on businesses and families have been disruptive, widespread, and unequal across communities (Wang and Kang, 2021). Early studies show that different regions and social groups faced differentiated risks of contagion and related consequences. Infection rates and the magnitude of socio-economic effects were significantly greater for vulnerable populations: women, children, low-income groups, ethnic minorities, and undocumented immigrants (Haase, 2020). Additional aspects of identities, market conditions, policies and geographical location may position SEBOs and produce further differences. Accordingly, understanding Covid-19 varied effects (positive/negative) and SEBOs' responses to them requires intersectional and positional analyses (Martinez Dy, 2020; Maestripieri, 2021).

Intersectional scholars examine the convergence of systems of inequalities (e.g. gender, class, race/ethnicity, family situation) that (dis)advantage individuals, families and communities by positioning access to opportunities (Romero, 2018). For example, Fabrizio et al. (2021) found that less-educated women with young children were the most adversely affected in paid work during the first nine months of the Covid-19 crisis. US self-employed women of colour experienced more negative Covid-19 business effects (Umoh, 2020); US Black women-owned childcare businesses were devastated by closures (Burnley, 2020). In Czechia, tourism and personal and social services, industries dominated by woman-owned businesses, were hard-hit by Covid-19 (Pelikanova et al., 2021). Longitudinal studies (Manolova et al., 2020) suggest that Covid-19 effects varied after initial closures ended. Thus, the salience of different inequalities may vary across situations, locations, and over time (Dudová and Křížková, 2023). Empirical analyses of Covid-19 effects must be sensitive to such dynamic interacting effects.

Geographical location also shapes Covid-19-related obstacles and opportunities (Wang and Kang, 2021). Different countries and regions within countries face diverse economic, regulatory and cultural contexts that influence business and family (Welter, 2011), with Covid-19 found to have affected countries differently and at different times. Country context as well as country regions and the timing of Covid-19 waves are all critical elements. Governmental responses also varied. Individuals' positions of (dis)advantage are not only shaped by social identities and their salience, but also by the specific historical times and contexts in which they are located (Yousafzai et al., 2019).

Martinez Dy (2020) employs the concept of positionality to analyse how entrepreneurship is embedded in a structural context that shapes lived experiences, opportunities and behaviour. She argues that the social arrangements that emerge from intersectionality give rise to positionality, which serves as a juncture between structure, culture and agency. Positionality challenges the meritocracy assumed in much entrepreneurial research by attending to the social embeddedness of entrepreneurship and the differential availability of concrete resources and conditionality of business opportunities. A positional perspective can further intersectional analysis of entrepreneurship's relation to structural disadvantage and inequality. The positionality of individuals and social groups in such social organizing structures as gender, race/ethnicity, immigration status, socio-economic class, and country context among others, obviously shapes opportunities and challenges within both family and business spheres, perpetuating social stratification and privilege/disadvantage (Martinez Dy, 2020).

The next section outlines the economic and cultural contexts of Czechia and the USA, and the general timing and impact of Covid-19 in each country. We also discuss relevant government policies implemented since the pandemic arose.

COUNTRY CONTEXTS

Czechia

Czechia was among hardest hit European countries during the pandemic. The number of deaths per number of inhabitants surpassed US levels (WHO, 2022). Czechia experienced above average school closures. All schools were closed on 11 March 2020 and were opening and closing as case numbers rose and fell until April 2021 (OECD, 2022). The huge increases in care demands caused by these closures fell primarily on mothers of young children (Dudová and Křížková, 2023), but they were never discussed in the debates surrounding pandemic policy. Parents, mainly mothers, suddenly had to assume the added care and educational work for their children. Among the government mitigating measures introduced around school closures at the beginning of Covid-19 was the so-called "crisis attendance allowance" (80 per cent of previous salary). This measure was introduced for all parents of children under 13 (under 10 after autumn 2020) who could not carry out paid work. SEBO parents were included in this measure for the entire period of school closure.

Personal services shops—excluding basic groceries and state borders—were closed by government after March 2020. Compensatory aid helped many businesses to overcome Covid-19. All SEBOs affected by this closure were eligible for a flat rate compensation (about US$1,000 per month), which was considered to be a quick help; social and health insurance contributions were waived for SEBOs for six months. These measures failed to differentiate between SEBOs with large operating costs and those with very low costs, yet, they were appreciated by recipients for their low administrative burden. Another programme targeted employee retention and office rental support, but this programme was introduced too late for many businesses (after employees had already been dismissed), and the application procedure and eligibility criteria were difficult. Some SEBOs feared they might have to return the subsidy. In further Covid-19 waves, the compensation bonus was reintroduced with more difficult requirements such as declaration of decreased earnings compared to previous periods (which was problematic for start-up entrepreneurs), and it could no longer be combined with the crisis attendance allowance. When schools reopened, many children were still in quarantine and SEBOs were ineligible for the attendance allowances received by employees (Dlouhá et al., 2014).

The USA

On 19 March 2020, California issued stay-at-home orders for all but essential businesses and personnel. Other states followed as cases expanded rapidly (AJMC, 2021). The definition of essential varied across states. In late May, a large number of US states reopened due to economic concerns and political confrontations over school closures and mask mandates (Scocca, 2022).

School closure policies varied considerably across states and districts, and changed significantly over time. Many districts moved to online schooling and provided equipment to do so, but these policies created hardships especially for working mothers of young children and those with limited economic resources (Viner et al., 2020). Covid-19 created awareness of the plight of working women, and support for enacting permanent national paid parental leave and childcare programmes increased (Fabrizio, 2021).

The US government created programmes to ameliorate the economic effects of Covid-19. The Payroll Protection Plan (PPP) made "forgivable loans" available to businesses if 60 per cent of the loans were spent on payroll and employee numbers and pay levels were maintained. Other programmes were directed at individuals. Three separate stimulus payments ($1200; $600; $1400) were made to eligible tax filers. Because the USA has no mandatory parental leave policy, the Families First Coronavirus Response Act allocated money for up to 12 weeks of paid parental leave. An advanced child tax credit reduced federal income tax, and gave parents early tax refunds (The U.S. Department of the Treasury, n.d.).

The first wave of the PPP programme was hurried and loosely regulated. There was much confusion surrounding the programmes regarding who was eligible and how to apply. Banks administering the programme offered immediate assistance to their best customers.

As a result, much of the money went to large corporations. In subsequent waves, more money went to small and midsize businesses, yet, sole practitioners, informal businesses, and undocumented immigrants were ineligible for assistance (National Public Radio, 2020).

METHODOLOGY

The study presented in this chapter is based on a project involving a collaboration of researchers in Czechia and the USA that examined Covid-19 effects on the two countries' women SEBOs. The methodology combined convenience and snowball sampling with purposive variations because our focus was on women SEBOs with care responsibilities in the two countries. Czech respondents were drawn across the nation, and US respondents were drawn from metropolitan areas in Arizona, California, Texas, and Missouri. Interview samples included 12 Czech (CZ) and 10 US women who defined themselves as self-employed or as small business owners, and had responsibilities for the care of children age 14 and under, and/or one or more elder relatives. The Czech sample comprised native-born respondents. The US sample included native-born and first-generation immigrant women. The sample varied based on business type, business and respondent age, family status, and in the US, immigrant status (Tables 10.1 and 10.2). We used a sampling strategy of maximum variation in order to make meaningful comparisons of core experiences and shared strategies (Neergaard, 2007). Although these samples were small and non-representative of all SEBOs, their purposive nature offered significant insights about business and family pivots during Covid.

Authors in the two countries conducted interviews in 2021 and early 2022 mostly online due to the pandemic and geographical distance restrictions. Following oral consent, most interviews were recorded and transcribed. If recording was not permitted, copious notes were taken. Interview schedules were structured around the following topics: respondent/business demographics, pre-Covid-19 business development, and business experiences during Covid-19 stages, changes in care responsibilities during Covid-19, and strategies for managing business and family during Covid-19. Interview summaries were prepared and shared among the researchers, and common thematic codes were generated and used for interview transcription/notes coding. Thematic codes included effects of Covid-19 on business and family, pivots in business and family, and respondent assessment of Covid-19 impacts on work–life balance. Interviews were coded according to these categories with sensitivity to emergent and intersecting themes of (dis)advantage. In the next section, our findings convey the intersectional and contextual comparison of business/ family pivoting in the two countries, revealing how individuals' social and geographical positionality shape pivot opportunities and strategies in business and family.

FINDINGS

Initially, respondents reported that they feared for their business' future. In each country, shutdowns produced many challenges. In response, SEBOs modified business operations. Day-care and school closures created increased care responsibilities for parents, which affected family relations. Those who cared for the sick, disabled, or elders faced increased health concerns. Respondents' struggles varied depending on business type, family situation, family support, and access to economic resources. In the USA, immigrant respondents outlined additional issues. Respondents pivoted business and family lives to meet challenges. Czechia had nationwide shutdowns; US responses varied across states.

Our findings below outline the pivots undertaken and the ways in which pivot opportunities were shaped by intersecting business, family, economic positions, and government programmes. In response to our research questions, this findings section comprises three parts: how respondents pivoted their (1) business and (2) families over time, and (3) how these pivots were shaped by the positionality of varied women SEBOs.

Business Pivots

We identified two types of business pivots that correspond to the literature (e.g. Manolova et al., 2020). These were *defensive pivots* to reduce risk, and *offensive pivots* to address new opportunities that emerged amidst Covid-19. Both are described below and summarized in Table 10.3.

Table 10.1   US women SEBO sample

Case #	Race/ethnicity	Age	Marital status	# Children (age of children), other care responsibilities	Business field	Years in business
#1	White	55	Married	1 (adult) & elder care	Food service	20
#2	E. European immigrant	40	Married	2 (10, 12)	Office space rentals	1
#3	Chinese immigrant	30–40	Married	2 (7, 12)	Restaurant	7
#4	US permanent resident/Chinese origin	30–40	Married	2 (2, 5)	Insurance	8
#5	Mexican immigrant	50	Married	3 toddler grandchildren & ill spouse	House cleaning	20
#6	US permanent resident/Chinese	30–40	Divorced	1 (13)	Vehicle dealership	7
#7	Asian American	43	Married	2 (14, 16)	Medical professional	17
#8	White	33	Married	1 (5) & elder care	Animal breeding/ training & auto shop	6–7
#9	Latina immigrant	49	Married	4 (11, 19, 21, 26)	Financial management	2
#10	White	70	Divorced	1 (adult child with disabilities) & elder care	Insurance & personal care	25

Source: Authors.

Table 10.2   CZ women SEBO sample

Case #	Race/ethnicity	Age	Marital status	# Children (age of children), other care responsibilities	Business field	Years in business
#1	White	47	Married	2 (17, 14)	Food service	7
#2	White	45	Married	2 (10, 5)	Tourism	21
#3	White	50	Married	2 (14, 15)	Personal care	23
#4	White	35	Married	1 (4)	Art production	15
#5	White	51	Divorced—solo mother	2 (17,14)	Tourism	11
#6	White	40	Divorced—solo mother	1 (11)	Tourism	11
#7	White	37	Married	2 (7, 4)	Personal counselling	7
#8	White	46	Cohabiting	1 (7)	Personal care, counselling, rental service	16
#9	White	64	Divorced	2 (adult) & grandchildren	Tourism	13
#10	White	32	Married	1 (4)	Manufacturing, retail	7
#11	White	40	Married	2 (9, 13)	Education	2
#12	White	41	Married	2 (6, 12)	Gastronomy	11

Source: Authors.

Table 10.3   Business pivots

Defensive	Offensive	
• Business closure • Business components closure • Employee reduction • Business put on hold • Change of business plans—halt on development	• Innovation in existing practice	• Rearranging work spaces • Purchasing safety equipment • Development of new working procedures (online sale or service provision)
	• Multiple business components	• Pre-existing multiple business components • Developing new components due to Covid-19

Source: Authors.

Defensive pivots to reduce risk

Both Czech and US SEBOs engaged in business pivots to reduce losses during the Covid-19 pandemic. Pivots included temporary closures, reductions in employees, supplementing business earnings through employment, cancelling planned expansions, and in the worst cases, closing the business, as summarized in Table 10.3.

SEBOs that required in-person customer service and large overheads experienced the greatest reductions in the early Covid-19 periods if they were deemed nonessential (March–May 2020). One US SEBO (US2) closed permanently because no one wanted to rent shared workspaces. A Czech hairdressing salon owner for 17 years (CZ3) with several employees closed at the beginning of Covid-19, when the state ordered temporary closures.

Employee reduction is a common defensive strategy in both countries. Czech women SEBOs in tourism (CZ2,5,6,9) and food service (CZ12) were examples. The Czech hairdresser (CZ3) mentioned above re-opened later as a sole proprietor. A US housecleaning business (US5) struggled because clients feared individuals who were non-family entering their homes. She eliminated one cleaning team. By late 2021, her business resumed but was erratic as Covid-19 rates fluctuated.

Flexibility was important to SEBOs' survival as they reduced employees and operating costs. One US "essential" business (US9) closed most days but said: 'We continued to go in once a week to accommodate clients who wanted to be seen.' Their employees were laid off during this period and received Covid-enhanced unemployment compensation from the government. A US food service SEBO (US1) said: 'With hindsight I probably reduced my employees more than needed, but I was afraid not to at the time.' A US car dealer (US6) stopped employing anyone during the pandemic. Another US restaurant owner (US3) had flexible rosters, which helped reduce staff as needed.

For SEBOs without employees, rents, or other significant operating costs (e.g. US4,10; CZ2,4,5,6,7,9), businesses could be *put on hold* at times. However, this pivot reduced earnings.

Two Czech tour guides (CZ2,5) took low-paid jobs to supplement business incomes and low state compensation. One mother (CZ5) said: 'Since there isn't any work, I tried to find something else [...] and now I've been employed since April [2021]. I still travel abroad occasionally [...] Right now [...] I have three tours, but that's just to earn some additional money because the salary [in the new job] is not very high.' A language school owner (CZ11) added a job as a swimming teacher. This income multiplication meant that she could counter Covid-19 effects and benefit from state support for employees: 'I actually have two jobs now, I'm definitely not happy about it, but I don't want to give it up because I see the potential in it.' In contrast, none of the US sample took jobs during Covid-19, although two respondents considered it, for example a solo mother (US6): 'Entrepreneurship comes with financial instability and unknowns which wear me out. I considered looking for new employment with better job security in the summer of 2020 [...] I did come across some jobs that I liked but they were not very well paid.'

For some SEBOs, Covid-19 dramatically changed future business plans: A Czech food business (CZ12) was forced to curtail expansion plans; funds had to be directed towards business survival. Two US food businesses (US2,3) closed components entirely during the pandemic.

Pivots towards new opportunities (offensive)
Most SEBOs went beyond defensive pivots to engage new opportunities that the pandemic created. These included innovations in existing practices and business diversification. Upon reopening, some SEBOs in restaurants and personal services *innovated* in varied ways: rearranging workspaces, purchasing safety equipment, developing new work procedures. One Czech gastronomy family franchise (CZ1) shifted partly to home delivery. One clothing manufacturing/retail franchise SEBO (CZ10) shifted to online sales, inventing new strategies to reach online customers: 'When the stores closed, we depended on e-shop orders. And I think that's where the social media helped us.' The language school (CZ11) shifted to an online format in the first Covid-19 wave, but this innovation did not last in subsequent Covid waves because of overload with online communication: 'The problem is, that the parents are fed up with the on-line schooling. Kids were on the computer for a long-time last year.' A psychotherapist SEBO (CZ7) shifted to online and outdoor therapy during walks: 'There are always options: to sit, to walk or online therapy.' A US restaurant owner (US1) said, 'We converted our outdoor table space to counter-ordering and self-seating. It worked great and we are keeping that arrangement.' Another respondent (US7) who owned a restaurant as a second

business shifted to technology that reduced the need for waiting staff. A restaurant owner (US3), an immigrant, utilized a popular instant messaging app and successfully reopened her business in an almost contactless format. This innovation increased her prestige in the business. Another respondent (US6) and her business partners rebounded their pre-owned car dealership by using disposable car seat covers and arranging video walkarounds and contactless test drives. Some US SEBOs in professional services shifted entirely to online work and escaped closure (US4,7,8,9,10), but this pivot entailed learning new technology. 'I had to learn Zoom for online meetings and that was very stressful at first' (US10).

As summarized in Table 10.3, apart from innovations in existing business practice, another innovation took advantage of pre-existing multiple business components or diversification after the Covid pandemic began. Having multiple business components before Covid-19 offered pivot opportunities during Covid-19. Respondents could shift their emphasis to more Covid-friendly business lines. One US respondent (US10) engaged in three self-employment income activities. During Covid-19, she terminated the in-person business and focused on two others. Several other US SEBOs had prior multiple components (US1,6,7,8), and shifted emphasis during the pandemic. In contrast, the Czech sample contained only one SEBO with pre-existing multiple components. She (CZ8) offered multiple services (i.e. massages, consulting, wedding dress rental), and reduced the massage component.

Some SEBOs developed *new business components* to seize new Covid-friendly opportunities. The Czech family restaurant franchise (CZ1) opened a new restaurant outside of the franchise. When her personal services business had to close during lockdowns, another Czech respondent (CZ8) started a food delivery business on a digital platform. A mother of a small child, self-employed in film-production (CZ4) diversified her business activities after experiencing reduced business during the pandemic. A US restaurant owner (US3) added a new service to her business, which was home delivery of frozen dim sum to customers.

Some US (US6,7,9) and even more Czech respondents (CZ1,2,6,8,11) described frustration with Covid-related demands. Within the Czech sample, long-term negative effects in terms of business reduction, temporary closures and decreased profits prevailed. Accordingly, despite defensive and offensive pivots, Covid-19 reinforced some Czech women entrepreneurs' (CZ10,11) financial dependence on male partners with few prospects in sight: 'My husband earns quite a lot, so [during Covid-19] I didn't necessarily have to go to work. Well, it's certainly not pleasant' (CZ11).

In contrast to the Czech sample, several US SEBOs described improved business during Covid-19 (US3,8,9). One animal training business (US8) said, 'People were at home and wanted to buy and work with their animals. Prices for animals also increased and stayed high.' Another respondent (US9) joined her husband's financial management firm because his business increased dramatically during closures and he needed help. 'People at home had time to worry about investments.' A food business SEBO (US1) said that because of modifications made during closure, the second year of Covid-19 was one of her best years. Although, some US SEBOs described increased precarity during the pandemic (US2,5,10), they also commented on positive business effects. This was not true for Czech SEBOs; overall their Covid-19 narratives were more negative.

Family Pivots

Table 10.4   Family pivots

• Temporary pivot towards increased male involvement in domestic labour
• Women's care acceptance
• Shared care work
• Renegotiation family pivot
• Grand parenting care pivot

Source: Authors.

In addition to business pivoting, Covid-related family issues forced pivots in domestic care arrangements, as summarized in Table 10.4. Respondents lost childcare options during the pandemic and had to find alternatives including taking children to work (US8; CZ10), hiring a caregiver (US3,6), getting help from grandparents and other family members (CZ4,9), and getting support from partners/husbands (US2,3,4,7,8,9; CZ7,10,12). One US respondent assumed care of her grandchildren (US5). Two US (US7,9) and eight Czech respondents had children who were being schooled online. Those with teenagers agreed that they required less supervision (US7; CZ1,3,5,11,12). However, those with children under 10 years of age had to devote their time and energy to online schooling assistance. One US respondent (US9) moved her daughter's school computer nearby: 'I didn't listen to everything, but I could tell she was working.' Another (CZ11) shared a computer she needed for work with her child for an online class: 'When my younger son was on my computer, I cooked and cleaned. Then I took the computer and I worked.'

During closures, some respondents reported that their husbands/partners assumed more of the domestic/care labour. For example, the respondent above (US9) said: 'During Covid, my husband worked more at home. He was able to be more involved with the kids.' They re-purposed a room in the backyard so their teenagers could entertain friends. However, when Covid-19 restrictions subsided, her husband, like the male partners of several Czech respondents, returned to the office. She was not upset when he returned to work since she viewed her role in the home as primary. Another US respondent (US3) and two Czech respondents (CZ7,10) described a temporary pivot towards increased male involvement in domestic labour during the shutdown that decreased when men returned to work.

For some respondents, Covid-19 uncertainty, closures, and business losses meant increased reliance on male breadwinners and women's automatic assumption of increased care burdens, particularly in Czechia (CZ1,2,3,4,8,11): 'My husband went to the office every day, but I was actually always at home, always with the kids, always afraid of what would happen' (CZ11). The Covid pandemic ended one US respondent's (US2) business, and she assumed primary childcare; her husband had taken on the primary care work during her business. Accordingly, with Covid-19, there was a gendered acceptance of increased care duties among women. We call this strategy *care acceptance*.

Not all respondents exhibited such acceptance. Several Czech respondents (CZ1,2,3,8,11) were quite frustrated by the increased care burden and the concomitant loss of financial independence during the pandemic, as illustrated by a quote: 'It's awfully depressing, I don't want to live like that' (CZ3). US respondents were concerned about the loss of financial independence (US2), and the strain on both finances and care responsibilities (US5). The US housecleaning SEBO (US5) was overwhelmed. She normally supervised her teams from home where she also cared for three toddler grandchildren. The negative effect of Covid-19 on her business, her care demands, and the fear that she or her husband would contract Covid stressed her out 'financially and emotionally' (US5). She pivoted by reducing care days for the grandchildren. A Czech SEBO (CZ9) reduced her business time in order to care for several grandchildren two to three days a week.

Some respondents described couple sharing of care arrangements both before and during Covid-19. Three US SEBOs (US2,4,7) shared care work with their partners. US4 emphasized an advantage of working from home: 'Doing business at home frees my husband up for helping me take care of our children at home.' Two Czech SEBOs (CZ10,12) described their division of care responsibilities as already equal before the pandemics. The time flexibility was seen as advantageous for both in CZ12 couple: 'My husband takes care of the kids a lot in the afternoon. If he had a regular job with normal hours, I would have some kid quarantined, sick, some online teaching all the time, totally crazy […] I'd probably […] have to shut down.' Although these respondents described their care arrangements as shared, detailed comments often suggested that the women did more.

Another US SEBO (US8) was renegotiating the division of home/care responsibilities in 2021. She added a business component that entailed more work away; he started a home-based SEBO, so 'Now he is home with our son more and he does dishes and laundry on days that I have to be at the ranch' (US8). She still assumed primary responsibility, but their care negotiations were ongoing. Respondents described this renegotiation family pivot as a long-term strategy. No renegotiation pivot appeared in the Czech sample.

Some respondents negotiated care help from other family members. Especially in the second wave when Covid-19 fears subsided but kindergartens were still closed, the film producer (CZ4) needed significantly more help with care from her parents than before Covid-19. We call this a *grand parenting care pivot*.

Position to Pivot

Table 10.5   Position to pivot

Socio-economic characteristics	Relation to Covid-19 rescue programs
• Economic resources • Family/partner support/dependence • Children's ages • Partner situation: partners at home/single mother • Immigration situation	• Eligibility for Covid-19 rescue programmes • Trust of Covid-19 rescue programmes

Source: Authors.

A variety of pivots in businesses and families were identified from our study. However, essential for understanding the various forces that shaped pivots was respondents' positioning vis-à-vis gender, business type, age, economic resources, family status, immigration status, and governmental support. These intersecting dynamics position respondents and frame pivot opportunities. These dynamics are described below and summarized in Table 10.5.

Access to economic resources and multiple business components provided a cushion to protect the SEBOs, allowing them to pursue business opportunities opened up by the Covid pandemic. Respondents with means and applicable skills could shift their business focus and develop new products appropriate for Covid contexts. 'After the initial shock, I knew I had some financial reserves so I was able to relax a bit and think about the best pivot strategies'(US1).

Resources also increased options for family Covid pivoting. Respondents with economic resources could afford homes with workrooms and play spaces for homebound children (US3,6,7,9). They could afford paid care, but Covid still added obstacles because care workers and employees had to be carefully recruited and better paid. Care from grandparents was important, but because of Covid, some feared infection and restricted this type of care. Women with pre-Covid-19 business successes and economic cushions were more confident about business survival. For them, Covid isolation was a positive time for family bonding: husbands were home and they could enjoy their children without feeling guilty about missing work (US1,3,4,7,9; CZ1,4). Even respondents whose businesses closed (US2; CZ3) said that because of their husband's income, they could enjoy time with children and planning their next ventures.

Covid-19 intensified the already gendered care burdens for women. Most US and Czech respondents accepted primary caregiver roles and worked around care responsibilities, a forced situation for single mothers. Women with older children and/or with romantic partners who shared care responsibilities reported reduced pressures. During shutdowns when romantic partners were home, there was more care sharing, and some couples negotiated more sharing before or during Covid-19. However, care acceptance was common among the women in our sample.

Resources also eased respondent concerns about their welfare when closures were prolonged. A US (US1) respondent said she was comforted knowing that she could retire if the business got too stressed. One Czech respondent (CZ9) was already retired so she had her pension as well as the state compensation to support her optimism that her business might recover. Another US respondent's (US6) business growth stalled after the shutdown, but she 'successfully created a steady passive income stream from pre-Covid rental property investments, and therefore could still keep the entrepreneurial career viable'. A Czech respondent (CZ1) said with frustration that her business survival was possible only because of financial support from her partner's parents. Those in both precarious financial circumstances and in-person businesses worried the most about their health and economic futures. Immigrants (US5,9) worried about family members in their home countries. One (US5) had to stop sending financial assistance to her family. A Czech SEBO in a precarious situation (CZ8) illustrated the problem of insufficient savings: 'We never had enough to […] save in stocks, so we could live on it for two or three years. But when you hit rock bottom and if I didn't have that guy (cohabiting partner), then—.' Family and partner/husband support facilitated several CZ SEBOs' survival (CZ1,3,8,10,11). This support facilitated business pivoting, but some respondents spoke openly about their dislike of the lost independence: 'I'm not happy about that because I'm used to being an independent unit and this doesn't really suit me' (CZ3).

Respondents were also differently positioned in their eligibility and willingness to trust Covid-19 rescue programmes. The US PPP loans were targeted towards businesses with employees, so sole proprietorships were ineligible.

Not all respondents with employees received loans (US2,5). The US respondent whose business closed said the loans came too late (US2). Mature SEBOs said they received 'a lot of support for equipment' (US9) and payroll (US1,9), but that applying for these monies was 'like a job in itself that required lots of time' (US1). US1 said, 'Still, without these loans I might not have survived.' Respondents were critical that many loans went to large corporations, not small businesses, but agreed that the second lending wave was better targeted. Some US respondents commented that they would have preferred the stimulus payments to be targeted to the poor (US3,7,9,10).

Several US respondents who were immigrants said they did not benefit from US government assistance. One (US3) said, 'What I received was like a windfall of extra money.' Two others did not consider government assistance essential to business survival (US4,6). 'My business and life would be the same without the money, and it should go to people who are in a really bad situation'(US3). Two Chinese immigrants (US3,6) argued that China's zero-Covid approach was good, and a Covid-free environment was more important for their businesses than government assistance. Another, who was a US permanent resident, did not apply for government assistance; she feared any aid would risk her eligibility for naturalization (US4). One respondent (US5) (a Mexican national) said her immigration status rendered her ineligible for loans.

The support programmes used by most Czech SEBOs were a daily compensation bonus and attendance allowance for those with children when schools were closed. In addition, the social and health insurance payments were waived in the first six months of Covid-19; this was highly appreciated, especially with regard to the universality of the allowance and its administrative simplicity. For those SEBOs without employees, these programmes were sufficient for several months to cover basic living needs (CZ2,4,5,8), and to keep the business running (CZ11,12). However, in later Covid-19 waves, SEBOs feared they were ineligible, or that they would have to return the money. Some decided not to apply again: 'It was so complicated because we were able to keep the shop open for a while. We couldn't prove the drop in revenue […] in the end, we didn't ask for anything' (CZ10). Programmes for small businesses focused mostly on employee retention, and entailed time-consuming and complicated application procedures. They started too late for those who had to decide about closure and firing employees (CZ3,8,10). One Czech SEBO (CZ1) used the SEBO programme to retain their one employee.

CONCLUSIONS AND POLICY IMPLICATIONS

In this chapter we combined business pivoting research with a social positionality perspective to explore how women's entrepreneurship and family life were affected during a major global turbulent era—the Covid-19 pandemic. Our findings suggest the importance of research on both SEBO business and family pivots and on the interactions between them as well as the relevance of social positionality for understanding women's entrepreneurship and family lives during the pandemic. We identified a variety of business and family pivots, and in this conclusion, we summarize how Covid-19 pivots were dynamically shaped by intersecting dimensions of inequality and the resulting social arrangements that positioned women SEBOs differently during the pandemic. We highlight ways in which experiences and pivots varied in two countries: Czechia and the USA, and the interplay between social structure and agency in each context. We end with a discussion of policy implications and avenues for further research.

Economic resources, children's ages, family support and partner situation, and immigration situation were among the most salient intersectional dynamics that positioned respondents for pivoting opportunities. Both countries had long closures of schools and economic sectors, and different state support policies that influenced businesses differently. In both countries, larger, more established businesses received the most state support. The US sample had more successfully established businesses prior to Covid-19 and fewer US respondents were located in the Covid-vulnerable industries of the Czech sample. Thus, interview narratives suggest more devastating impacts for the Czech sample.

State support programmes arrived too late for some SEBOs, especially those with large operating costs and limited backup resources. Conversely, SEBOs with low operating costs were able to suspend or reduce business operations and pursue employment and/or state support until the economy reopened. In some cases, the Covid-19 context brought opportunities for business innovation, diversification, or expansion. However, without adequate state support, some SEBOs had to invest spare resources in business/family survival. US government support was very generous to larger, established businesses who knew how to file all the applications, but many smaller and immigrant-owned SEBOs were excluded. Subsidy payments were welcomed by most, but not sufficient to cover living costs beyond a few weeks. In Czechia, state support covered only individual living costs for SEBOs; the "crisis attendance allowance" could be used to care for children when schools closed. In both countries, women in precarious SEBOs with limited financial reserves and small children fared worse.

Multiple business components and financial reserves offered a sense of security and pivot opportunities to some US SEBOs. Czech respondents started income-multiplying strategies only once the turbulence began and turned to diversification when previous income sources were reduced. Innovations in business operations, most often going online for contactless service provision, proved successful except for a Czech online language school that failed due to market saturation.

Reduction in business and/or employees increased economic dependence on partners/husbands for several Czech and one US respondent. Sometimes, family support strategies or financial investments in the SEBO facilitated business innovation and diversification rather than business reduction. Regardless, Czech women experienced any loss of independence quite negatively.

US culture encourages male participation in childcare and housework more so than Czech culture. Czech attitudes support the woman doing all or most of the care- and housework (Jurik et al., 2019). Increased care responsibilities with school closures were accepted by women with children under 14, and largely by Czech women. Women's care acceptance was reinforced by Covid-19 pandemic closures that challenged women-owned SEBOs' economic independence. Among US respondents, more male partners contributed to childcare and housework regularly. In the Czech sample, males contributed more, but often temporarily during shutdowns. In both samples, the family pivot towards renegotiated increases in male participation reduced the pressure on women SEBOs, although it was often reduced in later Covid-19 stages.

The US sample includes immigrants from four different countries. Intersecting dynamics such as pre-Covid business success, family support, country of origin, and immigration status are some factors that converged to differentially position these respondents and their pivot opportunities. Undocumented immigrants viewed themselves as ineligible, and permanent residents (e.g. US4) cited laws that made seeking government assistance a risk to future citizenship application.

Future Research and Policy Implications

Our findings reveal how positionality shapes the interplay between entrepreneurship and care arrangements and frames pivot opportunities in the two countries. The study focuses on only two countries, and in the case of the Czechia, only on the Czech (non-immigrant) population, which may have influenced the observed variability in the experiences of entrepreneurs. In addition, it focuses only on the pandemic period. Future research should incorporate Czech immigrant respondents and compare additional countries. It would also be useful to examine the longer-term impacts of the strategies chosen and the inequalities within them. The US sample may also have under-sampled precarious entrepreneurs. In both countries, larger and more varied samples would be recommended in further research.

The closure of schools and care institutions reveals how childcare and other family services are important for SEBOs' survival and prosperity. The long closures during Covid-19 made visible the problematic care infrastructure in the USA and Czechia, and highlighted how women's acceptance of increased care demands challenged their business ownership. Despite Czech state support for childcare and family leave, such systems are not sufficiently sensitive to the needs of working women, especially women SEBOs. The USA almost totally lacks state supports for childcare or family leave. Covid-19 raised interest in such programmes, but the government's Covid policies remained largely insensitive to the special care demands that the pandemic created for women. Care infrastructure, and the promotion of equal sharing between partners are essential for supporting employed women and SEBOs.

State business assistance programmes were not sensitive to the gendered needs of SEBOs in either country. They were slow, and eligibility was unclear, especially for immigrants. Benefit applications took considerable time. In Czechia, except for the first few months, financial support (i.e. income substitution or childcare support for young children) was not available to SEBOs. Loans in both countries targeted businesses' employee retention. In Czechia, it took months to introduce loans with complex application procedures. In the USA, large businesses/corporations quickly grabbed the first round of funding. Faster and administratively simple support measures targeted to specific needs of small SEBOs are needed in crisis situations such as the Covid pandemic.

Policymakers should learn from this experience and constantly compare policy effects on employees and SEBOs, especially for women and other socially marginalized groups in both countries. Temporary paid sick leave and care allowances for Czech SEBOs need to be made permanent. Universal paid sick and family leave and childcare supports are sorely needed in the USA for employees and SEBOs. Policymaking should include the voices of SEBOs and consider differences between and within gender groups.

ACKNOWLEDGEMENTS

Alena Křížková and Marie Pospíšilová wish to thank the Czech Science Foundation for support of their project Gendering the Pandemic (reg. nr. 21-13587S). Nancy Jurik wishes to thank the U.S. Fulbright Program and ASU SkySong's Office of Entrepreneurial Opportunities for funding support for this project. Authorship is equal. The study methodology conformed to all institutional review board-required informed consent and confidentiality guidelines.

REFERENCES

Abbate, T. et al. (2021). Pivoting in innovative startups during the COVID-19 pandemic. In J. Nesterak & B. Ziębicki (eds.), *Business Development in Digital Economy and Covid-19* (pp. 133–144). Warsaw: Institute of Economics, Polish Academy of Sciences.

AJMC [American Journal of Managed Care] (2021). A timeline of COVID-19 developments in 2020 (January 1). Retrieved from https://www.ajmc.com/view/a-timeline-of-covid19-developments-in-2020.

Al-Dajani, H. et al. (2020). 'Stay home' and work? Implications of COVID-19 and the UK governmental response for self-employed women. Retrieved from https://isbegen.wordpress.com/2020/03/27/stay-home-and-work/.

Anthias, F. (2008) Thinking through the lens of translocational positionality: An intersectionality frame for understanding identity and belonging. *Translocations: Migration and Social Change*, *4*(1), 5–19.

Burnley, M. (2020). Black childcare providers hit hard by Covid. The Fuller Project (September 15). Retrieved from https:// fullerproject .org/ story/ black -childcare -providers-hit-covid/.

Daniel, E., Reuschke, D., Henley, A., & Price, V. (2021). Doing it all: Self-employed women and unpaid domestic labour during COVID-19. Paper at Institute for Small Business and Entrepreneurship, October 28–29, 2021, Cardiff.

Dlouhá, M., Jurik, N., & Křížková, A. (2014). Genderové inovace v malém podnikání. Institucionální podmínky a dosahování genderové (ne)rovnosti u podnikatelských párů. *Gender, Rovné příležitosti, Výzkum*, *15*(2), 87–100.

Dudová, R., & Křížková, A. (2023). Czech parents under lockdown: Different positions, different temporalities. *Sociological Research Online*, *29*(1), 184–203. https://doi.org/10.1177/13607804231168249.

Elam, A. et al. (2019). Women's entrepreneurship report: Global entrepreneurship monitor 2018/2019. Retrieved from https://www.gemconsortium.org/file/open?fileId=50405.

Fabrizio, S. et al. (2021). Covid-19 she-cession: The employment penalty of taking care of young children. IMF working paper (March). Retrieved from https://www.imf.org/en/Publications/WP/Issues/2021/03/03/COVID-19-She-Cession-The-Employment-Penalty-of-Taking-Care-of-Young-Children-50117.

Ferreira, F. (2021). Inequality in the time of Covid-19. *Finance & Development* (June). Retrieved from https://www.imf.org/external/pubs/ft/fandd/2021/06/pdf/inequality-and-covid-19-ferreira.pdf.

Graeber, D., Kritikos, A. S., & Seebauer, J. (2021). COVID-19: A crisis of the female self-employed. *Journal of Population Economics*, *34*(4), 1141–1187.

Gromada, A. et al. (2020). Childcare in a global crisis: The impact of Covid-19 on work and family life. Unicef research brief. Retrieved from https://www.unicef-irc.org/publications/1109-childcare-in-a-global-crisis-the-impact-of-covid-19-on-work-and-family-life.html.

Haase, A. (2020). Covid-19 as a social crisis and justice challenge for cities. *Frontiers in Sociology*, *5*. Retrieved from https://www.frontiersin.org/articles/10.3389/fsoc.2020.583638/full.

Jurik, N. C., Křížková, A., Pospíšilová, M., & Cavender, G. (2019). Blending, credit, context: Doing business, family and gender in Czech and U.S. copreneurships. *International Small Business Journal: Researching Entrepreneurship*, *37*(4), 317–342. https://doi.org/10.1177/0266242618825260.

Kalenkoski, C. M., & Pabilonia, S. W. (2022). Impacts of COVID-19 on the self-employed. *Small Business Economics*, *58*(2), 741–768.

Li, F. et al. (2019). Key factors affecting sustained business operations after an earthquake: A case study from New Beichuan, China, 2013–2017. *Natural Hazards*, *104*(1), 101–121.

Madgavkar, A. et al. (2020). Covid-19 and gender equality: Countering the regressive effects. Retrieved from https://www.mckinsey.com/featured-insights/future-of-work/covid-19-and-gender-equality-countering-the-regressive-effects.

Maestripieri, L. (2021). The Covid-19 pandemics: Why intersectionality matters. *Frontiers in Sociology*, 6. Retrieved from https://www.frontiersin.org/articles/10.3389/fsoc.2021.642662/full.

Manolova, T. et al. (2020). Pivoting to stay the course: How women entrepreneurs take advantage of opportunities created by the Covid-19 pandemic. *International Small Business Journal*, *38*(6), 481–491.

Martinez Dy, A. (2020). Not all entrepreneurship is created equal: Theorising entrepreneurial disadvantage through social positionality. *European Management Review*, *17*(3), 687–699. https://doi.org/10.1111/emre.12390.

Mun, S. et al. (2022). Current discussions on employees and organizations during the COVID-19 pandemic. *Frontiers in Psychology*, *13*. Retrieved from https://doi.org/10.3389/fpsyg.2022.848778.

Neergaard, H. (2007). Sampling in entrepreneurial settings. In H. Neergaard & J. P. Ulhøi (Eds.), *Handbook of Qualitative Research Methods in Entrepreneurship* (pp. 253–278). Cheltenham: Edward Elgar Publishing.

National Public Radio [NPR] (2020). Here's how the small business loan program went wrong in just 4 weeks. Retrieved from https://www.npr.org/2020/05/04/848389343/how-did-the-small-business-loan-program-have-so-many-problems-in-just-4-weeks.

OECD (2022). *Education at a Glance 2021: OECD Indicators*. Retrieved from https://www.oecd-ilibrary.org/sites/41805c67-en/index.html?itemId=/content/component/41805c67-en#section-d12020e4325.

OECD/GWEP (2021). *Entrepreneurship Policies through a Gender Lens*. OECD Publishing. Retrieved from https://doi.org/10.1787/71c8f9c9-en.

Parker, K. (2012). *Women, Work, and Motherhood*. Retrieved from www.pewsocialtrends.org/2012/04/13/women-work-and-motherhood/.

Pelikanova, R. et al. (2021). Addressing the Covid-19 challenges by SMEs in the hotel industry: The Czech sustainability message. *Journal of Entrepreneurship in Emerging Economies*, *13*(4), 525–546.

Reuschke, D. et al. (2021). Testing the differential impact of Covid-19 on self-employed women and men in the United Kingdom. IZA Discussion Paper No. 14216. Available at https://ssrn.com/abstract=3813643 or http://dx.doi.org/10.2139/ssrn.3813643.

Romero, M. (2018). *Introducing Intersectionality*. London: Polity.

Romero, M., & Valdez, Z. (2016). Introduction to intersectionality and entrepreneurship. *Ethnic and Racial Studies*, *39*(9–10), 1553–1565.

Sadeghiani, A. et al. (2021). Theorising pivot in small and micro businesses. *Journal of Small Business and Entrepreneurship*. Retrieved from https://www.tandfonline.com/doi/abs/10.1080/08276331.2021.2014205.

Schilder, D., & Sandstrom, H. (2021). The pandemic exacerbated the child care crisis: The urban wire (October 28). The Urban Institute. Retrieved from https://www.urban.org/urban-wire/pandemic-exacerbated-child-care-crisis-how-can-states-reverse-trend.

Scocca, T. (2022). The argument over closing schools is still stuck in 2020. *The Washington Post* (January 15). Retrieved from https://www.washingtonpost.com/outlook/2022/01/15/schools-debate-closing-covid-pundits/.

The U.S. Department of the Treasury (n.d.). Covid-19 economic relief. Retrieved from https://home.treasury.gov/policy-issues/coronavirus.

Torres, J. et al. (2021). The impact of the Covid-19 pandemic on women-led businesses. Policy Research Working Paper 9817, World Bank. Retrieved from https://openknowledge.worldbank.org/bitstream/handle/10986/36435/The-Impact-of-the-COVID-19-Pandemic-on-Women-Led-Businesses.pdf?sequence=7&isAllowed=y.

Umoh, R. (2020). Black women were among the fastest-growing entrepreneurs, then Covid happened. *Forbes Magazine.* Retrieved from https://www.forbes.com/sites/ruthumoh/2020/10/26/black-women-were-among-the-fastest-growing-entrepreneurs-then-covid-arrived/?sh=4d1fab826e01.

Viner, R. et al. (2020). School closure and management practices during coronavirus outbreaks including Covid-19. *Lancet Child Adolescent Health, 4,* 397–404. Retrieved from https://www.ncbi.nlm.nih.gov/pmc/articles/PMC7270629/pdf/main.pdf.

Wang, Q., & Kang, W. (2021). What are the impacts of COVID-19 on small businesses in the U.S.? *Geographical Review, 111*(4), 528–557.

Welter, F. (2011). Contextualizing entrepreneurship-conceptual challenges and ways forward. *Entrepreneurship Theory and Practice, 35*(1), 165–184.

WHO (2022). WHO coronavirus (Covid-19) dashboard. Retrieved from https://covid19.who.int/.

World Bank (2022). Global economic prospects. Retrieved from https://www.worldbank.org/en/publication/global-economic-prospects.

Yousafzai, S. et al. (2019). The contextual embeddedness of women's entrepreneurship: Towards a more informed research agenda. *Entrepreneurship & Regional Development, 31*(3–4), 167–177.

Zavella, P. (1991). Reflections on diversity among Chicanas. *Frontiers: A Journal of Women Studies, 12*(2), 73–85.

Index